A Question of Character

Studies in American Literary Realism and Naturalism

A Question of Character

Scientific Racism and the Genres of American Fiction, 1892–1912

Cathy Boeckmann

THE UNIVERSITY OF ALABAMA PRESS
Tuscaloosa

1 2 3 4 5 6 7 8 9 . 07 06 05 04 03 02 01 00

Jacket Design by Gary Gore

∞

The paper on which this book is printed
meets the minimum requirements of
American National Standard
for Information Science-Permanence of Paper
for Printed Library Materials,
ANSI Z39.48-1984.

Library of Congress Cataloging-in-Publication Data

Boeckmann, Cathy, 1968–
A question of character : scientific racism and the genres of American fiction, 1892–1912 /
Cathy Boeckmann.
p. cm. — (Studies in American literary realism and naturalism)
Includes bibliographical references (p.) and index.

ISBN 0-8173-5297-x
1. American fiction—19th century—History and criticism. 2. Racism in literature.
3. American fiction—20th century—History and criticism. 4. Literature and science—
United States—History. 5. Characters and characteristics in literature. 6. Race
discrimination in literature. 7. Passing (Identity) in literature. 8. Afro-Americans in literature. 9. Eugenics in literature. 10. Literary form. I. Title. II. Series.
PS374.R34 B64 2000
813′.409353—dc21
99-6765

British Library Cataloguing-in-Publication Data available

Contents

Acknowledgments

The development of this project falls into two main phases, with people to thank in each of them. I'm grateful to my former colleagues at the University of California at Irvine for their mentorship and support. Steven Mailloux and Gabriele Schwab read early drafts and provided valuable commentary. Robyn Weigman offered some particularly thoughtful and challenging feedback that helped me understand more clearly what I was up to; I'm glad I sought her out. Lisa Carstens, Colette LaBouff, Grace Lovelace, Corrie Martin, and Clara McLean devoted their time to reading and editing my drafts; I thank them for both their time and their friendship. David Tokaji, far above and beyond the call of duty, read the entire manuscript, and I can't thank him enough for it. And I am especially grateful to Brook Thomas for his thoughtful criticism and encouragement during the development of this project and also in the face of countless other professional challenges. With so much good advice I have inevitably fallen short in incorporating it: any shortcomings in this project are my own and should not reflect ill upon any of these fine scholars.

During the later stages of preparing the manuscript for publication, I received some equally important support. Folks at the Georgia Institute of Technology—Andy McMurry, Daryl Ogden, Alex Reid, Greg Vanhoosier-Carey, and Kim Vanhoosier-Carey—were encouraging about the prospects of publication and gave me solid, strategic advice.

Thanks also to Curtis Clark and his colleagues at the University of Alabama Press, and to the anonymous readers who did such a fine job reviewing the manuscript. And above all, I doubt whether this book would have come into being at all without Michael Merrill's unflagging enthusiasm and gentle prodding. His campaign to make me see publication as a reality helped me be more self-confident and has already benefited me in ways far beyond the scope of this book. Thanks, Mike.

Financial support came from the regents of the University of California and the Humanities Office for Graduate Study at U. C. Irvine. The Dorothy and Donald Strauss endowed fellowship (a wonderful resource for students of literature at Irvine) was also instrumental to the successful completion of this project.

Special thanks to my parents for their kind "fellowship" support as well.

Portions of chapters 1 and 4 were published previously and appear by permission from *REAL: Yearbook of Research in English and American Literature* 11, edited by Winfried Fluck, copyright © 1995 by Gunter Narr Verlag.

Introduction

A Question: Why Character?

The theme of passing—usually when a light-skinned black individual passes as white—is rapidly becoming one of the most explored in American literature. Since the proscription against the serious study of minor nineteenth-century authors has eased, many critics have turned to figures who at one point were relatively obscure but who dealt with the paradoxes and tragedies of race, especially mixed race.[1] As of yet, much of the criticism touching upon this literature displays a similar set of interests. Most recent critical works concerned with mixed race and passing follow the links and connections between a series of conceptual or theoretical points with recognizable popular currency. Commonly, a chain of argument runs from remarks on the cultural manipulation of the supposedly natural signs of race to analysis of the overwhelmingly visual nature of popular culture.

For example, critics with an interest in identity are concerned with how the arbitrary distinction between black and white has been naturalized. This focus usually leads to a discussion of mixed race because the constructed nature of the racial binary becomes most apparent in the case of the biracial individual. Literature that explores mixed race and the troubled binary of racial classification often involves passing, so critics look at novels and narratives of passing to explore how race is a performance or a disguise rather than a natural category. Critics then often move from passing to a discussion of the conventions for visual assessment and to visual culture more generally. In her introductory essay to the anthology *Passing and the Fictions of Identity* (1996), Elaine Ginsberg cites Amy Robinson's assertion that "the 'problem' of identity, a problem to which passing owes the very possibility of its practice, is predicated on the false promise of the visible as an epistemological guarantee" (4). However, as many critics have pointed out, visual conventions and the faith in the truth that visual images provide are what allowed race to be naturalized in the first place. Thus, the critical argument circles back on itself and returns (perhaps rather incessantly) to the constructed quality of race.

The conceptual links between these points of argument that I identify run in both directions and can be explored from any entry point, in more or less any order. The topics that cluster around mixed race—the natural basis of race, passing, visual culture—are so conceptually linked that they are seldom considered in isolation. For example, in *Neither Black Nor White Yet Both* (1997), Werner Sollors turns his attention to fiction with themes of mixed race because he wants to understand "the cultural operations which make [races] seem natural or self-evident categories" (3). So he looks at many narratives of passing among the texts he examines, and he has also "chosen to illustrate [his] book, which is primarily concerned with *texts,* with interracial images" (9). Thus, text is supplemented with visual images, and the power of the visual is incorporated into the analysis. Similarly, in *American Anatomies: Theorizing Race and Gender* (1995), Robyn Wiegman is interested in how race became rationalized as a natural category, so she examines the epistemic shifts in scientific forms of vision that "locat[e] in the body an epistemological framework for justifying inequality" (2). This theoretical exploration of vision and science serves to introduce her examination of race and gender in American literature and visual culture.[2]

Like these critics, I am interested in the representation of blackness, especially when it is invisible, as is the case in the novel of passing.[3] In this book I am therefore engaged in an exploration of the negotiations that take place when the binary distinction of race is made unstable. I approach my investigation from the perspective, however, that the constructed nature of race has been well established. At the start of her introduction, Ginsberg cites an 1836 advertisement for a runaway slave named Edmund Kenney which warned that the slave might pass for white. Ginsberg follows it with commentary designed to introduce the anthology's focus as a whole: "That Kenney's legal status was an imposed, socially constructed identity is self-evident; that his race was also imposed and socially constructed is not" (1). In many contexts, of course, the constructed nature of race is far from self-evident. However, in the context of the critical work on passing and mixed race, I believe that it is. I work from the assumption that it is now more fruitful to investigate how the terms "natural" and "constructed" translate, or fail to translate, into the racial discourse of the nineteenth century, and then push analysis from there.

In this book I address the topics of race, passing, bodies, and American literature using an approach based in historical vocabulary. As my title makes clear, the controlling term in my investigation is not *passing* per se (though it does address that issue) but *character.* The notion of character formed the core of discussions of race in the late nineteenth century. In fact, questions of character were so important that a field of study known as characterology was devised to answer them.[4] In current usage *character* is a figurative term, signifying the imagined structure of an individual's moral and ethical orientations, but in the nineteenth century it referred to a quantifiable set of inherited behaviors and tendencies that were almost always racial. My focus on character responds to the vocabulary and concepts used to describe race in the period's fiction and nonfiction rather than to critical vocabulary. For example, our notion of culture does not accord with nineteenth-century usage. Wiegman suggests that her project sets forth the ways in which "specific racial categories are rendered 'real' (and therefore justifiable) through the naturalizing discourses of the body, those discourses that locate difference in a pre-cultural realm where corporeal significations supposedly speak a truth which the body inherently means" (4). By my reading of the late-nineteenth-century discourses of the body, there is no pre-cultural realm in their figurations. Wiegman here uses *culture* in the twentieth-century sense, and her readers understand her figuration to apply to that setting. However, for the racial theorists of the period I am looking at, culture is in and of the body in such an inextricable sense that the body *is* culture. I believe that making a distinction between our sense of culture and that of the late nineteenth century provides the means to pay closer attention to how race was both beyond the constructions of culture and a precondition for them.

In fact, nineteenth-century thinkers could not fail to recognize the instabilities in the categories of race, especially as they tried to measure visual signs that were often invisible to them. As a result, the need to locate the supposed essence of racial difference fell upon the concept of inherited racial character—a racial essence that is connected to the features of race but which can also be extricated from them. Nineteenth-century scientific racism elaborates on the links between physical signs, racial identity, and racial character with surprising flexibility. The concept of character defined a racial essence that was not visible and established a framework for how the individual inherits the traits of culture. Thus, the behaviors and institutions that distinguish civilization from barbarism were largely prior to environmental pressures, as they were part of the body's inheritance. In this sense, culture in the nineteenth century was more a synonym for nature than for nurture. In order to do justice to the literature of race in this period it is first necessary to understand its vocabulary. And as I understand it, the most important synonym for *race* in this period, and the term with the most complex conceptual framework, was *character.*

Characterizing Genre

I have introduced my critical focus in terms of its historical responsiveness, but in a practical sense responsiveness to historical vocabulary results in a shift in approach. Clearly, an emphasis on how the vocabulary of character functions in late-nineteenth-century fiction allows me to supplement the usual theoretical approaches to the topic of passing; such approaches are not conceptually positioned to examine the historical specificity of terms like *character* and *culture,* since they rely on theoretical vocabulary developed from contemporary understandings of race. However, a focus on character allows for a move beyond thematic approaches as well. Typically, thematic readings like Sollors's (whose book offers compelling explanations of why plots, motifs, and events repeat in work after work) do not develop connections between theme and the formal features of literary traditions. I have found that examining nineteenth-century racial vocabulary opens up a pathway—perhaps an unexpected one—to generic considerations.

Given that *character* was the modal term for race in the late nineteenth century, when novelists sought to depict both whiteness and blackness they were concerned very explicitly with the depiction of the character of their characters. The artistic demands involved with the handling of mixed-race characters especially exacerbate this concern. When race is securely visual it is depicted in passages of physical description, but when race is a matter of a nonvisible, inherited character it must be characterized. And characterization in this period was a fairly formal exercise: each literary genre had its own rules and conventions for the creation of character. The depiction of mixed race would therefore appear to be contingent on the parameters for characterization offered by the chosen generic form. At this moment, American literary discourse displayed a fair amount of self-consciousness about genre and its conventions. Specifically, one ground of contention between realists and sentimentalists in the late nineteenth century was over characterization. Literature was assumed to be the best location for the representation of national and racial character, and debates over the relative merits of sentimental, romantic, and realistic fiction were embroiled in discussions of which mode offered the best form of characterization.

Recognizing the conceptual importance of characterization as a feature of genre allows for a more complete picture of racial discourse in the period. As I have already noted, scientific studies of race were engaged in discussions of character; when literary debates are placed next to scientific ones, a shared vocabulary of character emerges. In the chapters that follow, authors accommodate the physically invisible blackness of their passing or light-skinned characters through appeals to character. Therefore, scientific and pseudo-scientific notions about the inheritability of race and the workings of character appear in these novels as features of characterization. As such, this investigation establishes connections between the genres current at the turn of the century and scientific discourses of race in order to establish the extent to which the period's generic debates reflect the period's racism.

Using character as the modal concept for race also provides the basis for the scope of my project. First, I place white supremacist novels along with more straightforward novels of passing because they all provide perspectives on the discourse of character. Second, I focus on the 1891 to 1912 time span because during this period the language of character was beginning to undergo an important shift in emphasis. In the last decades of the nineteenth century, character had become the stand-in for the visible signs of race that the novel of passing disrupts. But widespread cultural conviction in the inherited nature of character was beginning to falter as environmental theories of race were beginning to achieve some currency. As a result, the inheritability of character was insisted upon with vehemence at the same time that the concept of character itself was being expanded and molded to fit a growing interest in environmental forces, performance, and willed transformations of one's personality.

In my first chapter, I provide an overview of how the discourses of race and genre are connected by a shared interest in character. I begin with a summary of racial attitudes common in the late nineteenth and early twentieth centuries—attitudes which I refer to as scientific racism. Then I move into a survey of scientific and popular discourse to explain how the term *character* was used in the period and how it carried almost inevitable racial and evolutionary implications. Finally, I give an account of the generic categories and traditions that I will work with in the chapters to follow, demonstrating that sentimental fiction, the plantation romance, and literary realism all contain parameters for characterization that have their basis in a pseudo-scientific logic of character.

In my second chapter, I argue that in Thomas Dixon's novels *The Leopard's Spots* (1902) and *The Clansman* (1905) the historical romance offers a mode of physical description by which outer appearance is taken as a sign for inner character. Thus, the fixed character types of romance allow Dixon to make white skin a sign for superiority and strong racial character and black skin a sign for depravity and lack of character. Dixon then circumvents the crisis of the mixed-race character's white skin by suggesting that a seemingly white exterior signals "personality" rather than character, in effect making character solely a white possession. Dixon's novels provide the most extreme example of a post–Civil War tradition in which southern writers attempted to create a racial history of the South by using the sentimental romance to support an ideology of white supremacy.

The authors under investigation in the chapters that follow implicitly and explicitly respond to the conventions for characterization employed in southern romance fiction. As a result, a debate develops among the chapters over the South's politics and its romantic literary conceptions. However, I do not stage this debate in order to demonstrate that the literary techniques and generic innovations of Twain, Howells, Chesnutt, and Johnson are an answer to Dixon's historical romance. In fact, only Johnson's novel was published after Dixon's, and he is the only one to respond to him directly. Rather, I am interested in looking at how these four novelists respond to the tradition that Dixon represents: the tendency for southern literature to use the romance to justify and idealize its social institutions.[5]

For example, in the third chapter I argue that Mark Twain's *Pudd'nhead Wilson* (1894) mocks sentimental fiction set in the South, particularly the plantation romance and the tragic octoroon novel. However, since Twain's novel is also an example of detective fiction, the novel is at generic cross-purposes, especially since the genres place different amounts of emphasis on the relationship between body and character. To burlesque sentimental fiction, Twain makes physical appearance, character, and race ironically disjunct. However, in detective fiction the detective figure solves the crime on which the plot turns because he is able to show that the physical evidence of the crime points without question to the body of the criminal and his criminal character. Thus, I argue that the novel's inconsistency about its mixed-race murderer's racial character and Twain's own slippery position (which has puzzled critics) have their base in generic hybridity, the racial implications of which remain unappreciated without attention to character and genre.

In the fourth chapter, I examine how William Dean Howells's *An Imperative Duty* (1892) and Charles Chesnutt's *The House Behind the Cedars* (1900) employ different generic forms of closure as they critique the links between race and sentimental fiction. Both ostensibly present a more realistic account of the relationship between the mixed-race character's appearance and racial character. For Howells, *all* Americans are of mixed race in the sense that all European national types become mixed in the United States. Figuring the light-skinned mulatto as simply another favorable mix of inherited racial characters, Howells grants that racial character is visible but denies that it is necessarily inferior. With a white hero who can see mixed race in this supposedly realistic way, Howells replaces the sentimental tradition's act of renunciation (in which the mixed-race heroine must reject her white suitor to serve her race) with a marriage that ensures a comic ending.

Chesnutt's novel of passing displays a different understanding of race, character, and genre. He rejects the notion that black racial character can be read from the physical features of a light-skinned mulatto. He suggests that in the absence of visible blackness, the mixed-race character's racial identity and character are fixed by a self-fashioning story that he or she tells. Chesnutt's mixed-race characters accordingly try to incorporate the conventions of the racialized southern romance into the story of themselves in order to privilege their white southern blood. However, Chesnutt demonstrates that the white romantic story is not anchored (as southerners assume) by racial memory transmitted by blood but rather by the operation of white social power. When Chesnutt's heroine cannot wield this power because of her gender, the genre shifts to tragedy.

It is important to note that I do not argue that realism—or any fiction that stages a critique of sentimentalism—is in a fundamental way less racist than Dixon's novels. As I argue in chapter 1, realism was no less concerned than sentimental fiction with the proper representation of racial character. Realism is firmly implicated in character-characterization discourses, despite the fact that (or perhaps due to the fact that) the defenders and proponents of realism attacked other forms of fiction over the validity of their characterizations. Though some authors are more aware than others that genre is connected to characterization, each works from within an understanding of racial difference constrained by the notion of racial character.

Yet despite these very constraints, in the final chapter I argue that the first-person narration of James Weldon Johnson's *The Autobiography of an Ex-Coloured Man* (1912) marks a significant change in the way discourses of character and mixed race are aligned with genre. Johnson comments explicitly on the limits genre imposes on the representation of black characters. As his narrator notes, there are really only two acceptable genres for this purpose: a comic one whereby the black figure is made a buffoon, and a tragic one whereby social mistreatment renders him pathetic. As a result, Johnson's novel subsumes the two limiting genres of tragedy and comedy within the genre of the fictional autobiography in order to transcend them. In first-person narratives, the narrator's disembodied voice presents physical features only indirectly, disrupting the conventions of physical description that present both body and character in other genres; the character of the black narrator is enacted rather than represented.

In this last chapter, I also look at how the African-American literary tradition is in dialogue with the white canon. Specifically, Johnson comments on the limits for the representation of blackness in the white canon and employs a genre or mode from the African-American literary tradition that would push those limits. This sort of focus on African-American literature allows for a more complete sense of the intertextuality of American fiction. Johnson's novel, however, has even wider implications for American literature and art. In *The Autobiography,* the narrator fails to be a representative black man when he decides to pass. Johnson thus suggests that written representation necessarily involves a suspect racial collectivity that seeks to characterize the entire race on the basis of a single characterization.

In this way my investigation returns to its starting point. In the epilogue I look at Johnson's comments on *The Birth of a Nation,* the movie version of Dixon's novels. He suggests that visual representation is the most damaging form of racial representation. Nearly all of the novelists in this investigation voice a concern for the relationship between visual and written art; perhaps an aesthetic that privileges characterization over physical description cannot help but be drawn into more general discussions of representation and its inadequacies. And since the theories of racial difference in the nineteenth century evoke many of the abstract underpinnings of figurative language, my conclusion stages a more extensive exploration of the ties race has to language alluded to in the previous chapters.

In general, my project gives a glimpse of how genres can be racialized and how the conventions of literature, not just its themes, help to create race and to make it visible. The conventions of fiction make it a unique kind of discourse, but understanding how genres operate allows for a better understanding of how nonfictional discourses can also be bound by descriptive conventions. In addition, in this book I place the discourse of character squarely within the development of American literary realism. Though realism imagined that it did away with convention—it had no set plots and no distinct character types—it was still bound by the social and scientific conventions for the representation of character. I thus suggest that realism at the turn of the century was linked by way of these conventions to attempts to represent whiteness, blackness, and the presumed differences between them.

Finding the Sources

Though I have framed this introduction in terms of what sorts of approaches I wish to supplement through a reworking of their methods, there are some critical works that I drew upon in a more straightforward fashion. In particular, my study of race owes a significant debt to George Frederickson's *The Black Image in the White Mind.* I do not replay his arguments within the body of my chapters, but his book was the starting point for my research in the materials of the period.[6] The vocabulary and concepts of race would have remained far more obscure to me without his painstaking review of the historical record of significant writings on racial topics. Furthermore, Frederickson's bibliography and footnotes pointed me toward authors and commentators whose names have little contemporary currency but who nonetheless served as touchstones for their age. Many of these names appear in the next chapter.

The Black Image in the White Mind also contributed to the conceptual grounding of this book. Frederickson's main insight—that the key issue in the history of racism is how race is conceptualized and then how that concept is transmitted—helped shape my focus on characterization as a conceptual nexus bearing more cultural information than might at first be obvious. The account Frederickson gives for his project in the preface to his book could therefore serve well enough as an account of mine: "In large part this book is a study of the development of intellectualized racist theory and ideology as it was applied directly and programmatically to the 'problem' posed in the white mind by the presence of millions of blacks in the United States" (xvii). My book focuses on one particular nexus within that body of intellectualized racist theory—racial character—and then tracks its use in the articulation of the problem of race mainly in one particular segment of discourse—literature.

1

Scientific Racism, Character, and American Fiction

American discourse of the late nineteenth and early twentieth century is marked by an intense concern for the future of race relations. In the aftermath of Reconstruction, the debate over how the black and white races could be part of the same social universe often took a North-South cast, with white southerners declaring what they would and would not accommodate. In most cases such declarations were accompanied by an explanation of what exactly about the black race rendered it unfit for social congress. In Thomas Dixon's novel *The Leopard's Spots* (1902), a white southern reverend makes an observation of the second sort as he chastises a black preacher: "In the old days . . . I used to preach to your people. I saw before me many men of character: carpenters, bricklayers, wheelwrights, farmers, faithful home servants that loved their masters and were faithful unto death. Now I see a cheap lot of thieves and jailbirds and trifling women seated in high places. You have shown no power to stand alone on the solid basis of character" (311). This novel—a white supremacist polemic which was later adapted as the film *The Birth of a Nation*—concerns itself with a transformation which has supposedly occurred in the black population in the post-emancipation period: as the population has become pervasively immoral, it is implicitly unfit for participation in white social life.

While Dixon's larger point is manifest and obvious, the implications of the final sentence take some work to uncover. He identifies a moral transformation, but the transformation of the social and moral environment of the ex-slaves is not his ultimate point. Rather, Dixon alludes to what the transformation of the social environment of the ex-slaves reveals about *innate* racial tendencies. What to a modern reader might appear to be an observation about *nurture*—the moral standards supposedly adopted by post-emancipation black culture—is actually a pronouncement on *nature*—the innate, racial capacity for moral behavior. The capacity for moral character in Dixon's conceptual universe is an inherited racial property; while slavery held those in bond to high moral standards, ex-slaves could not stand alone in this regard because their race had supposedly not evolved the necessary character themselves. Thus this passage makes a scientific (or more properly pseudo-scientific) pronouncement about the evolutionary basis of racial character. And as Dixon explicitly wrote his novel as an answer to Harriet Beecher Stowe's *Uncle Tom's Cabin,* this passage ultimately illustrates what is often true in a larger sense of racial discourse at the turn of the century: scientific arguments about race were often staged as literary debates.

Dixon was only one of many observers, both northern and southern, who believed that character was the key to the race question. In *The Plantation Negro as a Freeman* (1889), Philip A. Bruce published his own account of what changes freedom had brought to the freedman. In his introduction Bruce asserted that "the truest lover of his country, as well as the most disinterested friend of the blacks, is he who will portray their character and depict their society, without partiality and without prejudice" (vii). Put together, these quotations from Dixon and Bruce illuminate the scope of the argument about character that I develop in this book. First, the emphasis on observation in both cases suggests that it was a pressing duty—even, as Bruce claims, a patriotic duty—to examine the nature of race as it manifests itself in character. As such, the study of character took on the trappings of science in its supposedly disinterested conclusions based upon close professional scrutiny. Second, both quotations demonstrate the importance of the literary or discursive characterization of those scientifically observed. Whether in the medium of fiction or nonfiction, character must be *portrayed* and *depicted.* The science of character, the art of characterization, and social policy converge: in the representation of racial character, the social implications of race—the ones which so concern both Dixon and Bruce—can be made clear to the widest audience.

Yet, at least in Dixon's case, the simplicity of this progression—from scientific observation to artistic expression and from there to social policy—symptomatically betrays a basic conceptual difficulty. Though Dixon suggests that the scientific examination of character is a matter of correct vision since moral decay is abundantly clear simply upon casual inspection, his other writing nonetheless demonstrates his keen awareness that moral and racial character is sometimes difficult to determine visually. Though one might expect that Dixon would avoid the question of racial ambiguity entirely, his novels feature mulatto or mixed-race individuals for whom visual inspection is not sufficient to determine character, let alone race. As I will demonstrate in the pages that follow, many other writers at the turn of the century sought to use a supposedly scientific inspection of race and character to answer questions about race relations and social organization. But rather than disregard the complicating factor of mixed race, discourse in this period returns with some frequency to the color line, to miscegenation, and to the qualities and features that supposedly place people on one side or the other.

Though the phrase "the color line" was rarely explained or qualified in the postwar decades, it actually had two distinct though related meanings.[1] The color line first of all represents the line of distinction drawn between the races which made political equality distinct from social equality. With this line in place, economic and civic congress between the races could be achieved without encouraging social intercourse. As Marion Dawson put it in 1901, in the postwar South social engineers endeavored to "maintain a social barrier across which no alien foot should come, and preserve at all hazards Anglo-Saxon ascendancy" (280). As this formulation suggests, defenses of the color line often took on a supremacist logic; the white race was superior, but it was necessary to prevent alien individuals from invading or defiling that superiority. And the implied threat to superiority in this and most other cases was the prospect of miscegenation. According to scientific understandings of racial difference, when white blood mingled with that of other races the resulting offspring were inferior to the white parent. If this happened on a larger scale, the race as a whole would be degraded. As William Benjamin Smith declared, the South—in its insistence on the strict social segregation of the color line—"stands for *blood,* for the *'continuous germ plasma' of the Caucasian race*" (5, emphasis in source).

Interestingly, the second meaning of the color line refers to the people who are the products of interracial mingling and who represent the discontinuity of Caucasian germ plasm. Individuals of mixed racial background were said to be "on" the color line, as if they existed in a space between the races. As a result, there is a wry and ironic aptness to the double uses of the phrase: the color line is the social barrier to intermarriage and interbreeding, and when that line is crossed the people produced are said to be on the line, as if in perpetual reenactment of the initial act of crossing. Yet despite the fitness of this metaphor, there is also clear disjunction and tension between the two meanings of the color line. In his essay "The Race Problem in the South" (1892), biologist Joseph Le Conte discussed the legitimacy of what he called the "race-line": "It will be objected again that the race-line is artificial, and therefore unjust and irrational . . . wholly the result of race-prejudice, and this in turn only a remnant of slavery. . . . But race-prejudice or race-repulsion, to use a stronger term, is itself not a wholly irrational feeling. It is probably an instinct necessary to preserve the blood purity of the higher race" (365). Since the color line was justified on the basis of a supposed instinctual desire to preserve the blood purity of the white race, the people on the color line stood as ironic testaments to the inconsistent influence of that instinct. All in all, if social segregation was necessary in order to prevent interbreeding, since science claimed it resulted in degeneracy and race-weakness, then the prosperity and achievements of people on the color line stood as direct rebukes to that science. In short, the people on the color line were in a position to threaten the science that justified the existence of the line in the first place.

A scientific racism based purely on outward physical signs would clearly be inconsistent. Though it has been commonplace for literary critics to describe scientific racism as naively dependent on statistics and measurements of visible characteristics, the discourse was capable of responding (albeit often no less inconsistently) to the complexities of racial ambiguity. Like Dixon's fiction, scientific racism often faced the fact of mixed race head-on. But in doing so, theorists of race and racial difference had to abandon a blind faith in statistics and measurements and turn instead to the much less quantifiable notion of character. The examples from Dixon and Bruce above demonstrate that by the turn of the century the language of race had begun to show a dramatic shift to a focus on character. For both authors, the crucial and determining issue was not race per se but rather the implications and conclusions that could be drawn from the manifestations of racial character: the question of race had become a question of character.

The notion of character clearly straddles the conceptual worlds of science and literature. Character is a building block of literature, and it intrudes itself upon scientific discourse in the basic requirement that an assessment of character be *characterized*—whatever conclusions can be drawn about character have to be given shape in descriptive language. Therefore, an emphasis on inherited race character brought racial theory into a close relationship with literary notions about characterization. And as different genres have different conventions for characterization, it also follows that different genres can be used to present race differently. In the United States, one of the central concerns in the turn-of-the-century debates about the relative worth of different genres was the determination of which genre did the best job of characterization. By implication, the aesthetic debates over realism, romance, and sentimental fiction were in some cases implicated in racial debates.

For some late-nineteenth-century literary theorists and critics, especially Hippolyte-Adolphe Taine, literature was linked to the revelation of character in an explicitly racial sense: Taine argued that fiction provides access to the essence of racial groups. Fictional discourse revealed character in ways that other forms of discourse could not. And since the activity of reading character was a pervasive obsession in the nineteenth century, such concerns gave literature particular prominence. In this way, in the discourse of character the discursive conventions of science and literature merge not only with each other but also with political concerns. One of the important reasons for characterizing race was to allow for scientifically based policy decisions. In this period, detecting and understanding racial character was inevitably a political activity. But determining how conventions for characterization in different turn-of-the-century genres met the challenge of mixed race and racial ambiguity—and thus made politically significant statements about racial character—first requires an understanding of the nature of racial science in this contentious period.

Neo-Lamarckian Culture-Evolution

Nineteenth-century commentators referred to the need to determine how black Americans could be included in political and social life as "the race problem." And since anthropologists and other social scientists commented on racial issues confidently while others expressed bewilderment, many saw the emerging natural sciences as a likely source for solutions to the so-named problem. Social scientists were confident in part because they took comfort in numbers and data in the face of the frightening complexity of racial issues. For example, the antebellum work of Dr. Samuel George Morton marks an early milestone in the statistical study of race in the United States and provided a foundation for what became known as the "American School" of physical anthropology. In *Crania Americana* (1839) Morton described the results of his measurements of the cranial capacity of skulls from a sampling of human races and populations. He claimed that if the skulls were ranked in descending order of brain size, Caucasian skulls could be placed at the top and the "Ethiopian" at the bottom; and since he assumed that brain size was a determinant of intelligence, his ranking was of the relative mental superiority and inferiority of the races represented in his study.[2]

This sort of statistical analysis of racial difference became even more prevalent in the later decades of the nineteenth century. As Stephen Jay Gould has noted, the fascination with and absolute faith in numbers was a defining feature of American anthropology.[3] Accordingly, in an article published in *Science* in August 1895, Daniel G. Brinton defined the science of anthropology in terms of its various "aims," chief among them the collection of statistical data. As he explained, the "first and indispensable aim of anthropologic science" is "collecting and storing . . . facts about man from all quarters of the world" (244). Not surprisingly, measurements of human physical characteristics relevant to making racial distinctions were of primary importance. According to Brinton, anthropologists desired "to know about a man, his weight and his measure, the shape of his head, the color of his skin and the curl of his hair. . . . [W]e would register all these facts in tables and columns, so that they should become perpetual records, to which we give the name 'vital statistics'" (244).

These statistics were given the status of fact and were assumed to be above argument. Demographic statistician Frederick Hoffman, at the start of his 1892 article "Vital Statistics of the Negro," explained the source of his faith in statistics: "A prominent writer has defined science as a knowledge and a classification of *facts,* and it is in the sense of this definition that I propose to present the so-called race problem" (529). It appears that the race problem, when studied scientifically, was merely a matter of collecting the right data. In 1896, Hoffman published the comprehensive results of his studies of the health, vitality, and moral conditions of freedmen in the South thirty years after emancipation. Titled *Race Traits and Tendencies of the American Negro,* it provided nearly three hundred pages of tables and text comparing the lung capacity and rates of respiratory, venereal, and other diseases for black and white populations. Hoffman concluded that since in each case the black groups were more unhealthy, his work gave "a most severe condemnation of modern attempts of superior races to lift inferior races to their own elevated position. . . . In the plain language of the facts brought together the colored race is shown to be on the downward grade, tending toward a condition in which matters will be worse than they are now" (312). Since Hoffman argued away the influence of environmental factors (such as crowded living conditions and diet), he was able to attribute his findings to African-American racial inferiority. The authority of the plain language of facts gave Hoffman the evidence he needed to conclude that the black race was degenerate and was rapidly becoming more so, despite emancipation and the policies of Reconstruction.

Vital statistics such as Hoffman's then usually made their way into the popular press as evidence marshaled in support of proposed solutions to the race problem. Professor John Straton of Mercer University in Macon, Georgia, made extensive use of statistics—including ones taken from Hoffman's book—in his essay "Will Education Solve the Race Problem?" In that article he defended the use of statistics directly: "Though the foregoing statistics, like all other statistics, are liable to the criticism of a lack of absolute finality as indicators of conditions and tendencies, still there must be some strong element of truth in them when they are so decisive; and judging from them, the educational work for the negroes does not seem to be realizing the expectations based upon it" (791). In this case, Straton confidently argues that his data suggest that a "hereditary factor" in the black race prevents education from having its usual beneficial effects; the policy implications for further investment in the education of African Americans are obvious. If the facts of science declare that education will not solve the race problem, why should southern states provide it?

Some commentators were even more explicit about the role the relatively new science of anthropology had to play in directing the management of race relations in the United States. In an essay titled "Science and the African Problem" published in the *Atlantic Monthly,* Nathaniel Southgate Shaler recommended that a learned "society" be founded to help students arrive at a "method of determining what shall be done at the outset of our effort to grapple with the difficulties which the presence of our African brethren has brought upon the state" (38). He suggested that the society should collect information in three main areas: "first, the history of the negro race; second, the present condition of the race from the point of view of anthropology . . . ; and, third, the social and civic quality of the race both in itself and in relation to the white people" (38). Clearly, the anthropological assessment of the condition of the race would make possible the determination of what civic quality the race possesses. In another example, Le Conte warned that "there really seems, in this country at least, to be serious danger of retrogression in politics unless we understand the principles of sociology and try to apply them to the art of government" (353). Though Le Conte evoked the authority of sociology, he made it clear that he was interested in "discussion of political and social questions from a scientific and especially an evolution[ary] point of view" (353).

As Le Conte's reference to evolution suggests, by the last decades of the nineteenth century evolutionary thought had become integral to anthropological and scientific understandings of racial difference. The social policy question of what relation the races should take to each other was driven by scientific understandings of the supposedly natural racial hierarchy that had formed during the course of human evolution. Previously, in the early part of the century, questions about how to arrange the taxonomy of races were tied up with the issue of whether the races were created by acts of separate creation. Morton, for example, had argued that the sizes of his different skulls suggested that the human races had no common ancestry, and had been created separately. This argument became known as "polygenism," in contrast to "monogenism," which hypothesized that the races had somehow differentiated after a common origin. Respected Harvard biologist and paleontologist Louis Agassiz defended Morton's polygenism, and as a result it had become the dominant biological theory of racial difference by the 1860s.[4] Another key defender of the polygenist argument was Josiah Nott, a southern physician who popularized the theory with a series of articles in the regional press and with the publication of *The Types of Mankind* (1854), which he wrote in collaboration with G. R. Gliddon.

The polygenist argument was widely accepted in part because it accorded with what Herbert Hovenkamp calls the "traditional" position on race, one that had long been part of Western thought. By this traditional account, the races were distinguished by characteristics that were innate and permanent. In order for races to have had common ancestors, as the monogenist argument claimed, races would have to be in some way mutable. In contrast, the traditional view of race held that biodiversity was created as is. As Hovenkamp puts it, traditionalists took the rule that "like begets like" as a theory of heredity; they argued that the "distinguishing features of each group were part of its permanent nature" (634). By this logic, racial characteristics were innate and unchanging, and their distinctiveness was arranged by the hand of God through the operation of the laws of nature. However, by the late 1860s and 1870s, scientific thinkers had almost completely abandoned the polygenist argument in favor of an evolutionary understanding of racial difference. As George Stocking explains, the monogenists had already "been forced into protoevolutionist speculations (occasionally even foreshadowing the mechanism of natural selection) in order to explain the increasingly evident reality of human diversity" (45). Therefore, once theories of evolution were adopted by scientific thinkers, a solid biological explanation existed for the progressive human development that had previously been hypothesized.[5]

Of course, the scientific turn to accept evolution was not accomplished without a fight, and the struggle over its theoretical validity is visible in the popular imagination and the popular press. Richard Hofstadter notes that from 1860 to 1870 attitudes toward evolutionary thinking expressed in the *North American Review* progressed from hostility to full acceptance. For example, in 1860 an anonymous reviewer of *The Origin of Species* "rejected Darwin's theory as 'fanciful,'" but in 1870 an article by Charles Loring Brace praised the inception of evolutionary thought as "one of the great intellectual events of the present century, influencing every department of investigation" (22). Yet despite the fact that evolutionary theory had won wide acceptance, it is important to note that it was not necessarily Darwinian evolution per se that was being applied. Most evolutionary thinkers, when discussing human evolution especially, did not use the mechanism for change that is central to Darwinian evolution. Darwin proposed that species change as mutation or natural variation results in "sports" whose differences are favorable to survival. These sports survive in greater numbers and eventually pass the variation on to the majority of the species. Since the appearance of such sports was given as more or less random, there was an element of chance in the process; an accidental variation could eventually become important to the species.

In contrast, the evolutionary thought that most appealed to the incipient social sciences in the United States employed a different mechanism for how the variations that would become traits were acquired and transmitted to future generations. The vast majority of scientific thinkers in the late nineteenth century believed evolution was a Lamarckian process—named for French biologist Jean Lamarck—whereby traits acquired during the individual life span could be passed on. By this theory, the individual organism strives to better itself, acquires a favorable trait, and then passes it on through heredity; under such a mechanism the individual willfully drives the forward motion of evolution. And as a consequence, anthropologists, with their focus on human evolution, were more concerned with forward-directed mental progress. As Charles Lofgren notes, "Until approximately the turn of the century, practitioners in the emerging disciplines commonly employed biological analogies which incorporated the teleological, progressive evolutionary viewpoint of Herbert Spencer, rather than the unpredictable development increasingly implied by biological Darwinism" (101). The evolution that most concerned commentators, both scientific and political, was the Spencerian evolution of the human race toward eventual perfection.

In fact, those who held to the Lamarckian mechanism in the late nineteenth century were a self-conscious and crusading group. As Stocking details, Darwin's natural selection had already been under attack for its lack of provision for racial progress in a directed and positive sense. And when August Weismann attacked the scientific validity of the inheritance of acquired characteristics in the 1880s, he galvanized a scientific debate that resulted in the detractors of natural selection and the defenders of Lamarck forming a school of neo-Lamarckianism. As a result, the last decade of the nineteenth century is marked by a particularly vigorous and dogmatic argument in defense of teleological evolution powered by the acquired trait.[6] These neo-Lamarckian scientists were attached to their theory most of all for what it allowed them to conclude about parallels between the cultural and physical evolution of the human race. As John Haller explains, with neo-Lamarckianism "both the physiological or purely biological structure of man and the aspects of his social life became part of the same cosmic development. . . . [E]xplanations of biological and social evolution became synonymous in meaning" (98). Evolution could work on culture as well as biology because each individual embodied that culture in his or her inheritance of the social behaviors, mental traits, and intellectual acuity acquired by one's ancestors. As Stocking puts it, "Lamarck's was fundamentally a theory of behavioral evolution,—or perhaps better, a behavioral theory of biological evolution" (238).

Thus, many scientists were convinced that the social behavior practiced by an individual during his or her lifetime was passed on to future generations as innate and inescapable biological features. And as that theory came under attack, scientists saw it as their duty to convince a larger audience. Not surprisingly, the best and most forceful examples of neo-Lamarckianism applied to human evolution appeared in the popular press. For example, Le Conte patiently explained to the layman that "one of the most important recent modifications of our philosophy of life, forced upon us by the theory of evolution, is the recognition of the fact that a very large part of every man's intellectual and moral capital comes by way of inheritance. . . . [T]he inherited bank account is continually growing from generation to generation by small additions from individual acquisition. The growing inheritance constitutes the evolution of the race" (366). Le Conte's chosen metaphor is apt for a Gilded Age audience presumably well acquainted with the way capital moves in the social environment, and it equates the evolution of the race neatly with the acquisitions of the individual.

As Lofgren explains, the logical consequence of the application of a Lamarckian mechanism to mental as well as physical evolution is the quantification of its effects into relative grades or levels: "Thus enamored of progressive neo-Lamarckian evolution, social scientists sought out stages. They typically conceived of different cultures and societies as occupying lower or higher places along a unilinear scale. Races received comparable positions, because of the association of 'race' with distinctive mental, linguistic, and cultural traits" (102). Though Lofgren's account is correct, it is important to note that he uses the term *culture* as we would now, not as it would have been used in the period. In the late nineteenth century, races received comparable positions not because cultures (plural) were ranked relative to each other, but because races were assumed to be in relative phases of development along a unified series of stages leading toward culture (singular). As Stocking argues, the word *culture* was not used in the plural until well into the twentieth century. For nineteenth-century social scientists, culture was Western civilization, and all other societies were on different rungs of the ladder that lead to the achievement of that singular civilization.

The theory of "culture-evolution"—whereby culture is the product of human evolution because humans have inherited more and more civilized cultural traits—is associated most directly in the United States with Lewis Henry Morgan, sometimes called the father of American anthropology. In *Ancient Society* (1877), Morgan delineated the many stages of culture-evolution and gave them names that today resonate rather ominously: "As it is undeniable that portions of the human family have existed in a state of savagery, other portions in a state of barbarism, and still other portions in a state of civilization, it seems equally so that these three distinct conditions are connected with each other in a natural as well as necessary sequence of progress" (32).[7] All human groups progress from savagery through barbarism, and then the "gradual evolution of their mental and moral powers" allows them to "[win] their way to civilization" (32). All three of these major phases are subdivided into lower, middle, and upper subphases. Morgan's divisions, and the work of others who shared his outlook, were received by Daniel Brinton as a revelation, a "discovery little less than marvelous, the most pregnant of all that anthropology has yet offered, not yet appreciated even by the learned" (243). As Brinton explains it, "this discovery is that of the psychical unity of man, the parallelism of his development everywhere and in all time" (243).

Though Brinton enthused about the unifying implications of this theory—that all human development is essentially the same—the racially divisive implications of neo-Lamarckianism and culture-evolution are clear. Since civilization was defined as the culture of western Europe, all non-whites and non-Europeans were in states of savagery or barbarism, or in lower grades of civilization. And in most instances where neo-Lamarckian culture-evolution arguments were evoked in the popular press, they were made to account for the evolutionary basis of African-American inferiority and for its intractability. As Nathaniel Shaler explained, "The negro is not as yet intellectually so far up in the scale of development as he appears to be; in him the great virtues of the superior race, though implanted, have not yet taken firm root, and are in need of constant tillage, lest the old savage weeds overcome the tender shoots of the new and unnatural culture. To those who believe that the negro is only a black white man, who only needs a fair chance to become all that the white man is, these pages are not addressed" (42). Since American social scientists generally accepted the evolutionary model of culture, the most important place to apply that model was to the relative position of African Americans. As Shaler illustrates, the traits of culture were assumed to be alien to the black race because they had not been acquired and passed on as part of the hereditary bank account.

In *The Crucible of Race*, Joel Williamson argues that the three main racial mentalities detectable in southern public discourse in this period can be distinguished from one another precisely in their approaches to the questions of racial inheritance posed by Shaler in the quotation above. Williamson demonstrates that the vast majority of individuals in the South would have agreed with Shaler's initial assertion of white superior development. Those with the "conservative" mind-set assumed black inferiority, and even if they did not use explicitly evolutionary vocabulary, they were nonetheless interested in making the social place of the black population reflect an intractable hierarchy. A small but vocal group of "liberal" thinkers opposed the conservative assumption of inferiority: "In the 1880s Liberalism felt that the capacity of Negroes to absorb white culture in America had not yet been fairly tested, and it refused to close them out brusquely and across the board somewhere far below the white man" (Williamson, *Crucible* 5). For these racial optimists Shaler clearly seeks to explain how difficult and protracted the process of cultural absorption and cultivation can be. In fact, his warnings about the dangerous "savage roots" are calculated to evoke fears of racial degeneration that define Williamson's last mind-set. Racial radicalists believed that the black race had made no real evolutionary progress as a result of contact with white culture and was actually rapidly regressing back to savagery now that the end of slavery had removed all temporarily "uplifting" contact.

In the abstract, the process of neo-Lamarckian culture-evolution would seem to guarantee that if blacks are placed in an environment which enables them to acquire desirable characteristics, they will pass these characteristics on to further generations and the race itself will evolve. Yet, as the evidence from the period demonstrates, few would concede this point. Hard-liners like Brinton felt that external conditions would have little effect:

> Some maintain strenuously that it is not ethnic or racial peculiarities, but solely external conditions . . . which are the factors of culture-evolution. While I admit that the question is still *sub judice*, I add that the position just stated seems to be erroneous. . . . I must still deny that all races are equally endowed—or that the position with reference to civilization which the various ethnic groups hold today is one merely of opportunity and externalities. (248)

Since, as Brinton argued, external conditions are not responsible for the success of a society's progress toward civilization, it would be illogical to conclude that a change in opportunity and externalities would result in further progress. And even when commentators admitted that evolution might take place, as Straton grudgingly did in the *North American Review* in 1900, such an end was going to be a long time coming, if at all:

> Are there not grounds, therefore, for thinking that the negroes are simply not able to take on this civilization in the true meaning of the term? Have they reached a state of development which demands or can support this

> higher status? . . . We must not confuse the rapid development of exceptional individuals with the evolution of a race. . . . [T]he evolution of a race comes slowly—a part of each new element of strength being transmitted by the laws of heredity from father to son and on to succeeding generations; and so, slowly and painfully, a race advances. (798)

Straton's allusion to the "true" meaning of civilization can only be understood in terms of culture-evolution, by which civilization is taken on as the result of neo-Lamarckian inheritance. And whether blacks can be afforded certain privileges of civilization—Straton's larger point—depends on whether cases of individual development can be shown to be racial and heritable on a much larger scale.

Measuring Cultural Progress

In the late nineteenth century, social scientists established that a racial hierarchy existed and demonstrated that progress along that hierarchy was the result of inheritance. However, as Straton's questions above suggest, the important issue for those interested in setting racial policy was whether true racial progress could be detected and substantiated. In Lewis Henry Morgan's formulation of culture-evolution, a society's relative place in the progress toward civilization was measured by looking at forms of subsistence technology, family organization, language, and other such markers. For example, according to Morgan, the middle phase of barbarism in the Western Hemisphere "commenced" with "cultivation by irrigation and with the use of adobe-brick and stone in architecture" (37). Thus, a society is best studied in its own native habitat, practicing its native arts.

However, the situation of African Americans in the United States was obviously more complicated. In the study of American blacks there was no recourse to native arts, since slavery had disrupted their practice irrevocably. In the United States, even prior to the resurgence of Lamarckian thought, the placement of African Americans relative to whites was often made on the basis of physical attributes rather than cultural ones. The attraction to physical measurements and vital statistics that flourished in the nineteenth century was conditioned by the prevailing conflation between grades of evolution and racial features.

For this reason, anthropological studies that focused more on details of physical appearance had always been designed to support the existence of a racial hierarchy and continued to be used as such even after the wide acceptance of the evolutionary science of culture.

Furthermore, any distinction between cultural and physical signs of racial status is essentially a false one; there never was a clear line drawn between physical evolution and mental evolution in the late nineteenth century, precisely because neo-Lamarckian thought posited that mental factors evolve in tandem with biological ones. Therefore, social scientists worked from the proposition that biological structures should show signs of progress analogous to the workings of culture-evolution. Just as human societies evolve toward cultural perfection, it was assumed that human bodies evolve toward physical perfection. And this equivalence in types of development quite often formed the logical basis for arguments designed to support or disprove the positions taken by racial radicals, conservatives, and liberals. For example, the radical regressionists' claim that the race was moving backward rather than forward could be demonstrated on the basis of physical degeneration or mental degeneration, but the two were usually argued in tandem. In *The Plantation Negro as a Freeman,* Bruce sought to lay before his audience the changes that emancipation had brought to the black population of the South. His conclusion: "Their character approximates . . . more closely to the original African type than the character of their fathers who were once slaves. This is due partially to the fact that the whole race is reverting to the original physical type, and therefore to the original moral [type]" (129).

Even those who did not wish to dismiss the potential for racial advance were constrained by the same conceptual vocabulary; they had to demonstrate a physical development that would suggest a mental one. For example, Shaler—in his discussion of how "modern anthropology" can shed light on the "African problem"—asserted that the study of the existing "mental and physical condition of the negro in this country" must be "based upon a careful application of anthropometry" (40). The science of anthropometry sought to create indices out of various measurements of the human body, such as limb lengths and proportions between body parts. Though Shaler wanted to look at the existing mental and physical condition of African Americans, it seems that physical anthropometry served as a foundation for the discussion of both. As he noted, "even a careful study of the crania . . . would give a beginning for the discussion" (40). A study of crania would serve to ground the discussion of both mental and physical conditions because the head allows for a conflation of the two phenomena, given that the brain is the physical site of mental processes. He reminded his audience of the real issue: "It should be remembered that the main problem with reference to the negro is as to his sensitiveness to influences which make for advance. Any evidence of real, deep seated organic advance under his American condition would be most welcome to all those who have his future and that of the state, which is a large part his, at heart" (41). Here it is clear that evidence of physical or organic advance would be taken as evidence of potential for advancement in a mental and a racial sense.

In another example, English commentator James Bryce claimed to have observed the physical advance to which Shaler alluded. Bryce cautioned his audience that "history and science tell us that social and moral advancement is an extremely slow progress, because it issues from a change in the physical as well as mental nature of a race" (643). However, when he contrasted his observations of the physical form of African Americans in 1891 with observations he made in a previous visit to the South, he argued that physical differences have arisen in American blacks, distinguishing them from African populations: "Compare the negroes even of the semi-tropical States with the negroes of the coast of Guinea or the lower Congo or Hayti, and the advancement is undeniable. Something may be ascribed to the difference of climate . . . but much is also due to the influence of the white people and, indirectly, to the spirit and tendency of American institutions" (643). Though Shaler and Bryce hold out a liberal hope—and question conservative and regressionist ideologies—their conclusions are no less logically suspect given that all groups shared a problematic conceptual framework. When placed together, the two men's arguments become tautological: Shaler argued that physical advance would prove that African Americans were capable of participation in American institutions, while Bryce argued that participation in American institutions had resulted in physical advance.

In a way, this tautology reflects the potential circularity of all evolutionary argument. As with the famous question of the chicken or the egg, it is hard to point to the prior cause in an evolutionary series. However, the logical confusion also results from the fact that social scientists in the nineteenth century never really made the causal lines of influence between mental and physical advance clear in their formulations. Even more important, there was much confusion over whether the physical traits could be said to be the *determinants* of the mental ones, or vice versa. Is mental superiority an effect of physical superiority, or are both simply the end results of parallel and somehow connected lines of evolution? Though that question was apparently never settled definitively, there is evidence that the determining effects of physical features were often insisted upon for blacks but not whites. As Lofgren explains, "Social scientists [did not] always [hold] that physical traits of races 'cause' non-physical traits"; he immediately adds, however, that "they most often asserted a causal connection between the physical and the non-physical in discussions of Negroes" (102).

The bottom line is that no matter how confused the cause-and-effect argument was—and no matter which social agenda it was marshaled in defense of—if mental and physical traits are linked then all signs of physical difference between whites and blacks can be used as evidence of mental and cultural difference. And in American letters physical difference is far more often taken to indicate mental inferiority. In Query VI of his *Notes on the State of Virginia,* Thomas Jefferson contradicts the Count de Buffon's characterization of the native inhabitants of the New World as "degenerate" on the basis of its lack of logical connection between mental and physical features.[8] Buffon asserts that the native American is nearly as large as the European, but deficient in mental and moral faculties. If, Jefferson asks, the elements and physical causes in the environment of the New World that would be expected to retard the native's physical development have somehow been suspended, "by what inconceivable process has their action been directed on his mind alone?" (926). Though this argument is staged in defense of one non-white racial group's capacities, Jefferson also uses the link between physical and moral natures to question the mental capacity of African Americans. Further into his discourse, Jefferson discusses at length the aesthetics of racial difference: "Is [color] not the foundation of a greater or less share of beauty in the two races? . . . Add to [this], flowing hair [and] a more elegant symmetry of form. . . . The circumstance of superior beauty, is thought worthy of attention in the propagation of our horses, dogs, and other domestic animals; why not that of man?" (933). Since blacks have not yet been the subject of the inquiries of natural history, Jefferson advances as "suspicion only" that blacks "are inferior to the whites in the endowments both of body and mind" (937). Given that it is logical folly to attempt to argue that the development of the two is distinct, Jefferson's rhetorical questions about physical and aesthetic differences of body imply that mental inferiority is easy to establish.

In the nineteenth century the discourse designed to establish white supremacy on an aesthetic basis was invigorated and refined by the development of evolutionary thought. Since Darwin had established the ape as a human ancestor, the location of "apish" physical characteristics in non-Europeans were often used to place such groups lower in the evolutionary hierarchy of races. It was commonly accepted that the profiles of humans, apes, and other mammals could be arranged by their relative amounts of "prognation" (the degree to which the jaw projects from the plane of the face) into a great evolutionary chain. The animal snout obviously showed the most prognation, while the human face showed the least. Since American anthropologist E. D. Cope had concluded in 1887 that "the Greek nose, with its elevated bridge, coincide[d] not only with aesthetic beauty, but with developmental perfection," all human populations could be ranked by their resemblance to Greek statuary (qtd. in Gould 116). Since the Anglo-Saxon face best matched the flat facial angles of Greek perfection, people of color were inferior because their faces were statistically "proven" to conform to angles less than perfect.[9]

Therefore, though it is not clear whether the face is the cause of mental achievement or simply an index to it, many nineteenth-century intellectuals believed that a race's worth could be read in the shape of the individual's face. And given that this belief was pervasive, physical descriptions of African Americans in the nineteenth century take on a heightened significance. Since facial and other physical characteristics were used to signal racial difference in scientific discourse, physical descriptions of African Americans in popular culture can implicitly carry scientific messages about the black race. I would argue that much physical description in the period was scientific, in that evolutionary understandings of race were contained within the language of physical description. If so, physical description was potentially political, since scientific understandings about race were used to justify political policy. Physical description could, in and of itself, stand as evidence for why certain social arrangements should not be attempted or for why certain social privileges should not be extended to black Americans. The scientific, the political, and the aesthetic all converge in passages of physical description.

The Problem of Mixed Race

Interestingly, the most powerful aspect of scientific racism—the use of physical difference to prove racial inferiority—was the least directly argued. The relationship between physical form and racial/cultural characteristics was never conclusively proven, but it was widely assumed. The indeterminable nature of this relationship was part and parcel of its power. Indeed, the way scientific racism approached the biracial individual provides the best example of how this fuzzy logic worked to its own advantage. Racial science was threatened by the physical presence of individuals who showed signs of both races in their physical makeup. The equation between outer and inner that was a cornerstone of white supremacy, and which was used to argue the absolute inferiority of African Americans, was unsettled by the mixing of physical signs of race. Specifically, those who would defend the relationship between light skin and racial superiority had to find a way to argue that though skin often gets lighter as a result of mixing, the qualities of the superior race do not necessarily follow. As a result, outer physical signs had to be relevant in the case of pure blood, but more or less irrelevant in the case of mixed blood. And the room to render physical signs irrelevant for those on the color line, if not for those on both sides of it, was provided for by theories of racial character.

Policy debates show that would-be racial theorists were interested in defining and assessing the mixed-race individual. Hovenkamp describes a legal brief submitted to the U.S. Supreme Court by the state of Kentucky in defense of a law that prohibited integrated schools. The brief asked the Court to take into account data about the deleterious effects of interracial breeding because such facts were "so notorious and universally known as to form a part of the common information of mankind" (631). The data cited was from an anthropometric scientist named Sanford Hunt who had supposedly demonstrated that the brains of mulattoes were smaller than those of both whites and blacks. Though Hovenkamp calls Hunt's study "esoteric," the suggestion that his conclusions were universally accepted and nearly self-evident was intended to put the data about mixed race past the pale of argument. Accounts of mixed race are nearly always stated with the utmost confidence and with appeals to common sense, as if race theorists hoped to persuade by the force or tone of their argument alone.

Yet the issue of mixed-race unions puts pressure on race theory, and discussions of mixed-race individuals are indirectly symptomatic of this pressure in their need to stifle the potential counter-arguments. For example, some contemporary scientists did recognize that crossbreeding could have positive results. Le Conte examined interbreeding at length, and since his theoretical framework for heredity was based on analogies to animal and plant husbandry, he had to extend that analogy to racial intermixture. As most crossbreeding produces stronger hybrids, Le Conte admitted that "there are valuable qualities in the lower races which ought not to be lost, which ought to be incorporated into the perfect ideal humanity for which we hope; and this can be done only, or at least most directly, by mixture" (374). However, Le Conte stopped short of endorsing interracial marriage; he argued that the mixture of radically different human types would not produce good results when the races were too dissimilar. Le Conte's argument found its echo in the popular press; E. W. Gilliam, writing for the *North American Review* in 1884, argued that "it is altogether probable that fusion between varieties of the same color is beneficial, but that fusion across the color line is lowering" (425).

The scientific consensus was that interracial products were inferior and to be avoided, though the arguments as to why this would be varied widely. In a forum on "The Future of the Negro" in the *North American Review* (also published in 1884), Charles Gardiner focused on the development of the brain and also cited Hunt's work.[10] Gardiner concluded that a "preponderance of white blood increases cerebral development, while the presence of one-quarter, one-eighth, or one-sixteenth produces a brain capacity decidedly inferior to that of the pure negro" (80). While Gardiner locates the deleterious effect in the brain, there were other scientific reasons why racial mixture would result in degeneration. For example, according to Joel Williamson, neurologists theorized that the electrical signals that control the functioning of the body and the nerves run in opposite directions in the white and black races. As a result, the products of mixed unions had confused signals and an inferior nervous system (*New People* 96).

As this scientific study filtered into the popular press, it merged with the prevailing understanding of mixed race, an understanding that had probably shaped the science in the first place. Williamson calls the popular understanding a "mythology of mulattoes" (*New People* 94). Within this mythology were pseudo-scientific assumptions that biracial individuals were physically weak and constitutionally frail, that they were flighty and effete, and that they could not reproduce beyond the third generation. The myth also assumed that given these weaknesses, the mixed-race population was in decline and would eventually disappear. Yet at the same time there were popular arguments that the mulatto's superior intelligence and cunning made him a super-predator, a brute who would attack and rape white women. As Mrs. L. H. Harris, resident of Rockmart, Georgia, argues in a May 1899 letter to the editor of the *Independent,* the black rapist is "almost always a mulatto . . . having at least enough white blood in him to replace native humility and cowardice with Caucasian audacity" (1354). The native black, according to Harris, is the cowardly, physically timid one, while mulatto criminality is the result of an inheritance of white assertiveness.

Whatever the source of these assumptions, they are clear opposites. Since the biracial individual was both lacking in sexual power and brutally sexually aggressive, it seems logical to conclude that he or she was a site for radical speculation provoked by uncomfortable mystification. As Williamson argues, the "myth of the mulatto demise" was a necessary comfort to an American society that found the presence of biracial individuals troubling. In the South especially, the end of the slave/free binary meant that much more pressure fell upon the black/white distinction. The mixed-race individual was a challenge to maintaining that distinction and to the scientific theories and myths that would require it to be maintained. As a result, the fact of mixed race was a source of anxiety, an example of how permeable the boundary was between races and of how often the white race had crossed it. Since healthy biracial individuals from families with many generations were rebukes to theories of racial mixing, there had to be the counterbalancing myth that the mulatto was weak and infertile. Or if those of mixed race were made the source of sex crimes in the South, it could better be argued that race mixing was the result of black sexual aggression rather than of white sexual abuses.[11]

Often at the center of these anxieties was the case of the mixed-race individual so light-skinned that the assumed physical signs of race were largely absent. Such people were rather literally on the color line, as they could be considered white or black depending on what side of a state line they found themselves. By the time Reconstruction had ended, most states had defined legally which people were to be considered black. While Delaware and Louisiana did not specify directly, seven states declared that any black heritage made one black, and seven states put the limit at one-eighth. As Williamson explains, despite the fact that the one-eighth rule was fairly liberal—it allowed some people to be legally white regardless of how they looked or what social worlds they inhabited—it was also largely irrelevant. The *de facto* situation in all southern states (except Louisiana, where social definitions of blackness were more fluid) was that a single "drop" of black blood was enough to make one black. If such a drop were known to a community, an individual was black, no matter how light-skinned.[12] In this extreme case, the exterior body was often in complete contrast to social positioning. Thus, the one-drop rule put tremendous pressure on racial scientists' attempts to equate mental and physical characteristics. Since it was not generally assumed that these white-black people were the inheritors of white cultural traits, the equivalence between form and inherited culture had to be completely abandoned. Clearly, such a radical disjunction between the physical and the mental was troubling to the theory of culture-evolution insofar as it assumed a parallel evolution of the two.

Accordingly, the disjunction between the body and racial aptitude presented itself as a place where racial theory could be challenged. Some commentators argued that the body was irrelevant and that humanity was uniform. As Oliver Johnson declared in the *North American Review*, the African American's "humanity, in spite of the accidents of birth, climate, and complexion, is identical to that of his whitest neighbor. He is endowed with all the natural elements, whether intellectual or moral, of a true manhood, and capable of the highest achievements in scholarship, culture, and refinement" (94). Johnson implicitly rejects the premises of scientific racism, denying that the aptitude for cultural development is an inherited trait and suggesting that the physical appearance of black people is but an accident of birth. Often such arguments discounting the importance of the physical signs of race were made by those on the color line; Charles Chesnutt—a white-skinned black man himself—enthusiastically stated in an article printed in 1900 that "recent scientific research has swept away many hoary anthropological fallacies . . . even color, upon which the social structure of the United States is so largely based, has been proved no test of race" (96). As both men argued, the fallacies of anthropology could be revealed and cast away once the emphasis on the body and the physical differences between races was dismissed and skin color was declared useless as a form of racial identification.

Thus it appears that when scientific racism was repudiated it was done alongside of, and perhaps in consequence of, liberating gestures dismissing the hegemony of skin color and the physical signs of race. Scientific racists, however, had an answer for the argued irrelevance of the body; they themselves were capable of pulling away from the physical basis of race in order to emphasize the mental. Specifically, racists indulged in a compensatory reification of the nonvisual implications of culture-evolution even while they insisted on the infallible visibility of race. For example, in an article published in *The Arena* in 1890, U.S. Senator John T. Morgan discounted skin but placed emphasis on the other inheritances of race:

> The social and political questions connected with the African race in the United States all relate to and depend upon the essential differences between the negro and the white man as they have been arranged by the hand of the Creator. Amongst these differences, the color of his skin, while it distinguishes the races unmistakably, is the least important. The mental differences and differing traits, including the faculty of governing, forecast, enterprise, and the wide field of achievement in the arts and sciences, are acutely measured by the contrast of the civilization of the United States, with the barbarism of Central Africa. (386–87)

Morgan, in his scientific account of race, was more ready to jettison the importance of physical difference, and thereby discount the idea of a correspondence between body and culture, than to suggest the irrelevance of racial difference in a larger sense. Though Morgan claimed that skin is an unmistakable racial marker, mental differences were given place of prominence as the key indicators of the essential differences between the races.

Racial scientists had all along been most interested in how the races differed in terms of cultural behavior—differences often referred to as racial temperament or racial character. The attempt to find anthropometric indexes for race had been important, since such indexes would offer the possibility for defining race numerically and would allow for the absolute determination of race that the color line required. Yet, according to Thomas Gossett, defining racial difference statistically had never been the real and ultimate scientific aim: "There was a fundamental fallacy behind this whole vast nineteenth-century search for methods to measure race differences. Many a racist awaited breathlessly some scheme of race classification which would withstand the testing methods of science and was prepared—once such a method was found—to pile mountains of *ad hoc* theory concerning the character and temperament of the races onto any discoveries concerning their measurable physical differences" (82–83). Scientists were frustrated that no clear mathematical/numerical formula for quantifying race difference could be produced. However, the scientific determination of the parameters of racial difference was merely the scaffolding on which the really important information—how the races differ behaviorally and thus culturally—could be hung. And ironically, while the scaffolding was subjected to the rigorous testing of statistical accuracy, the assumptions about racial character were unscientifically taken as givens.

As a result, the discussion of racial character could continue even without a firm basis in physical differences. In fact, Le Conte explicitly provided a scientific justification for the irrelevance of the body in discussions of race by replacing *form* with *character:* "Human evolution is spiritual, not bodily. Organic evolution is the change of form and making of new species, in order to come into harmony with an ever-changing environment. Man, on the other hand, changes the environment so as to bring it into harmony with himself and his wants; and, therefore, his evolution is not by change of *form* or making of new species of man, but by change of *character* and elevation of the plane of his activity" (371). Form is not of chief importance because the organic and the physical are irrelevant in the face of the importance of inherited traits of behavior. And the term used to stand for all of the invisible, nonphysical inheritances of race was *character.*

Thinking about race in the late nineteenth century had swung around on the question of skin color from Jefferson's insinuation that differences in skin color alone were enough to demonstrate that races were distinct, differently endowed, and in need of clearly defined lines of breeding. Perhaps the strongest demonstration of how much the semiotics of skin had changed comes from Bruce's discussion of how the moral character of the black man is best to be determined:

> Whoever seeks to judge the moral character of the negro . . . is very apt to be misled by the notion that he is merely a white man in disposition whom the Creator has endowed with a black skin. Plainly as his complexion distinguishes him from the whites, to the eye, it will be discovered . . . to be one of the smallest points of difference between him and the Anglo-Saxon. Remove all trace of that color with which Nature has painted his rugged countenance, wash away every stain that darkens it, and the moral traits that seem to be peculiar to his race would cause him still to occupy an original and unique position. (139)

Where the impact that color and physical difference had been for Jefferson a force of argument, for Bruce the impact that race makes on the eye is misleading and to some extent irrelevant. Rather than seeing black skin as the sign of related mental deficiencies, Bruce sees the African American as a racial deficient no matter what color he is painted—even with white skin, his racial character would not change.

All of the previous examples, whether from scientific or popular discourse, show a remarkable flexibility. The neo-Lamarckian evolutionary process, combining Darwin's biology with Spencer's sociology, allowed scientists to focus on either mental or physical evolution and to dissociate the two if necessary. The argumentative fuzziness in the causal connections between physical and mental evolution was absolutely necessary and, ironically, allowed scientific racism to remain logically coherent. When faced with paradoxes of the visibility of race, race theorists could switch their focus from body to character and make character the operative term for race. As a result, the answer to the political question of what social position the black race was to take in post-Reconstruction America could be predicated on any number of grounds. For some the body was a sign of black racial inferiority, while for others it was the more or less inconsequential vehicle for racial character—a character that needed to be read for its evolutionary implications. Addressing the race problem required one to read messages from a body that could take a number of different causal or determining relationships with racial character.

The Concept of Character

Character, then, became the bottom line in nineteenth-century arguments about race, as the frequent references to racial temperament or racial character illustrate. As such, the term *character* had an important explanatory power. As George Stocking demonstrates, it was used in all the places where we would use the term *culture* today. Since *culture* was a singular term, the phrase that was used to refer to the manifold differences in the forms of social behavior was simply *racial character.* Herbert Spencer, the most influential culture-evolutionist of the period, explained cultural difference as follows: "It needs only to contrast national characters to see that mental peculiarities caused by habit become hereditary. We know that there are warlike, peaceful, nomadic, maritime, hunting, commercial races—races that are independent or slavish, active or slothful" (qtd. in Stocking 240). As Spencer argued, culture-evolutionists believed they could observe racial differences by examining differences in what they called national character. The terms *nation* and *race* thus blur into each other, since any population that was assumed to have inherited the same characteristic behavior was eligible to be called a race in a biological sense. In Spencer's day, race was less a matter of shared physical characteristics than one of shared mental peculiarities. And these peculiarities apparently could be characterized by a descriptive word or two that captured the essence of that nation's character.[13]

Accordingly, the science of anthropology—the science of human difference—was interested in characterizing character. In "The Aims of Anthropology," Daniel Brinton echoed Spencer's language nearly exactly when he argued that "there is in some stocks and some smaller ethnic groups a peculiar mental temperament which has become hereditary and general." He went on to declare that the "patient and thorough investigation of these peculiarities is, therefore, one of the most apposite aims of modern ethnology" (249). The existence of innate mental temperaments, according to Brinton, means that "in this sense we can speak of the *Volksgeist* and *Völkergedanken*, a racial mind, or the temperament of a people, with as much propriety and accuracy as we can of any of the physical traits which distinguish it from other peoples or races" (249). Given that racial character is as distinct a phenomenon as physical difference, anthropologists were interested in developing the means to identify and quantify differences in character. Brinton trumpeted the importance of a field of investigation to which his German contemporaries had given the name "characterology": a science devoted to the concept of character and to the development of techniques to read and quantify it (249).

The manipulation of the notion of character was perhaps anthropology's most expansive impact on social policy. As Brinton explained, characterology is the "branch of anthropology . . . which offers a positive basis for legislation, politics and education, as applied to a given ethnic group" (249). The study of character offers a scientific basis rather than a philosophical one for the direction of legislation: "These peculiarities [of character], as ascertained by objective investigation, supply the only sure foundation for legislation; not *a priori* notions of the rights of man, nor abstract theories of what should constitute a perfect state, as was the fashion with older philosophies" (249). And as Brinton had already noted, some races have characters "of a nature to disqualify them for the atmosphere of modern enlightenment" (249). The new evolutionary and hereditary understanding of civilization allows for Enlightenment notions of government to be replaced by anthropological understandings of which people have the character to be allowed to participate in enlightened government and which do not.

Accordingly, discussions of African Americans and the American political situation in the popular press often evoked character along with other scientific assumptions about national and racial character. Nathaniel Shaler notes that "English, Irish, French, Germans, and Italians . . . [may] mingle their blood and their motives in a common race, which may be as strong, or even stronger, for the blending of their diversities" (37). Thus the European nations are given the status of races, which can combine blood and national characters to create a European super-race. But Shaler does not believe that the mixture of black and white will be as viable, since the individual who results from such a cross "has not the vital energy and the character required for the uses of the state" (37).

Accordingly, those who would defend the rights of African Americans to be active participants in the workings of the state were required to enter into discussions of the temperaments of the races of Europe and the extent to which black character was deficient in comparison. In the *North American Review,* Richard T. Greener characterized both Europeans and African Americans:

> Intemperance, a low standard of morality, an emotional rather than a reflective system of religious ethics, a partial divorce of creed and conduct, and a tendency (by no means confined to negroes) of superficial learning and of the less desirable elements of *character,* fitness, or brain, to force their way to the front, are evils which every honest negro must deplore, while sadly admitting their existence. But he who draws from these facts a wholesale inference derogatory to the entire race had better obliterate the histories of France, England, Germany, and Russia, or eliminate from their pages the scandals of social life, the vicious priesthoods, the bribery and corruption in high places, the venality, immorality, and degradation which have *characterized* these more favored races at various stages of their development. (93, emphasis added)

Here Greener balanced his description of African Americans, including a tendency toward the less desirable elements of character, against his description of the races of Europe. The discussion was thus placed on the level of character, national and racial. In order to mitigate the impact of the assumed tendency of blacks to demonstrate lesser fitness or character, Greener had to remind his audience that the white "races" have exhibited and been characterized by the same traits.

It should be noted that in the above examples it sounds as if commentators often conflated the general notion of racial character, as in the inherited mental peculiarities of a race, with character in the individual sense of having a "strong" or "good" character. The former would seem to be an innate tendency, while the latter is assumed to be at least in part the result of a conscious effort to be moral and ethical. The strength of one's character was an obsession of the nineteenth century, and I would argue that racial character and individual character were largely overlapping categories. It seems reasonable to expect that questions of personal character would blur into questions of racial character in a neo-Lamarckian intellectual setting; if traits of the individual are inherited, then personal character could itself become racial.

For example, it was widely assumed that blacks were of low character and, therefore, that the racial character of blacks was correspondingly lacking. In an essay titled "The Race Problem" (1890), U.S. Senator Wade Hampton of South Carolina began his discussion with the "pregnant fact" that "the white and black races are essentially different, not only in physical organization but in mental characteristics" (133). Hampton then noted that this observation was not intended to apply to "those of the race in this country . . . who have proved their capacity to be numbered among our reputable, estimable, citizens. There are many of our native born blacks who profess high characters and great ability, men who deserve all praise" (133). Yet Hampton pulled back from this optimistic note and asserted that these black men of good character are "the exceptions which prove the rule, which, from time immemorial, has shown that they are incapable of self-government" (133). The demonstration of high character by some black individuals is enough to exclude them from the general characterization of the race as incapable of self-government. Even though the exhibition of personal character is given as an example of an exception to racial character, the important point is that the two forms of character are implicitly related to one another.

The blurring of individual and racial character in scientific discourse is visible first of all on the level of vocabulary and illustration. As noted before, Le Conte explained the notion of a racial inheritance through the use of a metaphor drawn from the movements of capital and commerce. He suggested that each person is born with a certain amount of "moral capital" which is his or her share of the inherited bank account of racial character. Furthermore, when the acquisitions of the individual are deposited to this same account, racial character evolves. Significantly, in the same article Le Conte illustrated *personal* strength of character using the same metaphor he used for racial character. In his discussion of whether African Americans are worthy of the ballot, he suggested that a test of education and property be devised to keep all uncultured individuals, both white and black, from voting. He explains that "in uncultured men generally, and especially in lower races, there is no better, I might almost say there is no other, evidence of character necessary for the exercise of the ballot than the steady industry necessary to accumulate property. Mere book education, on the contrary, though easily acquired by the Negro on account of his quick apprehensiveness, has little effect on character, and is but a small guarantee for self-governing capacity" (377). The very best evidence for the development of character is the acquisition of money and its investment in property. It appears that while the race builds its character by saving into metaphorical accounts, the individual demonstrates character by saving into actual accounts. Put bluntly, personal character, acquired through the acquirement of capital, became capital itself.

Le Conte's choice of the economic metaphor was conditioned by a larger, societal conflation of the economics of racial and personal character. Richard Hofstadter has demonstrated that part of the appeal of Spencerian evolution—and the competition between races theorized under the rubric of social Darwinism—was based on an appeal to "a kind of naturalistic Calvinism" (10). He explains that in the prevailing late-nineteenth-century economic ethic, hard work and hard saving were nearly moral necessities, while leisure and waste were signs of moral laxity. Hofstadter mentions William Graham Sumner as a proponent of this social Darwinist economic ethic, claiming that Sumner "expressed an inherited conception of economic life . . . under which economic activity was considered as a field for the development and encouragement of personal character. Economic life was construed as a set of arrangements that offered inducements to men of good character, while it punished those who were, in Sumner's words, 'negligent, shiftless, inefficient, silly, and imprudent' " (10–11). Though Hofstadter means to suggest that Sumner inherited this ethic from Calvinism, it would be quite appropriate to stress the importance of inheritance for this economic formulation. Personal character is added to the stock of racial capital. Literal capital becomes metaphorical capital as it passes through the framework of neo-Lamarckian thought.

The shared economic metaphor of capital is only one of the ways in which character becomes racialized in nineteenth-century discourse. In 1899, Orison Swett Marden published a short book titled *Character: The Grandest Thing in the World* in which he attempted to "name certain deep-rooted dispositions which are essential in the mental make-up" of those who would seek to achieve greatness of character (7). In his rambling discourses on character, Marden evoked the same language as Le Conte, using economic metaphors to describe the value of character. He asked his audience, "What is character but the poor man's capital? Is not character an available piece of property? Is it not estimated as moral security, the noblest of possessions?" (33–34). In consequence, he also reckoned the value of character far above that of money or property, suggesting that character has a far nobler purpose in its long-term effects on civilization: "Who would not prefer to be a millionaire of character . . . ? Whoever uplifts civilization is rich though he die penniless; and future generations will erect his monument" (39).

In this and other examples it is possible to argue that Marden merely linked character to civilization, and thus to race progress, in a loose and unevolutionary sense. However, Marden also transformed personal character into racial character in more recognizably evolutionary language. Specifically, he claimed that the man of exceptional character, who is "head and shoulders above his fellow-men," in effect shows that "Nature has not lost her ideal of great-heartedness, and after a while even the average man will over top the highest wave of noble manhood yet given to the world" (15). Forward progress in the level of character exhibited by the average man is here made a sign that the future man will have even greater character and that character is both a factor in and a result of the evolution of the human race toward perfection.

In this treatise on character, Marden paid considerable attention to the mutable and plastic nature of character. He devoted himself to the premise that every individual has the power to strengthen and shape his or her own character. Yet, though character can be built, there is also the suggestion that it is an inheritance: "Every one, however humble, is daily and hourly altering and molding the character of all with whom he mingles, and exerting a power that will reproduce itself through countless generations" (48). Though the mechanism for the transmission of character is not explicitly Lamarckian, character is given as something that is both acquired and enduring. In effect, since Marden dedicates his book to the prospect of progress, he cannot help but be influenced by the evolutionary thought of the period. When he explains that "the main business of life is not to do, but to become" and that "action itself has its finest and most enduring fruit in character," his doctrine of "becoming" seems to be a clear consequence of the shift from a static picture of human nature to a dynamic one.

Another example of the popular discourse of character is D. Starke's self-help book *Character: How to Strengthen It.* Starke used more obviously evolutionary language and concepts, with much more direct racializing implications. His book was an edition of Funk and Wagnalls's "Mental Efficiency Series," and like Marden, Starke was giving guidance to people interested in building character. However, Starke defined character much more concisely than Marden, calling it "the resultant of a complex effort to exert the will directed upon a single point—the mastery of the self" (15). And, in this quest for self-mastery, Starke claimed that "the obstacles we meet with are nothing less than our lower instincts" (15). He meant by this that the strengthening of character reflects the movement of the individual beyond those instincts that govern the behavior of those who are not as evolved: "People weak of character yield readily to the solicitation of the moment. . . . They have not learned to make a distinction between the race-instinct and the emotions whose principle rests in the attaining of a higher evolution" (61). Growth of character is analogous to, and evidence for, the evolution of the human race.

The question of which race is superior could thus be settled on the basis of character. Since the white race was assumed to have achieved greater self-mastery and to have produced more individuals of exceptional character, its supremacy was clear. And since the black race was assumed to be ruled by the lower instincts and generally speaking less possessed of high character, its inferiority was also clear. In this respect, the surface of the body counted for very little. As Straton argued, the surface was no longer the place on which to discuss issues of race: "Are there not ethnological tendencies that lie deeper than all of our surface discussions? We have given the negro Latin and Greek and looking glasses and steam engines, and have observed as a result a seeming advance; but below the surface it appears there has been going on this ethical and even physical decay" (797). The problem becomes how to chart and measure the racial decay or inferiority that does not manifest itself on the surface. Put another way, how can one tell when a race or individual exhibits the kind of advance in character that should be taken note of by those who have power over social arrangements? L. H. Harris notes in her letter to the editor that African Americans "can in the quaintest dialect imitate the highest ideals of character; but the negro never confounds his ideals with the humdrum of existence" (1354). Character is the bottom line in discussions of race, but since character can be imitated, it is unclear how the concept can be used as a solid basis for racial policy.

Furthermore, the emphasis on character began to divorce the notion of racial character not only from the surface of individuals but from the assumed biological basis of race itself. As Williamson argues, "Blackness had not become a matter of visibility, not even, ironically, of the one-drop-rule. It had passed on to become a matter of inner morality and outward behavior. . . . [I]n sum, 'Negro' became an *idea*" (108). The separation of character from appearance led to problems of detection and to a need to reestablish a connection between inner and outer that would ensure reliable information about character. And it is in the discourses of character that we find this mechanism of reconnection.

Pseudo-Sciences of Character

The nineteenth century was not the only age interested in character. Individual character—a person's unique temperament and personality—had always been a locus for speculation about the differences between people and the nature of individuality. And, virtually since the inception of Western discourse, speculation about the extent to which character could be read from the physical details of the face and body has been the province of physiognomy. According to Gossett, the science has a long history, beginning perhaps with the treatise Aristotle composed on the subject. Physiognomy later became widely influential in Europe in the late eighteenth century when Johann Caspar Lavater published lavishly illustrated volumes of instruction so that people could read the signs of character in the facial features of their own acquaintances (Gossett 70–71).

As Carsten Zelle has argued, physiognomy has always filled "the need for a knowledge of people that confers superiority" (43). Physiognomy promised to make the invisible aspects of character visible and allow persons trained in physiognomic principles to make predictions about behavior that would allow them some edge. The potential of physiognomy, especially when granted the trappings of science, seems particularly far-reaching. As Ellis Shookman explains, the ability to read people and catalog their differences was a precondition for many of the nineteenth-century sciences that took the human body as a starting point. Specifically, Shookman notes that "Carl Gustav Carus with his craniology, and Alexander von Humboldt with his physical anthropology owed a great deal to Lavater" (5). Thus, Continental influences on American anthropologists at least partly contributed to their intense interest in reading race and the physical signs of race as essential markers of all human difference.

The problematic visibility of racial character is part and parcel of a larger concern in Western thought: the extent to which inner and outer can be said to exist in a causal or determining relationship and how this relationship can be used to some advantage by one who understands it. When race is aligned with character, and character with physiognomic correspondences between the face and body, the physical differences between races become the outer manifestations of inner differences in mental tendencies and levels of inherited ability. But the physiognomic premise behind the anthropology of the late nineteenth century was just as vulnerable to problems of the color line as other racial doctrines. The light-skinned black person who looks white is just as much of a sticking point for a racialized physiognomy as he or she was for physical anthropology. I have previously argued that the concept of character provided the means by which scientific racists could discount the importance of physical differences while holding fast to racial hierarchies. In similar fashion, the nineteenth-century modifications of physiognomy also provided a way to circumvent the problems of the unreliable surfaces of blackness.

Physiognomy was supplanted in popularity, especially in the United

States, by the newer pseudo-science of phrenology. Though phrenology built upon the premises of physiognomy, it provided a better and more subtle link between the outer and the inner. In short, phrenology was able to establish less tenuous lines of cause and effect between outer and inner, and gave direct access to the deep organs of character that are unaffected by the only sometimes visible surface signs of race. Phrenology is best defined as the systematic attempt to match sections of the brain, as mapped out on the surface of the skull, with characteristics of personality and intellect. As documented by a tract written by one of the fathers of American phrenology, Orson Fowler, the tenets of phrenology derive from the basic insight that the brain is the organ of the phenomena we describe as "mind," and from there follows a logical if somewhat specious chain of argument. Since humans can perform an almost unlimited number of tasks of mind at once (seeing, feeling, reasoning, speaking, etc.), phrenologists concluded that the brain must be comprised of a "plurality of innate and independent faculties."[14] Since physiological functions are generally the product of separate biological structures, the phrenologists concluded that each of these faculties of mind must correspond to separate sections of the brain, sections they called "organs." The size of these organs would then reflect the power and frequency of use of the corresponding faculties, phrenologists argued, since "other conditions being equal, *size* is always the measure of power" (Davies 179). And, they continued, if an organ in the brain is enlarged, the skull above it must be proportionately elevated. This last insight provided phrenology with its interpretive authority: "If we can ascertain what portions of the brain are employed by the various faculties, and also how much larger one portion is than another, we can also ascertain even the *minutiae* of a person's character and talents" (179).

Phrenology was originally the brainchild of German physician Franz Joseph Gall, who in the late eighteenth century arrived at the theory of cerebral location. As historian John D. Davies notes, though phrenology may have later come to resemble physiognomy in its popular applications, phrenology at its birth was a materialist reworking of physiognomy's fuzzy lines of causation. While Lavater's physiognomy was only metaphorical in outline—the appearance of the body and the features give symbolic expression to the character and disposition of the soul—Gall's theory of mind was less causally vague than the older science. As

Davies puts it, "Gall reversed the premises of physiognomy in a peculiarly materialistic fashion: character and intellect, he maintained, were simply the sum of the combined functions of the brain. Character *was* the brain" (7).

The shift from the face—the site for most physiognomic readings—to the skull and brain represented a gesture toward a more reliable way to read character. As Zelle argues, Lavater himself had wanted to make his "hermeneutics of character as reliable as possible" and for that reason had been interested in the firm parts of the body like the skull and skeleton (45). But the significance of the skull goes beyond its firmness; its status of being of the body and yet not mutable or subject to the modifications that affect other bodily parts made it a safe site for racial determinations. As Robyn Wiegman has argued in *American Anatomies,* the move from the exterior signs of race to interior ones—such as the brain—was no less an expression of the conviction that the body was incontrovertibly the expression of racial difference than were studies of skin color: "The move from the visible epidermal terrain to the articulation of the interior structure of human bodies thus extrapolated in both broader and more distinct terms the parameters of white supremacy, giving it a logic lodged fully in the body" (31).

And, as Wiegman also notes, the shift in the scientific discourse of race to the sometimes nonvisible, internal organs of race involved a shift in the techniques of observation: "While the visible must be understood as giving way to the authority of the invisible recesses of the body, to organs and functions, the full force of this production of racial discourse was nonetheless contingent on . . . newly developed techniques for rendering the invisible visible" (31). Thus Wiegman cites the invention of various calipers and craniometers that "overcame the limited specificity of the 'naked' eye" (32). The ability of scientific racism to document racial difference thus was coextensive with the technologies that made difference visible or allowed it to be represented in the statistical, numerical data that the calipers provided. In a very similar way, Lavater's physiognomy was historically contemporary with new techniques for representing the face, namely, the silhouette. Lavater himself invented a device that would make silhouettes as accurate as possible. As Brooks and Johnson suggest, Lavater wanted to "make observation more controlled and scientific by using a specifically invented piece of apparatus" (8). Just as Lavater sought to make his science more scientific by giving his attention to the hard surfaces of the body, he also sought to perfect the representation of facial individuality. In this respect, attention to character is apparently tied to the forms of observation and measurement that make data available and also to techniques for the representation of the body.

In Lavater's case especially, the examination of the human body for messages about character is inextricably connected to the arts. As many of the commentators on Lavater have noted, he was especially interested in artistic representations: "He recommended the study not only of living men and women, death masks and skulls, but also of paintings and busts of historical figures" (Brooks and Johnson 8). Lavater seemed to believe that even in cases when a painting or bust was not a good likeness, it could still contain the "essential and fundamental character" of the person represented. He also argued that even if the artist did not know what the person represented looked like, so long as he was acquainted with the subject's character, the resulting art would "necessarily bear a close relationship to the original" (8). As such, art was placed in a kind of mystical and rather inexplicable relationship to science. In the former example it appears that art can reveal character even if the physical details—the ones assumed to correspond to character—are wrong. Therefore, art has some mysterious ability to represent character that makes the physical details of appearance nearly if not completely irrelevant.

In nineteenth-century discourse there is a clear echo of this close relationship between art and character. Scientific discourse had been forced to shift from the surface of the body to racial character as the site for racial determinations. This move would seem to make the visual representation of race more or less impossible, since the invisible signs of character could not be depicted in an artistic medium that displayed only the outer and unreliable surface. However, once the language and concepts of the pseudo-sciences of character are incorporated into the discussion, character becomes both visible and representable. Written description can translate physical details into messages about character, making character—and implicitly racial character—visible once again.

For example, nineteenth-century phrenology, like Lavater's physiognomy, relied on portraits and on the character expressed within them.

The Fowler brothers—who ran a business providing physiognomic readings for a fee—published the *American Phrenological Journal* from 1838 to 1911. In its pages the brothers printed character sketches of prominent Americans from life or from their likenesses in sketches and photographs.[15] Significantly, a large number of these prominent Americans were writers; in the character sketches of novelists the features of the face, the qualities of character, and the qualities of prose representation are all entangled. For example, a discussion of Stephen Crane in the December 1900 issue declared:

> Stephen Crane had an excellent example of a large development of the organ of Hope. His forehead showed that the faculty is well represented, and his writings indicated the faculty of Hope along with large Spirituality and keen imagination. . . . Any one who has read Stephen Crane's remarkable imaginative work called "The Red Badge of Courage" will readily see that he could not have written the work without possessing in a marked degree that quality before mentioned. . . . [T]he power of analysis and discernment of character were noticeable features in his literary talent. (13)

The features of Crane's writing are just as much evidence of his character as is his forehead. In addition, his writing indicates that he has a certain "phrenological" talent in that he is able to discern character in his own representations. In this way, though fiction was not a new art or technology for representation, in the nineteenth century it was given particular status as a vehicle for character and as a means for its nonvisual expression.

Character and Literature

In the nineteenth century, American literature formed the basis for discussions of racial difference and of how various races should be characterized. Of course, it is not unusual for literature to function this way. The visual image—and all representation including the literary image—has been well established as a place where types are defined and perpetuated. Sander Gilman, in the context of his discussion of racial images in late-nineteenth-century art and medicine, has commented on the "essential iconographic nature of all visual representation" (205). Gilman claims that almost all artistic representations rely on the icon, or ideologically charged *representation,* rather than mimetic *presentation.* Accordingly, the iconographic nature of representation results in a situation where "the representation of individuals implies the creation of some greater class or classes to which the individual is seen to belong. These classes are in turn characterized by the use of a model which synthesizes our perception of the uniformity of the groups into a convincingly homogeneous image" (204). The representation of the individual is iconic because it implicitly seeks to establish the individual as representative of a type. Gilman also asserts that the conventions that govern artistic representation are the equivalent of an ideology in that they serve the purposes necessary for the typing and characterization of both individual and group.

During and after Reconstruction, popular literature and visual art were marked by ideologies of iconic representation. In his evaluation of images of African Americans, Henry Louis Gates, Jr., observes that popular visual representations were themselves part of the discourse that established black racial inferiority. Thus, Gates documents an awareness in the late-nineteenth-century black intellectual community that "the features of the race—its collective mouth shape and lip size, the shape of its head (which especially concerned phrenologists at the turn of the century), its black skin color, its kinky hair—had been caricatured and stereotyped so severely in popular American art that . . . nothing less than a full facelift and a complete break with the enslaved past could ameliorate the social conditions of the modern black person" (130). The conventions for popular representations of black features echoed the connections between facial characteristics and racial characteristics made by anthropologists and by the pseudo-sciences of character. Certain stereotyped features in caricature were clear signs of inferiority. In this respect, the physical representation of African Americans in fiction and elsewhere was seen as having a direct bearing on social conditions by way of its reflection and manipulation of popular conceptions of race.

Though Gates is interested in the representation of blacks in the era of Reconstruction, the interplay between popular representation and racial attitudes in American literature dates back to well before the

Civil War. In fact, literary debates in American fiction have occasionally hinged upon the question of racial representation. In her study of race in American fiction up to 1867, Dana Nelson notes that frontier novelists—James Fenimore Cooper, William Simms, and Robert Montgomery Bird—used race as a touchstone in their discussions of the relative merits of realism and romance. In his 1831 introduction to *The Last of the Mohicans,* Cooper promised a realistic account of Native Americans while he also asserted his intent to give a "poetic" depiction of North American life. Similarly, Bird's introduction to *The Yemassee* seeks to establish the "American romance" as a national style superior to British fiction while also offering a correction to what he saw as the unrealistic and "vulgar" depictions of "red men" in other fiction. As such, the debate over genre and style coheres around the question of the proper characterization of race. And as Nelson remarks, while each author sought to give romantic accounts of their white characters, they reserved "realism" for their non-white characters and thus used styles of characterization to emphasize racial difference.[16]

The literary situation in the South in the early decades of the nineteenth century shows some important similarities. As James Kinney has argued, the beginnings of a literature in the antebellum South that addressed race were coextensive with the need to draw a distinction between white and black in order to defend slavery. Before 1824 very little novel-length fiction was written in the South, and none of it included African-American characters. Then, with either George Tucker's *The Valley of the Shenandoah* (1824) or John Pendleton Kennedy's *Swallow Barn* (1832), the "plantation tradition" in southern fiction began. The novels which represent this tradition are set, predictably enough, on southern plantations. The mode of these novels, often called "plantation romances," was largely pastoral as they romanticized and idealized the plantation lifestyle. And the defense of the plantation lifestyle clearly was intended to be a defense of the system of slavery upon which it was based.[17]

As the attacks on slavery began to mount in the 1830s—the first issue of William Lloyd Garrison's *Liberator* was published in 1831—the plantation novels helped to articulate the southern defense of slavery. That defense was based in large part on the ideological manipulation of characterization. Specifically, plantation fiction was structured around a binary: the contrast between the southern gentleman, often called the southern Cavalier, and the blacks under his command. As historian Lawrence Friedman has explained, southern society was encapsulated "in the person of the generous and cultivated cavalier gentleman planter. Boasting an ancestry traceable to the most exclusive English stock, holding large estates, and enjoying a seemingly carefree and easy-going life style, the Cavalier stood for a refined, contented agrarian South" (57).[18] Along with the Cavalier, a cast of black slaves was described in terms designed to heighten the difference between his physical perfection and their physical asymmetry. As Catherine Starke has demonstrated, the physical description of black slaves in Cavalier fiction often was written with a "comic intensity" that moved it toward caricature (31). The Cavalier's physical graces were due to his superior stock and marked him as noble and good, while black features were given as signs of the mental, moral, and racial inferiority that supposedly justified enslavement.

Antebellum southern literature relied on casting black characters into stock patterns—the passive slave, the buffoon, the brute—because the whole southern system that literature defended rested upon a theory of characterization. For example, the debate in the last years of the war over whether the South should allow blacks to be soldiers was implicitly staged on the premise of racial character. Specifically, Georgia Governor Joseph E. Brown declared that "Whenever we establish the fact that [blacks] are a military people, we destroy our theory that they are unfit to be free" (qtd. in Friedman 14). The thought that blacks could be called a military race threatened the theory behind slavery. Implicitly, that theory involved the characterization of blacks as a race incapable of the strength of character that soldiers must possess. Accordingly, General Howell Cobb declared that "If slaves will make good soldiers, our whole theory of slavery is wrong—but they won't make good soldiers" (qtd. in Friedman 14). As such, the general's comments reveal a conscious effort to determine characterization in order to protect slavery.

Just as the potential for characterizations that would undermine slavery's theory of character was controlled, literary and popular characterizations were tailored to fit the South's idea of black character. For example, southern newspapers often printed accounts during the war of slaves who refused to leave their masters even when offered freedom. According to Friedman, during the war it apparently served the purposes of the South to engage in "characterizing blacks as a loyal and obedient race" (4). However, he notes that these accounts of "docility" were misleading and suggests that these characterizations were designed to assuage a sense of moral guilt among slave owners. Even more, such characterizations were designed to define "acceptable norms for Negro behavior" (5). Friedman concludes that "though Southerners frequently characterized their slaves as servile and loving, their characterizations must not always be accepted at face value. . . . Often [they] merely underlined the Southerner's desire for Negro docility" (5–6). Characterizations thus betray southern conceptions of the racial character that would best suit their social organization. Southern fiction was designed to present black racial character through the medium of fictional and popular characterization in ways that conformed to the logic of southern social institutions. As a result, southern fiction was drawn in bold strokes and was given to strategies of juxtaposition.

However, there was another current in antebellum fiction that was not designed to support the same set of southern mythologies. Specifically, in the antebellum decades the "tragic mulatto" or "tragic octoroon" genre contested the plantation romance's representation of slavery. In this genre, the heroes and heroines were not southern Cavaliers but rather mixed-race individuals, often slaves. And in direct contrast to the plantation tradition, the tragic mulatto novel nearly always contained at least a partial critique of the institutions of slavery. The genre's protagonists are the stunningly attractive light-skinned children of miscegenistic affairs. As such, the genre was well positioned to expose the horrors both of enforced concubinage (usually set in the brothels and boudoirs of New Orleans) and of the situations created when white men are the owners of their own children. Tragic mulatto fiction also usually subjects its heroes and heroines to dramatic reversals in fortune. Often they are sold into slavery when a kindly white father dies suddenly; sometimes they are not even aware that they have black ancestry. These protagonists face threats to their dignity and morality and are often faced with difficulties of the heart when white lovers must be told of their racial "stain."[19]

Interestingly, although tragic mulatto fiction was often written by abolitionists—for example, Richard Hildreth's *The Slave; or Memoirs of*

Archy Moore (1836)—it did not radically revise the conventions for characterization common to the plantation tradition.[20] The mode of characterization and physical description that dominated the plantation tradition follows the logic of *kalokagathy*, the ancient belief that beauty is good and ugliness is evil. Obviously, the physical contrast between owner and slave serves to support the former's moral right to rule over the latter. Similarly, in tragic mulatto fiction the physical beauty of the protagonist—often elaborated upon in lavish terms for pages at a time—is designed to have the same symbolic effect. The tragic mulatto is good because he or she is beautiful.

It appears that while the justification for slavery in plantation fiction was based on physiognomic grounds, abolitionists simply sought to attach positive connotations to the outer appearances of black individuals rather than reject the logic whereby outer is connected to inner. Much as Gates suggests above, there was a contemporary conviction that the features of African Americans had to be revalued, given that they had been so successfully associated with negative traits of character. For example, the black press sought to establish black faces within the logic of kalokagathy by defining black beauty and then equating it with morality and worth of character. In a fascinating article titled "Rough Sketches: A Study of the Features of the New Negro Woman," published in *The Voice of the Negro* in 1904 (and cited by Gates in his analysis), John H. Adams makes an effort to establish the links between sketches of black female faces and positive moral qualities. Adams introduces the sketches with the claim that they "represent the colored woman today as she impresses herself in the world as a growing factor for good and in her beauty, intelligence and character for better social recognition" (325). Adams suggests that the social recognition of the character of black women is a logical consequence of, if not identical to, the recognition of their physical beauty.

In effect, Adams adopts the same characterizing strategy as the tragic mulatto genre. In that genre, the protagonists are beautiful, and as the reader is forced to acknowledge it, he or she is also forced to acknowledge the goodness of an African American. And when the beautiful protagonist is threatened by the institutions of slavery, slavery becomes a threat to the transcendental goodness promised by physical beauty. In this way, a single mode of characterization or set of conventions for characterization—kalokagathy—is employed to support competing ideologies. Pro-slavery and anti-slavery arguments were staged in fictional genres that had essentially similar descriptive modes. Whether the fiction was romance and thus concerned with masculine notions of honor and codes of behavior, or was sentimental and concerned with the moral questions of domestic drama, the passages of physical description ran along similar lines.

The most famous sentimental anti-slavery novel, of course, is Harriet Beecher Stowe's *Uncle Tom's Cabin* (1852). That novel adopts many of the conventions of tragic mulatto fiction, as it follows the trials of George and Eliza Harris in their flight from slavery to freedom, and as it depicts the forced and attempted concubinage of Cassy and Emmeline to Simon Legree. Despite the fact that the novel depends heavily on a suspect physiognomic kalokagathy for its moral and physical characterizations (suspect for its complicity with southern defenses of slavery), Stowe sees her fiction as a progressive force, a new evolution in the morality of art. In her preface, Stowe explains that her motive in writing *Uncle Tom's Cabin* is to represent "a race hitherto ignored by the associations of a polite and refined society; an exotic race, whose ancestors, born beneath a tropic sun, brought with them, and perpetuated to their descendants, a character so essentially unlike the hard and dominant Anglo-Saxon race, as for many years to have won from it only misunderstanding and contempt" (v). Stowe thus accepts both the differences in racial character between white and black and their inheritability as givens. However, her book seeks to counteract the negative effects of these different characters:

> But, another and better day is dawning; every influence of literature, of poetry, and of art, in our times, is becoming more and more in unison with the great master chord of Christianity, "good-will to man."
>
> The poet, the painter, and the artist now seek out and embellish the common and gentler humanities of life, and under the allurements of fiction, breathe a humanizing and subduing influence, favorable to the development of the great principles of Christian brotherhood. (v)

Though Stowe's poetics seem drawn from the eighteenth-century doctrine of please and instruct, she believes that her "day" represents a previously unreached watermark in the moral influence of fiction. Implicitly, her fiction is more Christian because it represents the "common and gentler humanities of life" that transcend racial character and which establish the brotherhood of all people.

Therefore, though Stowe's fiction relies on the notion of racial character as a precondition for its existence, she ushers in what she sees as a new novelistic aesthetic that seeks to mitigate the effects of character by transcending it. She therefore claims that her mode of fiction (what we would call the sentimental mode) is a developmental step in the evolution of fiction toward Christian goodness and perfection. And progress in fiction toward greater moral influence is an implicit sign of progress—what Stowe calls a "general movement"—on the level of the race as a whole. The teleological progression of fiction that Stowe implies came into prominence in the decades that followed as evolutionary theories gained wider acceptance. Critics of literature came to believe, as Stowe seems to, that as a race progresses so does its characteristic fiction. American novelists in the early decades of the nineteenth century used theories of characterization to describe what was distinct about their fiction for nationalistic reasons (as the frontier novelists sought the creation of true American fiction) and for ideological reasons (as the plantation romance sought to defend slavery). With Stowe we begin to see such discussions take on the influence of evolutionary thought for the sake of Christian goodness.

Though not all of the novelists who followed Stowe and entered into the debate over characterization would share her religious focus, they would continue to emphasize evolutionary progress. The influential figure in the late nineteenth century who best illustrates the conceptual connections between progressive development and fiction was Hippolyte-Adolphe Taine. In his introduction to *History of English Literature*, published in translation in the United States in 1871 and given wide notice in the popular press, Taine explained his elaborate theory of the relationship between race and literature. He began with the premise that literature is "a manifestation of a certain kind of mind" or is the "mold" or "imprint" of the person who wrote it (1, 2). Accordingly, the study of history, according to Taine, needed to recognize that literature could assist in the reconstruction of the mind of historical man. Taine argued that the "visible" man who had previously interested historians is only a symbol for the *real* subject of history, the inner or "invisible" man (6). This language makes clear the explicit physiognomic and phrenological logic undergirding this theory of literature. As Taine put it, people "arrange words and imagery according to the necessities of their organs" (2). Therefore, literature is a point of access to these organs and thus to the "mass of faculties and feelings" that make up the mind of man (7).

The next step in historical analysis, in Taine's system, is to explore the causes which shape the mind of man and result in the ideas that inform his institutions and his literature. According to Taine, these causes are racial since there is a "system in human sentiments and ideas . . . [and] this system has for its motive power certain general traits, certain characteristics of the intellect and the heart common to men of one race, age, or country" (13). This system is the source from which literature, the arts, and all cultural products spring. Accordingly, the literatures of the different ages and nations of the globe are representative of the race, national character, and historical placement of the people who composed them. The underlying cause for the different forms these systems take is the unique "primitive psychology" of each race (13). As Taine argues, in the developmental stages of language creation the individuals of a race must form a "general conception" of each object and concept. Differences in these general conceptions are the root of all human difference:

> If the general conception . . . is a mere dry notation (in Chinese fashion), language becomes a sort of algebra, religion and poetry dwindle, philosophy is reduced to a kind of moral and practical common sense. . . . If, on the contrary, the general representation in which the conception results is a poetical and figurative creation, a living symbol, as among the Aryan races, language becomes a sort of delicately-shaded and coloured epic poem, in which every word is a person, poetry and religion assume a magnificent and inexhaustible grandeur. (14)

As Taine saw it, differences in racial character are visible in the literatures of a people because that literature reflects differences in the most basic aspects of perception by the racial mind. And difference is of course synonymous with inferiority; Taine vaingloriously asserted that the Aryan mind is the most finely and figuratively attuned.

Taine's theory of the racial mind of course only makes sense within a neo-Lamarckian framework. Taine defined *race* as "the innate and hereditary dispositions which man brings with him into the world, and which, as a rule, are united with the marked differences in the temperament and structure of the body" (17). Though he did not insist that inherited racial qualities alone account for human difference (he also discussed the effects of surroundings and historical positioning), Taine did give them a place of prominence. He predictably referred to racial continuity in terms of character, noting that man's "character is more stable" than the effects created by other circumstances since its "impression is made upon him" by "numerous repetitions, and is transmitted to his progeny by a more ancient descent" (18).

Taine's system thus suggests several separate but interlinking lines of connection between racial character and fiction. First of all, character is visible in literature because "when the work is rich, and people know how to interpret it, we find there the psychology of a soul, frequently of an age, now and then of a race" (34). In addition, literature is the place where the relative richness and complexity of the abstract basis of racial character can be measured through relative levels of symbolic and figurative content. And finally, history must seek to emulate literature, in that the best writers of fiction have always been able to capture the essence of a people and their character. Since racial character cannot be quantified, the best that can be done is to give a "literary impression" of it (23). In fact, whereas other common metaphors for the workings of character, like Le Conte's, were based on economics, Taine's very conception of character can be called literary. He claimed that "at any moment we may consider the character of a people as an *abridgment* of all its preceding actions and sensations" (18, emphasis added). The racial history of a people becomes the history of their language, and the key to that history—racial character—is the abridged version of that vast document. Most importantly, because of Taine's racial theory of literature (and others like it), commentators like James Bryce were able to use literature as evidence of racial endowment. As Bryce declared, "The peoples of western Europe, peoples naturally more gifted, as their primitive literatures prove, have been played upon for some two thousand years by various civilizing influences, and have had many centuries of experience in the arts of government" (648–49).

In this way, by the last decades of the nineteenth century character had become connected to fiction and to evolutionary thought. Not surprisingly, then, while Stowe's sentimental fiction conceived of itself as the best and most progressive fictional response to a theory of racial character, the enemies of sentimentalism were no less interested in the connections between literature and character. Specifically, Taine's theories are commonly regarded as a major contributing factor toward the development and articulation of literary realism. Just as Taine recommended that history pay attention to the inner causes of racial character, he suggested that literature was rapidly becoming the best place to represent it through attention to the character of its characters. As Sherwood Cummings explains, Taine's philosophy is "easily translated into a rationale and method for realistic writing" (69). In order to show the racial character or racial mind, as Taine thought literature should, novelists could painstakingly depict controlling ideas and patterns (sometimes explicitly racial ones) through the behavior of their characters. In this sense, literary characters became the most promising vehicles for the representation of character, and characterization became a direct link between theories of character and the characters of fiction.

In his study of the writings of William Dean Howells and the development of literary realism in the United States, Everett Carter notes that the rise of realism was as much an attack on sentimental fiction and its modes of characterization as it was a coherent movement with specific artistic aims. He describes Howells's work as editor at the *Atlantic Monthly* as primarily a crusade to free America from the kind of fiction in which "sentiment, stereotype, and striving for effect were the major literary techniques" (41). According to Carter, the kind of fiction that Howells opposed was peopled with characters who were mere caricatures with little depth: "Since the characters were types well known to any reader of fiction, there was little need for honest revelation of character through incident, and therefore, the author could simply hold up the convenient signpost—the villain's black mustache, the heroine's blond beauty, and could expect the conventional response" (40). In the fiction Howells objected to, characterization was created by bodily signposts, and body parts were synonymous with traits of character. Carter defines Howells's general target as "sentimentalism" or "the telling of the currently popular lies about life in order to satisfy the prejudices and preconceptions of the audience" (49). It is clear that these lies and expectations included techniques of characterization where body and character are equated.

In fact, Howells viewed the process whereby sentimental fiction would be pushed out by more realistic treatments as an evolutionary inevitability. Howells was one of the many prominent critics of literature in the late nineteenth century who believed that literature was a progressive evolutionary force and took as their starting point Taine's observation that literature is a reflection of the progress of the race that writes it.[21] As Donald Pizer argues, theories of the national and racial roots of literature like Taine's are easily extended into an evolutionary syllogism: literature reflects races and societies; those races and societies are in progressive flux; therefore, if race and its societies evolve, so must the literatures that they produce. When Taine's theories were paired with the progressivism of Spencer and Fisk, critics concluded that if evolution is progressive, then this literary evolution is a progressive force as well, creating successively more perfect forms of literature. Pizer notes that other evolutionary critics had refined the analogy between biological and artistic evolution in specific ways that influenced Howells's thinking on Taine and literary progress. Significantly, T. S. Perry, author of *English Literature in the Eighteenth Century* (1883), adopted John Addington Symond's argument that "literary genres occupied the position of species within the broad pattern of progress and that each genre passed through a life cycle of birth, maturity, and decay" (qtd. in Pizer 95).[22] This formulation allows for the progressive direction of literary evolution to be punctuated by the occasional literary dead end; abandoned genres are figured as species that were no longer able to compete.

Viewed in this context, it is clear that Howells believed that sentimental fiction was the literary equivalent of an endangered species, and his critical mission was to help the fledgling realistic mode to drive it into extinction. Many critics in the late nineteenth century took the fidelity with which a genre represents society as a sign of its evolutionary fitness. As Pizer explains, "The progress in any literary form was . . . not only a growth in technique and form, but also a more truthful representation of the life of its time. Decay occurred when this latter function was neglected or when another genre more able to perform the task arose" (96). In Howells's collection of critical essays published in 1891, he argues that realism appeals to civilized tastes, while other literary forms are atavistic. He goes so far as to argue that if people continue to revere survivals from past epochs, such as the historical romance, they risk missing the true function of modern fiction and are "in danger of becoming permanently part of the 'unthinking multitude,' and of remaining puerile, primitive, savage" (qtd. in Pizer 101). For Howells, the technique of presenting character through stale and predictable types was a sign of retarded racial development. All in all, Howells figured the freedom from old genres as a new way of seeing character. By his account, the new realists showed a "disposition to regard our life without the literary glasses so long thought desirable, and to see character, not as it is in other fiction, but as it abounds outside of all fiction" (qtd. in Pizer 101). As such, the proper presentation of character is one of the tenets of Howells's realism. Howells explicitly criticized characterization that operated as a closed system with characters drawn from a pool of already-existing types and with a fixed set of associations. Rather, he encouraged authors to engage in actual observation so as to present character as it exists in everyday experience.

As a result of these confluences between theories of race and theories of fiction, it becomes possible to argue that the genres of fiction popular in the late nineteenth century were implicitly racialized. I do not mean to suggest that sentimental or romance fiction in all ages and in all countries contains a theory of character or is racially motivated. However, at the particular historical moment and in the political climate I am considering, the sentimental and romance genres—which experienced a resurgence in popularity at the turn of the century—betray a physiognomic logic of characterization that lends itself to the depiction of racial character and difference.[23] And as hard as realism sought to distinguish itself from the sentimental genres that it believed it was supplanting, it was no less concerned with character.

Therefore, the confluence of scientific discourse and literary commentary that brought about the conceptual connections between character, characters, and characterization resulted from a shared and pervasive concern to represent the invisible aspects of racial character. Just as the mixed-race individual puts pressure on race theory implicitly—inspiring scientific discourse to explore the depths of racial character and its invisible organs rather than skin-level features—the desire to explore aspects of racial character pushes a literary theory like Taine's toward the depths of the racial mind and away from the visible man. The mixed-race individual thus stands at the intersection of these two related discourses; the nineteenth-century preoccupation with the mulatto is symptomatic of the fact that the conceptual frameworks of literature and science were both formulated in ways that made the paradoxical representation of the invisible or inner character possible.

As a result, in novels concerned with race and the representation of mixed race, the language and concepts of both science and fiction cannot be far from the surface of the narrative. The period from the late nineteenth century through the early twentieth was a transitional one marked by ideological and conceptual shifts: neo-Lamarckianism was being threatened by incipient theories of environmentalism, an emphasis on skin color was giving way to an emphasis on character, *de facto* segregation was giving way to *de jure*, the color line was being drawn and defended with more violence, and sentimental and romance fiction were fighting off threats from the literary realists. In fiction from this period the mixed-race character becomes a lightning rod for discussions of these scientific, political, and even aesthetic transitions. I would argue that it is necessary for the contemporary critic of literature to refrain from seeing realism as an aesthetic progression beyond sentimental fiction, since such a formulation buys into what is often a racist logic of artistic development. The literary developments of the turn of the century are less the story of growth and progress and more a case of a number of different generic responses to crises in science, in social organization, and in the theoretical language used to describe them both.

2

Thomas Dixon and the Rhetorical Mulatto

At the start of book two of the white supremacist novel *The Clansman*, Thomas Dixon introduces the character Silas Lynch, a politician modeled on Frederick Douglass. Though Lynch is a mulatto who has "acquired the full physical characteristics of the Aryan race," the narrator notes that "his dark yellowish eyes beneath his heavy brows glowed with the brightness of the African jungle. It was impossible to look at his superb face, with its large, finely chiseled lips and massive nose, his big neck and broad shoulders, and watch his eyes gleam beneath the projecting forehead, without seeing pictures of the primeval forest. 'The head of a Caesar and the eyes of the jungle' was the phrase coined by an artist who painted his portrait" (93). Paradoxically, Lynch's physical features make it impossible to look at him and not see pictures of the primeval forest, although those features are inherited from the "Aryan" race in full. In fact, despite the narrator's claim that Lynch's features are Aryan, the description includes several anthropologically and culturally specific "Negro" features, including lips, nose, projecting brow, and large forehead. Though Lynch's skin is white, the narrator makes it clear that his blackness is nonetheless visible, if not positively unmistakable. Dixon has abandoned the marker of skin color, but his rhetoric of race still insists on a logic of racial visibility.

In addition to falling back on a facially oriented scientific racism for its description of physical features, this passage also evokes the conventions of art and artistic representation in order to make blackness visible.[1] The reference to portraiture betrays a self-referential awareness of the rhetorical task of transmitting a word picture; Lynch is characterized by an artist and then inscribed by the narrator into the characters of written language. When Dixon insists that those who observe Lynch within the fictional universe cannot look at him without forming a visual connection with the jungle and all that it denotes and connotes, he provides within the text a reading of his own description—an account of what his character's face "speaks" both to other characters in the novel and to his readers. Thus Dixon attempts to create a kind of closure around his character. He simultaneously provides both a physical description and a physiognomic reading of physical features.

Yet despite this interpretive closure, the description of Lynch also comes with a set of extratextual political implications. Both of Dixon's novels that I will discuss in this chapter, *The Leopard's Spots* and *The Clansman,* are set in the era of Reconstruction, and both use preexisting figures as templates to recharacterize. In the case of *The Clansman,* Dixon reworks the historical figures of Douglass and radical Reconstructionist Thaddeus Stevens. Even more significantly, in *The Leopard's Spots* Dixon sets out to recharacterize literary characters. As if writing a sequel to Harriet Beecher Stowe's famous novel, he chooses a handful of characters from *Uncle Tom's Cabin* and places them in the post-Reconstruction South.

I am interested in connecting the two issues that the passage above raises. First, the fact that Lynch is both fully physically white and visibly black suggests that Dixon is lured into paradox by the need to make the blackness of a light-skinned mulatto visible. Second, the fact that Lynch is a historical person indicates that Dixon's descriptive aims include historical recharacterization and that his fiction is concerned with characterization in a more general sense. In particular, Dixon seeks to redraw black racial character in response to a conviction that northerners could not understand the South and its reaction to Reconstruction unless they could see African Americans as white southerners see them. As such, Dixon's novels reflect the turn-of-the-century trend in southern fiction to focus on Reconstruction and characterization. He uses the arena for characterization which fiction provides in order to illustrate the reasonableness and the scientific validity of the premises of white supremacy.

In keeping with these aims, Dixon uses a genre well suited to establishing links between appearance and character and to situating characters in a historical context. Both novels are identified by the author as historical romances, a particularly appropriate genre for representing a period in southern history when race was a contested issue. Specifically, the parameters for characterization in romances of the South, especially as established by the plantation romance, allow for the pointed illustration of racial contrasts. Yet, of course, mulattoes like Lynch are hard to fit into the color-coded binary of the plantation romance. This chapter ultimately takes as its central concern the ways in which Dixon negotiates the tensions between his own ideology of the absolute visibility of race (an ideology illustrated by his insistence that it is impossible *not* to see Lynch as "African"), the descriptive requirements of prose romance, and the artistic demand of representing mixed-race characters.

In the first section of this chapter I provide some background into southern attitudes toward Reconstruction and the intellectual sources for Dixon's beliefs about the racial implications of political organization and the democratic process. I then outline the logic of character Dixon professes to in both his fiction and nonfiction against the backdrop of his first novel, *The Leopard's Spots.* In that novel Dixon advances a physiognomic correspondence between character and appearance at the same time that he hints at how appearance can be manipulated. His second novel, *The Clansman,* picks up on and develops the fear of miscegenation that marks both novels. *The Clansman* presents a trio of mulatto characters who present complications to the physiognomic logic of character which Dixon accommodates by exploring conceptual alternatives to character and by evoking the invisible aspects of racial identity. Thus, in the final section I explore the contradictions which arise from *The Clansman*'s aesthetic of the invisible, contradictions inconsistent with the genre of prose romance and which ironically undermine the efficacy of written characterization to contain and transmit racial messages.

Clearly, Dixon's insistence on the always visible nature of race is not logically consistent. As this chapter will argue, in the case of the light-skinned mulatto Dixon makes adjustments to the logic of character in order to preserve his ideology of visibility that end up undermining the physiognomy that structured this ideology in the first place. However, my point is not simply that Dixon's logic of racial visibility is inconsistent; surely all arguments in defense of absolute racial visibility are ultimately illogical. Rather, my point is that Dixon's fiction illustrates how the ideology of racial visibility and the ideology of genre play out in the shifting language of character at the turn of the century.

Southern Characterizations

The main turn-of-the-century southern concerns about the race problem are listed in a program for a conference held in May of 1900 by the officiously named Southern Society for the Promotion of the Study of Race Conditions and Problems in the South. The conference featured panels addressing "The Franchise in the South," "Popular Education in the South," "The Negro in Relation to Religion," "Lynching as a Penalty," and "The Negro and the Social Order." In the explanatory note that precedes the published collection of these addresses, the society made clear its motives for publishing the addresses and its resolve to continue to publish papers subsequently submitted to the executive committee on the race question: "The object of these publications is to create, within the South itself, a popular literature on the subject—a literature representative of the soil and the people, a literature which will interpret the South both to the world and itself" (5). Here the society indicated that a body of discourse was needed to contain and transmit the southern perspective on the race question, much like the discourse that communicated the pro-slavery argument to northern audiences decades before. But this call for a representative literature also signaled a heightened interest in representation itself and the need for the South to take over the narrative presentation of its own behaviors, motives, and reasoning on the race question. The stakes were high. This literature, born of the very essence of what is southern about its land and its inhabitants, would stand for the South and would allow a self-alienated South to understand itself.

Thomas Nelson Page also noted the vital need for southern self-representation in his essay "The Negro Problem" published in *The Old South* (1892). Page claimed that the only way to prevent the "impending disaster" of misrepresentation of southern motives for secession was to "establish the real fact . . . the true and ultimate cause of the action of the South," and in doing so to perpetuate the "true and splendid story of the real position of the South[,] . . . wrest fame from defeat and establish her true place in history" (279). Though Page singles out Civil War history, the story that he wanted told more than anything was an account of the actions of the South in Reconstruction and after. In the last decade of the nineteenth century, many southern states were attempting the wholesale repeal of the franchise for black voters and the institution of *de jure* segregation where it had previously been *de facto.* The point of the re-presentation of historical events was to make these acts sensible and logical responses to the "Negro problem." The Civil War and Reconstruction re-presented became evidence for the wisdom of current policy. As Eric Sundquist notes in *To Wake the Nations,* the argument worked in both directions: "The problem of segregation—the theory, the fact, and the living reality of segregation—was the defining legal and social experience of the late nineteenth century for many Americans, not least for what it implied in retrospect about the meaning of the Civil War" (11).

By Page's account, settling the debate over the grounds of the race problem was the key to finding a national answer. But first, both North and South had to agree on the question. "The chief difficulty in the solution of the question," he claims, "exists in the different views held as to it by the two sections" (284). According to the northern view, a view ironically typified for Page by native-born southerner George Washington Cable, the issue was "whether American citizens shall not enjoy equal rights" (287). From this perspective, southern states were engaged in a blatant attempt to deny basic rights to American citizens. However, the southern view was that such actions were designed to prevent race conflict and eventual doom for the white race in the South. According to Page, what creates these different views is the interpretation of African Americans and their motives: "The North sees in the negro's attitude only the proper and laudable aspiration of a citizen and a man; the South detects therein . . . a menace to all that the Anglo-American race has effected on this continent" (312). Only one common ground could be appealed to in order to adjudicate this discrepancy, according to Page: "There underlies the whole matter the indubitable, potent, and mysterious principle of race quality" (313).

If, as Page claimed, the turn-of-the-century argument over the race problem hinged on the interpretation of race "quality," or racial character, the re-presentation of Reconstruction became vital. Reconstruction emerged as an indication of the inevitable results of full black participation in the political process. By Page's argument, the corruption and waste of Reconstruction governments was a sign of black political incapacity, a message that told Americans what the race's reaction to political power has been and will be. Thus, if the story of Reconstruction could be told and interpreted as a convincing condemnation of black character, the franchise could logically be denied on the basis of the weakness of that character. Furthermore, if the race question as a whole were re-posed as one of racial character rather than as one of social justice, other issues besides the franchise could be settled accordingly.

As the proceedings of the Southern Conference suggest, southern contributors to public discourse on race were doing just that. In his welcoming speech, E. B. Joseph, mayor of Montgomery, instructed the participants that all issues under consideration were to be treated from the theoretical perspective of racial character: "You are here to put in motion currents of public thought and conscience, which in the end will determine and shape the proper adjustment of conditions and rights of races. . . . In your deliberations, you will be confronted with the fact that human wisdom cannot recast nature, nor change race characteristics, or the conditions with which an all-wise Creator, for purposes of his own—but dimly seen and understood by human vision—has surrounded the pathway of the two races" (19).[2] Of course, if racial characteristics are taken to be the unalterable backdrop for any thought on the race question, the key issue appears to be who gets to characterize them; contrary to Mayor Joseph's claims, the power to "recast nature" often lies in the human ability to represent it.

Not surprisingly, the literary genius of the South was bent on the representation and characterization of key events in southern history.[3] Even more importantly, authors addressed the issue of racial character by creating characters who illustrated the southern view of African Americans in contrast to the one established by abolitionist literature. For example, Joel Chandler Harris in his introduction to *Uncle Remus* (1880) notes, "I trust I have been successful in presenting what must be, at least to a large portion of American readers, a new and by no means unattractive phase of negro character—a phase which may be considered a curiously sympathetic supplement to Mrs. Stowe's" (40). Thomas Dixon, however, took a less supplementary tack in his attempts to recharacterize. According to his biographer Raymond Cook, Dixon became interested in the representation of the South as early as 1887, when he heard a lecture in Boston entitled "The Southern Problem" which angered him so much that he stood up in the middle of the address to call the speaker a liar and a fool. Apparently a man easily incensed by public performances, Dixon in 1901 left a dramatic version of *Uncle Tom's Cabin* vowing to "tell the 'true story' of the South if it was the last act of his life" (Cook 105). Accordingly, in *The Leopard's Spots* Dixon rewrote the literary character of blacks established primarily by the influence of Stowe's novel. After the book's publication, he responded directly to critics who were alarmed at his use of Stowe, asserting, "It may shock the prejudice of those who have idealized or worshipped the negro as canonized in 'Uncle Tom.' Is it not time they heard the whole truth? They have heard only one side for forty years" (qtd. in Harkins 121).

Dixon was particularly well positioned to recharacterize Reconstruction politics from a white supremacist point of view. He had been an exemplary student at Wake Forest College and at age nineteen won a scholarship to attend Johns Hopkins.[4] According to Joel Williamson, in the 1880s Johns Hopkins intended to provide an atmosphere "congenial" to southern scholars (*Crucible* 153). In the single year that Dixon spent there as a student of history and politics, he was exposed to the scientific racism of the so-called Anglo-Saxon historians based in those departments. This school sought to classify political institutions nearly biologically, as organisms that could be ranked in an evolutionary hierarchy marked by different amounts of progress toward self-government. The democratic system was placed at the pinnacle, and its roots in historical time were traced back to the proto-democratic organization of Germanic tribes. According to Richard Hofstadter, historian Herbert Baxter Adams held seminars to disseminate the "picture of the big, blond, democratic Teuton and . . . the Teutonic genealogy of self-government" (174). And since the capacity to self-govern was assumed to be an inheritable trait, these seminars promoted the notion that the Teutonic capacity was passed on to Anglo-Saxons, who were to develop self-government into its most sublime form.

For these historians, self-government was the Anglo-Saxon's birthright. Hofstadter cites nineteenth-century historian James K. Hosmer's *Short History of Anglo-Saxon Freedom* (1890): "Anglo-Saxon freedom in a more or less partial form has been adopted (it would be better perhaps to say imitated) in every nation in Europe . . . [but] to that race alone is it thoroughly congenial" (174). Since Europeans could only imitate the Anglo-Saxon racial trait of democracy, non-white races were decidedly even less fit for self-government. Though the Anglo-Saxon historian's account was explicitly based on an evolutionary framework, it sought to isolate one branch of human development and bless it alone with the highest development of human freedom. If democracy were the end result of all human evolution, it could be argued that other groups simply needed to get there. However, the Anglo-Saxon historians were certain that their evolutionary hierarchy was frozen and that only Anglo-Saxons had the democratic capacity. Accordingly, African Americans should be excluded from the political process owing to evolutionary retardation.

In his fiction, Dixon connected his training in the construction of racist history with the premises of physiognomy. Specifically, he believed that the insights provided by physiognomy had the status of historical evidence. In a published defense of *The Clansman* against claims that he had misrepresented the history of the Ku Klux Klan by painting Klan leaders as heroic men rather than criminal vigilantes, Dixon cited the physical beauty of such leaders as proof that they were virtuous. In the journal *Voice of the Negro,* an article titled "Mr. Thomas Dixon, Jr., the Physiognomist" noted that "by publishing the pictures of some of the prominent leaders of the Ku Klux Klan" Dixon "asks the world to forget their awful misdeeds and accept them as paragons of excellence because of the comeliness of their features" (790). And, the article continued, "to further strengthen his defense . . . in contrast to the handsome portraits of some of its members, Mr. Dixon has published the picture of colored men, 'the lowest type of Negro'" (790). In this way, Dixon used the very features of the Klan as a testament to the purity of their motives and to the accuracy of his historical characterization of them, while the features of African Americans were sufficient to testify to the historical reality of the racial evil the Klan was combating. Apparently, Dixon had imbibed the picture of the tall, blond Teuton and associated physical features with political capacity and, by extension, with moral qualities. As such, in his fiction Dixon used the very features of his characters to launch political arguments, all in the generic context of a romance of the South.[5]

The Leopard's Spots and the Solid Basis of Character

The Leopard's Spots falls roughly into two halves. The first takes place during the period of Reconstruction directly following the end of the Civil War, and the second takes place closer to the turn of the century. Dixon recasts the events of Reconstruction and its aftermath and places recognizable characters from Stowe's novel against that backdrop in order to recharacterize them. The novel's original title was "The Rise of Simon Legree," a play on the title of William Dean Howells's popular novel *The Rise of Silas Lapham* but also a nod to the dominant obsession with examinations of the race question and the events of the war. Looking back over the last thirty-five years of southern history, commentators at the turn of the century shared an interest in asking who had risen, who had declined, and who would rise again.

The central character in *The Leopard's Spots,* Charlie Gaston, does not come from *Uncle Tom's Cabin.* Yet the novel is designed to emphasize his characterization just as clearly as it emphasizes the characters of the figures borrowed from Stowe. As the book begins, Charlie is a young boy waiting for his father to return to their home in North Carolina after the surrender. But his father has been killed in battle, and the boy watches his family and town slide into ruin as the twin menaces of freed slaves and Reconstruction politics begin to grip the South. The second half of the novel begins twenty-five years after the beginning of the first, so we see how Charlie was formed by his radical Reconstruction experiences. Charlie eventually becomes governor of the state as the Klan helps white southerners restore civic order and Democratic rule. The structure of the novel, with its lapse in time, allows Dixon to show how his hero's character was formed and what influences went into creating it. In this novel, characterization, as much as dialogue or plot, allows for the transmission of racial and political messages; character is a theme in *The Leopard's Spots* since characterization contains messages about character in the abstract.

The most important tension in Dixon's characterization of Charlie is between what he has inherited and what is self-made or self-formed through experience. Yet despite this tension, a singular logic is advanced: physical features correspond to qualities of character. From the start Charlie is fixed for the reader by his resemblance to his father; the resemblance suggests that Charlie adheres to the ideals and heroism of that man and generation. But the fixed, inherited nature signaled through physical resemblance is nonetheless shaped by self-exertion. Charlie's love interest is Sallie Worth—an aristocratic belle in the style of the Old South. When he gives her a school medal as a sign of their mutual devotion, he tells her, "This is the first medal I won at college . . . the first victory of my life. It was the force that determined my character. It gave me an inflexible will. . . . Every line cut on its gold surface stands for a thousand aches of my body. Every little pearl set in it grew in a pain of that struggle which set its seal on my inmost life" (288).[6] Body, material object, and inner mental life blur together in this token. Dixon uses it to suggest that emotional or intellectual experience is a determinant of character and that character can be externalized or represented in a symbolic, visual setting.

Interestingly, the affair between Sallie and Charlie best demonstrates Dixon's belief that character is signaled in external, bodily signs. When Charlie begins to woo Sallie, he requests an evaluation of his physical appearance from Mrs. Durham, a friend of the family and wife of the important character Reverend Durham. Her response is remarkable for its rhetorical and conceptual similarities to the description of Lynch in *The Clansman.* In both passages there is an insistence on what is visible and what the visible speaks:

> She answered, slowly regarding him. . . . "You are tall . . . and your muscular body gives the impression of power. You have black hair, dark-brown eyes that look out from your shaggy, straight eyebrows with a piercing light. . . . They suggest reserve power and brain capacity. . . . You have deep vertical wrinkles between your eyes just where your straight eyebrows meet . . . they mean habits of thought, like your stooping shoulders. . . . But the best feature of all your stock is your eye. Your big brown eyes are about the only perfect thing about you. There's infinite

> tenderness in them. Now and then they gleam with a hidden fire that tells of enthusiasm, thought, will, character, and dauntless courage." (238–39)

In this curious passage, Mrs. Durham takes over the function of the narrator by constructing a passage of physical description that is not merely part of the novelistic apparatus but is foregrounded as the means by which the theme of Charlie's character is advanced and developed. In this case, as with Lynch, the force of character is told in the eye, though in this case the eye speaks character rather than the jungle. All in all, there is a direct and complete correspondence between physical features and the projection of character and characteristic behavior: a muscular body gives the "impression" of power, eyebrows "suggest" brain capacity, and gleaming eyes "tell" of character and courage.

When Dixon begins to introduce characters from *Uncle Tom's Cabin,* he relies on the same physiognomic principle. For example, Simon Legree's appearance is a sign of his character:

> [Legree] was looking more at ease now than ever in his life. . . . He was a little older looking than when he killed Uncle Tom on his farm some ten years before, but otherwise unchanged. He had the same short, muscular body, round bullet head, light gray eyes and shaggy eyebrows. . . . His eyes, well set apart, as of old, were bold, commanding and flashed with the cold light of glittering steel. His teeth, that once were pointed like the fangs of a wolf, had been filed by a dentist. But it required more than the file of a dentist to smooth out of that face the ferocity and cruelty that years of dissolute habits had fixed. (86–87)

In *The Leopard's Spots,* Legree is a leader in scalawag circles and sees his fortunes rise as white southern living standards and hopes fall. Since he is still the villain, he is largely unchanged from the way Stowe described him (her description is no less physiognomic in its equation of Legree's appearance with his villainy).[7] Though Dixon suggests that Legree has sought to control how others read his face by having some cosmetic dentistry done, there are messages that his appearance cannot help but transmit, messages that are fixed in his features by years of dissolute behavior. In this sense physical features mirror and predict the tone of his conduct, but they are also the result of it. There is enough plasticity in human features, it appears, for Legree to have literally molded himself through the very force of his own low character.

The claim that Legree shaped his own face is ironic, given that the novel's title is a reference to the absolute immutability of racial characteristics. At the novel's conclusion the Reverend Durham, who gives voice to the novel's political and social philosophy throughout, engages in a debate with Charlie as he plans his inaugural address. Charlie wants to call for industrial education for African Americans, while Durham believes they must be removed to Africa. Durham chastises Charlie, saying, "Even you are still laboring under the delusions of 'Reconstruction.' The Ethiopian cannot change his skin, or the leopard his spots" (463). This indirect quotation from Jeremiah 13:23 serves as a summary statement of the novel's general conflation of appearance with behavior, whereby black skin is an outer sign of inner inferiority; since skin cannot be changed, neither can inferiority be amended by education or any other means. So, strangely, while Legree's face is plastic and shows its villainy as the sign of his chosen life of dissipation, the black individual's skin is a fixed, unalterable fact. In another scene, Mrs. Durham declares that "human nature can't be reconstructed by the fiat of fools who tinker with laws" (263). Thus, throughout the novel "Reconstruction" in a political sense is aligned with the notion of "reconstruction" in a racial sense. The word becomes a blanket term for all misguided efforts to ameliorate the conditions of blacks which ignore the fact that black racial character cannot be changed.

In fact, the novel flatly suggests that the notion of character is misapplied to blacks. In Dixon's published discourses on the theological "mistakes" of Robert Ingersoll, he alludes to the evolutionary theory that shapes his racism (and also structures his fiction).[8] In his discussion of Ingersoll's position on the Christian concept of free will, Dixon makes clear that he accepts the theory of evolution, but with his own interpretation of its implications and workings: "The supreme decree under which the material universe has been evolved and made what it is was the law of the survival of the fittest. Under the full operation of this law we have produced a self-made world. The highest creation is that which is thus made to create itself. It partakes then of character. The only man that is a real man is the self-made man. The only man who has character is such a man. This is the highest development of manhood" (85). This argument is loosely coherent and vaguely circular, but it articulates a Spencerian, human-centered version of evolution in which the evolutionary process is fueled by the exertion of will. According to Dixon, survival of the fittest is only possible with human participation in the selection process. In this sense, man makes himself "fit" and thereby creates himself and his race through self-guided evolution. The concept of character is central to human fitness because it is the quality that allows humans to use their will to operate in evolution.[9]

Dixon goes on to define this vague term *character* in the ensuing discussion of the necessity for humans to choose between good and evil in a Christian universe. By his argument, if man did not have the ability to choose between good and evil he would not be a man, but rather a "machine . . . driven by force" in "a world of mechanics": "In such a world . . . it would be impossible to produce character. Character is the result of the free play of the dual forces in the moral world—good and evil. Character is the choice of good in the face of evil. Character is the highest possible product within the attainment of man" (86–87). The causation remains fuzzy, but the general outline is clear: humans evolve because they make themselves. The fittest survive, but fitness is really a matter of self-making through moral choices. Both the ability to make moral choices and the fitness that results from having made them are called "character." Character is thus intrinsically tied to the notion of human progress, and since it affects the ability to make moral choices, it has a religious significance as well.

However, as *The Leopard's Spots* demonstrates, African Americans have not shown the ability to shape their own character. While Dixon's nonfiction uses an evolutionary framework to inform the Christian who is worried about free will that he exerts it in the process of evolution, his fiction uses the same framework to warn the nation of the danger that blacks pose to this evolution. In the passage I used to frame the first chapter, Reverend Durham suggests that African Americans possess very little in the way of character as he condemns a black preacher over the state of his congregation: "In the old days . . . I used to preach to your people. I saw before me many men of character: carpenters, bricklayers, wheelwrights, farmers, faithful home servants that loved their masters and were faithful unto death. Now I see a cheap lot of thieves and jailbirds and trifling women seated in high places. You have shown no power to stand alone on the solid basis of character" (311). In this novel, the fact that freed slaves commit crimes of any sort is proof that African Americans do not have the inner resources needed for moral decision making that whites have; outside the white-controlled framework of slavery, they cannot make moral choices between right and wrong and thus cannot maintain character. Moreover, as Charlie outlines in a campaign speech, the history of Africa signals that the race has always lacked character: "The African had held one-fourth of this globe for 3,000 years. He has never taken one step in progress . . . except as the slave of a superior race. . . . He has had one hundred years of trial in the Northern states of this Union with every facility of culture and progress, and he has not produced one man who has added a feather's weight to the progress of humanity" (441). Black history does not show the evolution toward civilization that white history does. And by Dixon's evolutionary theory, the lack of a solid basis of character is the ultimate reason for the lack of racial progress.

The most chilling example of how Dixon uses Stowe's characters to illustrate his theory of race and character is the reworking of Tom himself. In Stowe's novel, Tom is a Christ figure, a man martyred by the institution of slavery. His endurance under Legree's abuse is an expression of what would certainly be called strength of character—he adheres to his Christian beliefs, making a clear moral choice. However, Dixon could not grant a black Tom this kind of strength of character. Rather, in *The Leopard's Spots* the reworked "Tom" character is the poor white farmer Tom Camp who returns from the war with one leg. As critic Thomas Riggio notes, Tom Camp, like Stowe's Tom, lives alongside white aristocrats without envy, speaks with a dialect that signals his lower status, and quotes the Bible with notable piety.

However, the suffering that Tom Camp endures only has implications for white racial character. As Dixon argued in *Dixon on Ingersoll*, "Character is produced through suffering. Christ, we are told, was made perfect through suffering. Suffering seems to be the only power that levels all distinctions and binds the heart of the race in the primal unity of its divine strength" (87). In *The Leopard's Spots* the "race unity" that suffering produces in its Uncle Tom equivalent is explicitly white racial unity. Tom Camp has emerged from his suffering in the war with an abiding race feeling: "I always hated a nigger since I was knee-high. . . . And then I had to leave my wife and baby and fight for four years, all on account of their stinkin' hides, that never done nothin' for me except make it harder to live. Everytime I'd go to battle . . . it seemed to me I could see their black ape-faces grinnin' and makin' fun of poor whites. At night when they'd detail me to help the ambulance corps carry off the dead and wounded, there was a strange smell on the field . . . [that] always smelled like nigger to me. It made me sick" (28–29). Tom Camp's battle suffering has made him metonymically associate the war with the need for an economically based racial antagonism between poor whites and blacks and for white solidarity in the South. As Riggio notes, through this recharacterization "Dixon envisioned a new suffering Christ image for America. . . . [He] displaced the pious ex-slave . . . [and] created a white Uncle Tom, a poor white crucified both psychologically and economically by the black man" (67). Black suffering has been replaced with white suffering, the strength of character of a black figure with the strength of character of a white figure. And the white character that suffering builds forms alongside a racial unity that would deny character to any other racial group, regardless of commensurate suffering.

So apparently the character that Durham claims he saw in black congregations before the war, or any progress that black characters exhibit in the novel, is a temporary or illusory rise that has no basis in moral fitness or racial progress. As another character notes, "Put [the Negro] on a continent alone and he will sink like an iron wedge to the bottomless pit of barbarism" (264). The influence of white civilization on black populations in the United States apparently results in a temporary improvement in behavior, but were this influence removed the race would sink into barbarism, the level of culture-evolution below civilization. The appearance of civilization that results from education is thus only a surface emendation.

Interestingly, this sort of scientific racism translates into a logic of false appearances. According to Mrs. Durham, when she sees "these young Negro men and women coming out of their schools and colleges, well dressed, with their shallow veneer of an imitation culture," she feels like "crying over the farce" (265). The Ethiopian cannot change his skin, but the metaphor for his change under the influence of education is nonetheless visual: blacks wear education like a veneer, a whitewash layered over an unchanged core. As the language Mrs. Durham uses suggests, the educated black becomes a rhetorical mulatto of sorts, an unreliable body that transmits mixed signals with a visual blackness and a performance of whiteness.

In addition, like mulattoes in the popular imagination at the turn of the century, educated African Americans in *The Leopard's Spots* are caught between two levels of status and have no real place in postwar America. The reworked character from *Uncle Tom's Cabin* who best illustrates this phenomenon is Eliza Harris's son—"handsome and almost white"—whom Dixon renames George Harris, Jr. (314). Harris is referred to in an early chapter by a northern female philanthropist who is looking to prove the capabilities of African Americans: "I am conducting an experiment of thrilling interest to me which will prove that their intellectual, moral and social capacity is equal to any white man's. . . . I am collecting specimens of Negro boys and sending them to our great Northern Universities. . . . The most interesting of these students I have at Harvard now is young George Harris. . . . This boy is a genius, and if he lives he will shake this nation" (49). Dixon mocks white philanthropy as clinical experimentation and shows in his construction of Harris's destiny that southern "humanitarian" interest is actually more sympathetic and accurate in its predictions. Harris becomes an example of Mrs. Durham's view of black education. She argues that "education increases the power of the human brain to think and the heart to suffer," and as a consequence, "sooner or later these educated Negroes feel the clutch of the iron hand of the white man's unwritten laws on their throats. They have their choice between a suicide's grave or a prison cell." Her conclusion is that "the South is kinder to the Negro when he is kept in his place" (265).

Harris's story follows this outline exactly. He becomes utterly placeless as he is rejected by his northern patron when he asks to marry his daughter and is prevented by his education from finding happiness in menial labor, the only type of job that northern racists will allow him. As a Harvard graduate, his impressive performance of white culture makes him even more of an outcast than the segregated black, and his failure to find work leads to "a life of crime," depression, and eventually suicide. Harris is the tragic mulatto of *The Leopard's Spots;* denied marriage, he is left to wander and to die.

If Harris's story were told in the spirit of outrage, it would serve as a rebuke of the color line. However, in this case he is characterized as irrefutable proof of the concluding assumptions of Dixon's racial theory. As already noted, Dixon's character analysis demonstrates that blacks are evolutionarily unfit to stand as equals with whites in the political process. In the novel, the freedmen show up on election day with wheelbarrows to carry away their portion of the "franchise." Thus Dixon shows that blacks only farcically imitate white culture and institutions. And when he provides George Harris with the education needed to perfect the performance, he proves his assertion that political and other forms of civic equality will lead to expectations of social equality. As Mr. Durham says to Charlie, "You cannot seek the Negro vote without asking him to your house sooner or later. If you ask him to your house, he will break bread with you at last. And if you seat him at your table he has the right to ask your daughter's hand in marriage" (244). The real threat of political equality and education, and the last step in Dixon's argument, is that they create rhetorical and actual mulattoes like George who then wish to marry whites and create more mulattoes who will destroy civilization.

Fear of miscegenation is finally what the entire novelistic argument hinges on, a fear based on the premises of scientific racism. Mr. Durham explains: "The racial instinct is the ordinance of our life. Lose it and we have no future. One drop of Negro blood makes a Negro. It kinks the hair, flattens the nose, thickens the lips, puts out the light of intellect, and lights the fires of brutal passions. The beginning of Negro equality as a vital fact is the beginning of the end of this nation's life. There is enough Negro blood here to make mulatto the whole Republic" (244). Black blood has the power to remake white physical appearance and character. Thus, miscegenation is a direct threat to the features that speak white superiority because it can recharacterize them. Miscegenation destroys character in a parodic reversal of the novelistic language that constructs physical description by flattening, kinking, and perverting the set of signs that guarantee racial superiority.

The white characters in *The Leopard's Spots* are well aware of the theories that underlie the prohibitions against miscegenation. For example, George's patron appeals to the so-called science of racial contact: "I happen to know the important fact that a man or woman of Negro ancestry, though a century removed, will suddenly breed back to a pure Negro child, thick-lipped, kinky-headed, flat-nosed, black-skinned. One drop of your blood in my family could push it backward three thousand years in history" (398). The drop of black blood and its atavistic, de-evolutionary properties hangs over the entire novel as a threat to the vision of whiteness constructed in passages of description. The final message of this polemical novel is that the threat of miscegenation must be held in mind when addressing the race problem. In *The Leopard's Spots,* the fight against a future "mulatto America" is raised again and again to unite the South against African Americans and against Republican government. However, in Dixon's next novel, the mulatto is evoked as a common enemy for an even grander purpose: to unite the entire nation.

The Clansman and the Racial Soul

The Clansman reworks the same historical materials presented in *The Leopard's Spots.* Both novels depict the effects of Reconstruction on the South and the origins of the Klan, and both seek to characterize African Americans as a threat to Anglo-Saxon purity in order to make miscegenation the most serious postwar issue. Furthermore, both seek to prove the claim that blacks are animal and inferior by focusing on how the physical features of blackness signal the race's degenerate qualities. However, *The Clansman* takes all this one step further by implying that the main impediment to national unity is the North's failure to recognize these truths. Accordingly, *The Clansman* advances a vision of the means by which North and South can be united. At the novel's start, two families, one northern and one southern, are thrown together by the chaotic events at the end of the Civil War. The northern family is headed by Senator Austin Stoneman—a literary rendering of Thaddeus Stevens—who leads radical Reconstruction in Congress. The southern family is headed by Dr. Cameron, a parallel character to Reverend Durham in his espousal of anti-Reconstruction racial theories. The way the younger members of these families are brought together through marriage reflects Dixon's vision for healing post–Civil War America.

The novel's action is similar to *The Leopard's Spots;* black misuse of government and sexual aggression toward white women during Reconstruction prompt white southerners to unite, and the Klan restores Democratic political control. In this context, we see Stoneman battling with President Lincoln and later Johnson over their resistance to his punishing plans for the South under Reconstruction. We also meet Stoneman's mulatto cohorts: his housekeeper and mistress Lydia Brown and his political ally Silas Lynch. Lynch is in many ways the most important character for arguments about racial character. He stands as an example of how this second novel begins to stretch the logic of character and visibility advanced in the previous one by advancing the theme of the mulatto as a performer of white culture who transmits only a surface message. As a mulatto who looks physically white, Lynch poses a problem for the assumption that inner qualities like racial character are invariably visible in physical features. Dixon's depiction of Lynch is significant since the link between outer appearance and inner racial qualities—physiognomic kalokagathy—is central to his argument for northern and southern unity.

For example, the events that bring the Camerons and Stonemans together are precipitated by the recognition of the nobility of a handsome face. In one scene, a military doctor tells Stoneman's daughter Elsie about the moment Ben Cameron and her brother Phil Stoneman met in pitched battle against one another. Ben had been shot after valiantly fighting his way up to the Union troops: "Your brother sprang forward and caught him in his arms, and as we bent over the unconscious form, he exclaimed: 'My God, doctor, look at him! He is so much like me I feel as if I had been shot myself!' They were as much alike as twins—only his hair was darker. I tell you Miss Elsie, it's a sin to kill men like that. One such man is worth more to this Nation than every Negro that ever set his flat foot on this continent!" (8). The two men's uncanny physical resemblance leads the doctor to the conclusion that white Americans should be united in their sense of their own racial worth against the Negro who is their physical inferior, as signaled by his "flat foot." The recognition of a facial/racial resemblance translates into a recognition of the racial worth equated with it and leads to an erasure of sectional loyalties.

Additionally, the acknowledgment of shared worth as men is made possible by the recognition of explicitly animal qualities in black faces and bodies. As James Kinney has documented, Dixon employs animal imagery in his descriptions of African-American characters, using the language of scientific racism to suggest that the race is not entirely evolved. Dixon's most infamous achievement is his creation of the black rapist, Gus, upon whom he seems to have unleashed his bile: "[Gus] had the short, heavy-set neck of the lower order of animals. His skin was coal black, his lips so thick they curled both ways up and down with crooked blood-marks across them. His nose was flat, and its enormous nostrils seemed in perpetual dilation. The sinister bead eyes, with brown splotches in their whites, were set wide apart and gleamed apelike under his scant brows. His enormous cheekbones and jaws seemed to protrude beyond the ears and almost to hide them" (216). Here the shaping of features reaches a kind of apotheosis. The exaggerated protrusions begin to erase humanity altogether as the jaws almost "hide" the ears. The remark that Gus's face has ape-like qualities is almost mild in comparison to the suggestion that Gus's neck evokes the "lower orders" of animals. And Gus certainly fulfills the animal potential that his features prophesy when he rapes the Cameron's youthful neighbor, Marion Lenior. As Dixon describes it, Gus is an animal at that moment: "A single tiger-spring, and the black claws of the beast sank into the soft white throat and she was still" (304).

In another scene, Dixon suggests that Phil Stoneman, as a visitor from the North, is actually in a better position to read the messages of the black face; by implication, all the North really needs to do is take a close look at physiognomy in order to understand the South's position. Phil views Uncle Aleck, a former slave of the Camerons who, due to radical Reconstruction, is now a member of the North Carolina legislature: "Besides being so bow-legged that his walk was a moving joke, he was so striking a negro in his personal appearance, he seemed to the young Northerner almost a distinct type of man. . . . His receding forehead was high and indicated a cunning intelligence. . . . The animal vivacity of his small eyes and the flexibility of his eyebrows . . . expressed his eager desires" (249). Aleck's features are so exaggerated that they mark his distance from the Anglo-Saxon "type" of humanity. And the features of his face, some explicitly animal, telegraph threatening personality traits such as the cunning intelligence that will perhaps allow him to fulfill his "eager desires."

Not surprisingly, according to Stoneman the main task of Reconstruction as it undoes slavery is to take the animal out of the Negro. As Stoneman explains to Lynch, "If anything could reconcile me to the Satanic Institution, it is the character of the wretches who submit to it and kiss the hand that strikes. . . . The man who is mean enough to wear chains ought to wear them. You must teach, *teach*, TEACH, these black hounds to know they are men, not brutes!" (206). This plan of action actually makes sense from the perspective of Dixon's comments on character. In his discourses, manhood is an act of will, a freely chosen act of self-making. By that logic, character would be marred by the willing assumption of slavery, but its effects presumably could be countered by education and self-mastery. In short, one would think that by teaching brutes they are men, character could be established.[10] But as always, Dixon refuses to advance his own arguments on behalf of African Americans. Dr. Cameron directly refutes Stoneman's calls for the education that will allow blacks to become men and thus use their votes wisely: "His race is not an infant; it is a degenerate—older than yours in time. At last we are face to face with the man whom slavery concealed in its rags. Suffrage is just the new paper cloak with which the Demagogue has sought to hide the issue. . . . Is civilization a patent cloak with which law-tinkers can wrap an animal and make him a king?" (291). Education is misguided because the race is not in a childhood state where it has the potential for change. For Cameron and Dixon, slavery was not a cause of brutality but rather a screen that made the brutal features of the Negro hard to read. In the end, African Americans cannot be changed except in the most superficial ways, and whites must unite in their recognition of that fact.

In addition to its importance for uniting white men in their opposition to black "brutes," the equation of outside appearance with interior worth is also important to the novel's ultimate message of unity. The final act that unites all at the novel's conclusion is marriage, and that union is also shown to be based on an inner/outer logic. The most significant reversal in the novel is Elsie Stoneman's repudiation of her father's politics and her ensuing romantic attachment to Ben Cameron. At first, Elsie is "a bitter partisan of her father's school" and believes with northern prejudice that "all Southerners [are] savage brutes" (56). But the youth and beauty of the Rebel soldiers she sees in the hospital are enough to shake her convictions and convince her of the reality of southern manhood. Ultimately, the attraction between man and woman that becomes an emblem for political unity is based on falling in love with "character" through the intimacy that the body invites. Elsie finds that Ben's "handsome boyish face, his bearing, his whole personality, invited frankness and intimacy," and that "each day [she] saw new and striking traits of character which drew her" (113). This physical and emotional attraction eventually inspires Elsie's political conversion: "She began to understand why the war, which had seemed to her a wicked, cruel, and causeless rebellion, was the one inevitable thing in our growth from loose groups of sovereign states to a United Nation. Love had given her this point of view" (149). Elsie's conversion is made possible by her recognition of the links between Ben's body, character, and politics.

Marriage is important to Dixon's purposes, but the views on marriage held by Ben's mother, Mrs. Cameron, complicate the binary of inner body and outer character in ways that Dixon eventually loses control over. When Dr. Cameron is in jail, Mrs. Cameron apparently receives messages from him by transcending her body: "By a mental telepathy which had always linked her life with his[,] her soul had passed those prison bars. If he had written the pitiful record [of his conditions] with a dagger's point on her heart, she could not have felt it more keenly" (102). Marriage becomes a mystical union of souls that allows for extra-bodily perception. Accordingly, just as Mrs. Cameron transcends her body to "visit" her husband, the unity that her marriage creates is really a spiritual one. Mrs. Cameron advances this theory rather directly in a letter to her son: "They say that those who love and live the close sweet home-life for years grow alike in soul and body . . . I find it so. People have told me that your father and I are more alike than brother and sister of the same blood. In spirit I'm sure it's true" (118). Though the two share a physical resemblance that suggests common blood, the important connection is the unity of spirit. By implication, the marriages between the Stoneman and Cameron children re-create this spiritual transcendence and thereby act as the means for a divided nation to be made whole. As Walter Benn Michaels notes, applying this logic to the novel as a whole, "The identity of soul that brings the Stonemans and Camerons together transcends biology, replacing the natural unity of the family with a spiritual unity that, unlike the family, is genuinely invisible" (190). The novel thus moves from physical resemblance to invisible connection, with marriage and "brotherhood" as symbols for the unity that lies above the visible.

Thus, in *The Clansman* Dixon explicitly goes beyond the visibility of race to explore its invisible aspects. As Michaels argues, the context for this move is the historical confusion over how to enforce the laws of segregation in the aftermath of *Plessy v. Fergusson* and other similar cases. In *Plessy*, race is defined as something that is visible despite the fact that Homer Plessy was not visibly black, and also as a matter of racial instincts, although those instincts could not be considered visible either. Michaels explains that these inconsistencies were not seen as embarrassments to racist lawmaking; the slippage between skin color, race, and racial instincts was actually exploited as legalized discrimination and disenfranchisement were defended as a discrimination between characteristics rather than races. These characteristics actually had the biological authority of color since they were assumed to be biologically inherited.[11] In this way, race was grounded in the extra-visible, and mulattoes were no longer a threat to the color line since they were in a sense recolored by the pervasive association of race traits with the visible aspects of race.

As for white southerners, Dixon assumed that they were united through the invisible qualities of their shared blood. For instance, when her husband is imprisoned, Mrs. Cameron finds courage as "the heritage of centuries of heroic blood from the martyrs of old Scotland began to flash its inspiration from the past" (101). Similarly, the Klan is formed when Scottish blood boils up and a "gale of chivalrous passion and high action . . . swept the white race" (341).[12] However, this white blood is not necessarily connected to white physical features. Michaels reads the white sheets of the Klan as the "representation of an essentially invisible racial identity that can't be seen in people's skins (it couldn't be seen in Homer Plessy's), but can be seen in the Klan's sheets" (190). Thus the sheets are the visible sign of an invisible identity that a body cannot be an adequate sign for, at least not since mixed race had demonstrated how misleading the body could be.

Nonetheless, it is clear in Dixon's (and the Klan's) use of the sheets to make this invisible identity visible that white supremacists are uncomfortable with the notion of a "genuine" racial invisibility. The white sheets signify a spiritual identity that the white body could not be counted on to transmit, but Dixon the physiognomist would really rather that it could. The white sheets become a sign for Dixon's inconsistent desire that race always be visible and for the underlying vulnerability of his ideology. On the surface of this novel, bodies never fail to speak, and they are explicitly able to speak the soul—by implication the racial soul. As one character says, "Beauty is a sign of the soul—the body is the soul!" (301). As such, white bodies speak superiority and black bodies speak inferiority. However, Dixon must deal with characters who frustrate this logic and explain what messages the mulatto body speaks, especially a beautiful white-skinned mulatto body. By Dixon's own logic, if miscegenation stands as a threat to the white body because it erases white physical features, it also stands as a threat to the racial soul because the body is the soul. The most terrifying message of the mulatto body is that it speaks the instability of the white body, in part because it highlights the shaky relationship between body and racial identity, but most of all because it represents a white body transformed into a black one with the racial soul defiled accordingly.

At the nexus of the inconsistencies in Dixon's racial arguments—race is the soul not the body, but the body is the soul, so race is once again the body—are the mulatto characters of Silas Lynch and Lydia Brown. Dixon handles his inconsistencies by essentially leaving mulatto characters outside the racial logic of visibility. He deliberately asserts that Lydia Brown, Stoneman's mulatto mistress, is enigmatic. The first description of her conveys little more information than she is a "tawny brown woman with restless eyes" (191). In fact, her name is her epithet. She is referred to as "the brown woman" or the "strange brown woman," suggesting that she is odd and off-putting. She is also explicitly animal, described as a "leopardess" and as possessing an "animal beauty." But beyond that she is unknowable. When Stoneman meets with his henchmen and gives them instructions for his vision of Reconstruction,

Stoneman is visibly elated but Brown is unreadable: "The woman's face wore the mask of a sphinx" (100). Presumably, the mulatto face foils the physiognomist impulses of the narrator, so that her unreadability, or ability to mask her true face with an unreadable one, is part of the theme of mulatto evil. As sphinxes, mulattoes can hide the evil intentions that supposedly pure characters—both white and black—cannot help but signal.

Stoneman also tests the breaking points of Dixon's descriptive logic. Following the model of Legree, as an evil threat to white supremacy Stoneman is visibly villainous; he is an ugly, clubfooted cripple. Furthermore, the narrator notes that "audacity [is] stamped in every line of his magnificent head" (57). In fact, Stoneman's "whiteness" must be called into question since his professed strategy of revenge on the South is to use miscegenation to debase the racial soul of the Scotch southerners so that they will never be a threat to the North again. Dixon thus uses Stoneman as a physical sign for the evils of miscegenation. For example, when an ailing Stoneman makes an appearance on the Senate floor, carried in by "two gigantic negroes" who set him down and then "[crouch] down on their haunches beside him," the scene becomes a racial tableau:

> Their kinky heads, black skin, thick lips, white teeth, and flat noses, made for the moment a curious symbolic frame for the chalk white passion of the old Commoner's face.
>
> No sculptor ever dreamed a more sinister emblem of the corruption of a race of empire-builders than this group. Its black figures, wrapped in the night of four thousand years of barbarism, squatted there the "equal" of their master, grinning at his forms of Justice, the evolution of forty centuries of Aryan genius. (171)

As with the description of Lynch, a reference to art signals Dixon's desire that the reader accept the symbolic meaning for this visual image provided by his narrator. Specifically, though the impact of the emblem is created by the contrast between the black, barbaric "symbolic frame" and the "chalk white" face of Aryan genius within it, the emblem sends a single message, one of racial corruption.

In other places in the novel, Stoneman's face transmits the same message as it becomes a sign for the threat to the features of whiteness that miscegenation poses. According to the narrator, Stoneman's face betrays his excitement with "the nostrils of his eagle-beaked nose breathing rapacity, sensuality throbbing in his massive jaws, and despotism frowning from his heavy brows" (99). Though his nose is not flat, his nostrils give signs of animal passions, and his jaws are massive like black characters'.[13] Stoneman is thus figured as less than white and nearly animal. His mouth closes so tightly that "the lower lip protrude[s]," he has a "huge ape-like arm" (133), and his deformed foot seems to "grip the floor as the claw of a beast" (143). All in all, Stoneman is rhetorically mulatto, and his white features are coupled with features that are coded as black.[14] And as a mulatto, Stoneman shares another important quality with Brown. Specifically, he is difficult to read. Though his features speak of his evil clearly enough to us, other characters have trouble reading him. His doctor tells him, "The study of man has become a sort of passion with me, but you are the deepest mystery I've yet encountered . . . the secret of personality resides in motives, and I can't find yours either in your actions or words" (185). Stoneman's actions—as the sign of his will and thus the sign of his character—are hard to pin down. Stoneman's "strange contradictions of . . . character," later noted by the narrator, are echoes of the rhetorical mulattoism that makes his motives unreadable.

As a consequence of this unreadability, the mulatto has no fixed place in a novel governed by the logic of visible character. In fact, Brown seems to conduct herself, like the educated blacks in *The Leopard's Spots,* as if she were performing her position in white society. At Stoneman's meeting of henchmen, Brown "[takes] her seat opposite Stoneman and preside[s] over this curious group with the easy assurance of conscious power. Whatever her real position, she knew now how to play the rôle she had chosen to assume" (94). Her behavior is designed to thwart the observing eye, mask her motives, and communicate misleading messages about her relationship to Stoneman and his politics. Thus, as a mulatto she has mastered the art of the veneer by turning it into a role, and—unlike the placeless George Harris—she has found a position of power that allows her to parlay this performance into political results.

Thus, we come close to the center of this novel and to the mechanism behind the threat to Anglo-Saxon purity. Mulattoes can use their very unreadability to become active agents in the defilement of the white race. Ironically, this becomes most clear at the moment in the novel when Lynch becomes completely readable. While Lynch addresses the Reconstruction (and thus black) state legislature, Dr. Cameron witnesses the scene:

> In the first masterful tone of his voice the doctor's keen intelligence caught the ring of his savage metal and felt the shock of his powerful personality—a personality which had thrown to the winds every mask. . . .
>
> He held the surging crowd in the hollow of his hand. They yelled, laughed, howled, or wept as he willed.
>
> Now he painted in burning words the imaginary horrors of slavery until the tears rolled down his cheeks and he wept at the sound of his own voice. Every dusky hearer burst into tears and moans. (274)

The substance of Lynch's speech is that the horrors of slavery authorize African Americans to wage war against the white race so that blacks can be equal to whites and "take their daughter[s] in marriage" (275). At this moment, Lynch becomes an uncomfortable parallel to Dixon himself. Lynch recharacterizes the past—"the imagined horrors of slavery"—in order to exhort his audience to unite and wage a race war over the issue of miscegenation. He is also much like Charlie Gaston, the inveterate speechmaker in *The Leopard's Spots,* who is nominated for governor after a stirring speech that ignites a similarly frenzied response from his audience.

The real threat of the mulatto lies in the particular way in which Lynch produces this power over his audience. Lynch's power in oratory does not come from strength of character, as Charlie Gaston's does. Rather, after throwing away the "mask," he reveals himself as possessed of a "powerful personality." Historian Warren Susman has argued that the notion of character fulfilled certain functions in nineteenth-century culture: it provided a method for the mastery and development of the self and a standard for presenting the self to society at large. However, at the turn of the century another version of self-mastery and self-presentation began to appear more frequently in books and pamphlets. The concept of "personality" served the same functions as character, but was more concerned with self-realization than with self-mastery.

While character was associated with moral control and dignity, according to Susman "from the beginning the adjectives most frequently associated with personality suggest a very different concept . . . *fascinating, stunning, attractive, magnetic, glowing, masterful, creative, dominant, forceful*" (277, emphasis in source). Character is all about being good, but personality is all about notoriety and power. In a striking example of this shift, Orison Swett Marden—the author of *Character: The Grandest Thing in the World*—published a book titled *Masterful Personality* in 1921. In the first book, Marden's purpose was to give name to "certain deep-rooted dispositions" necessary for character, but apparently in the second the deep roots of character were just as significant as the "mastery" of personality. In addition, Funk & Wagnalls's "Mental Efficiency Series" (which had published Starke's book *Character: How to Strengthen It*) issued a volume on personality subtitled "How to Build It" (Susman 277). Here the associations are clear: character is something you already possess, something you strengthen, but personality is more of a construction, something you build.

The main feature of character had always been its relationship to fixed principles. As Susman explains, in the culture of character "the highest development of self . . . meant fulfillment through sacrifice in the name of a higher law, ideals of duty, honor, integrity. One came to selfhood through obedience to law and ideals" (280). For example, Charlie strengthens his character, but it is also rooted because it is in accord with an inherited, fixed moral code. In contrast, the self-making of personality does not accord to anything particularly rooted. Rather, "the social role demanded of all in the new culture of personality was that of a performer. Every American became a performing self" (280). To shape one's personality, one perfected techniques of presentation and appearance such as elocution, habits of grooming, and the use of beauty aids, all in order to "impress and influence" (280). So while for Dixon moral character shows in the face from within, the new vision of personality involved a control over the surface of the face from without. Personality was part of a conscious performance that would influence people regardless of the moral core of the self.

Comparing the places in these novels where Lynch unmasks his personality and Charlie demonstrates his character, it becomes clear that

Dixon feared the self-projection and self-making implied by the culture of personality. Dixon paints himself into a bit of a corner in *The Clansman.* He creates a black character who has access to power, and who has the ability to move ignorant black masses through speechmaking. However, since he must distinguish this power from the speechmaking made by Anglo-Saxon practitioners of democracy, Dixon attributes the effectiveness of black speech to personality. Though blacks might not have the ability to stand with whites on the basis of character, he argues that they can manufacture a mastery over others built through the allure of their personalities. However, the character/personality distinction creates the same internally inconsistent logic that ostensibly preserved the ideology of racial visibility. The unreadability that Dixon attributes to mulattoes in order to redeem his equation of body and soul undermines the physiognomy that was the basis for the equation in the first place. In the same way, the personality that he equates with mulatto characters in order to preserve the whiteness of the affective powers of character also undermines physiognomy in that it allows for bodies to transmit messages that are not rooted in character at all. In fact, the power that comes from personality is not "visibly" different from that which comes from character and can have exactly the same power over an audience.

In *The Leopard's Spots,* the Reverend Durham tells Charlie on several occasions that "the future American" will "either be an Anglo-Saxon or a Mulatto." And if the Anglo-Saxon triumphs in his drive for racial purity, all Americans will continue to signal their national and racial worth unambiguously in the way their bodies speak their character. However, by evoking personality, Dixon has employed a vision of self that presents a much more immediate threat to white inner/outer logic than the prospect of total miscegenation. The culture of personality, which comes into being with a weakening in the culture of character, allows all people access to a form of self-making and self-projection which as a surface performance ultimately makes their characters impossible to read. In the culture of personality, physiognomy proves useless because physical features are manipulated in order to transmit crafted messages; this new ethos allows the individual to change his or her body and take control over what it speaks. In a sense, all people become mulattoes. Dixon's fear of the mulatto thus translates into fear of a shift in the national vision of the self. Dixon's desire for racial purity becomes a nostalgic desire for a rooted self that apparently was no longer considered by some to be the modal type of the American.

The Romance of the Body

Dixon identified his novels as historical romances in their subtitles: *The Leopard's Spots* is "A Romance of the White Man's Burden—1865–1900," and *The Clansman* is "An Historical Romance of the Ku Klux Klan." As such, he chose perhaps the most rooted of all prose forms available to him. Since the romance relies for its action on the existence of a code (a moral standard with a corresponding code for behavior), it allows for narrative detail to be morally and ideologically grounded. The plot of the romance hinges on a breach of this code that is healed by the conclusion.[15] In Dixon's fiction, a threat to the code of American democracy and Anglo-Saxon purity surfaces in Reconstruction. Eventually, that threat is met when an even older code, the code of honor of the Scottish clans, is evoked. The Klan comes into existence because the descendants of the Scottish clans have inherited the racial tendencies that make a defense of white supremacy inevitable.

In romance, descriptive details are incorporated into the logic of the code. The way characters look is a sign of their allegiance or opposition to norms for behavior. Certain visual signs indicate villainy, others heroism, and both are defined by adherence to the code. Accordingly, romance is usually allegorical, and characters embody the qualities they are associated with. Dixon's insistence that good characters are beautiful and that evil characters are ugly resonates with this part of the tradition. Dixon thereby aligns the descriptive conventions of romance with his own form of scientific racism, since his physiognomist theories insist on the same kind of fit between appearance and essence. In this way, the historical romance suits Dixon's purpose rather neatly: as "historical" it allows Dixon to situate the action in a historical crisis, and as "romance" it allows him the perfect framework for his physiognomy.

In addition, the historical romance suits Dixon's purposes because of its particular plot shape. Typically the historical romance, as established by Sir Walter Scott, involves a conflict between two different groups separated by an ethnic or national difference. In Scott's romances of the

British Isles this conflict is resolved by a marriage between groups which cements their underlying ties of blood and ends the conflict. However, this convention does not hold for historical romances set in the United States, since the central conflict is often between white and non-white racial groups. Therefore, the form was reworked by James Fenimore Cooper so that the two races meet violently but in a context of assumed hierarchy. The resolution of the conflict is made possible by a restoration of the proper hierarchy which was temporarily disturbed.[16] Dixon neatly combines the two versions of romance: a racial relationship is established between North and South—and thus between Puritan and Scot—through a marriage precipitated on a recognition of shared racial identity. At the same time, an assumed racial hierarchy is reestablished with the suppression of the Negro.

In Dixon's novels, scientific notions about race are transmitted through the creation of character by way of the conventions of prose romance. But in order for these notions to be received as political messages, the reading of character must be internally determined or simultaneously presented; Dixon's particular version of the scientific truth about racial character needs to have a context within the narrative itself to be transmitted reliably. For example, the story of George Harris could be read as a sign that white racism is what keeps educated blacks from achievement, but with the commentary by other characters it becomes a story of the imperfect imitation of character that white racism will not accept. Or, as with Silas Lynch and his fully Aryan features, simultaneous descriptive information tells us that he is unmistakably African. In both cases, some authority embedded in the text provides a reading so that race, appearance, and character are correctly equated.

Significantly, in Dixon's novels the weather is always party to the emotional register of an important scene, and as overblown objective correlative it indicates how a passage is to be received. In *The Clansman* it rains at Lincoln's funeral, and when the Klan's campaign to take back the South coincides with a freakish storm, the narrator notes that "the events of the night were sufficiently eloquent. The movement of the clouds in sympathy was unnecessary" (344). Even if in this case the event speaks its own symbolic significance without help of symbolic weather, the descriptive strategy is clear. Visual details are chosen and provided in order to add up to a reading of the action transpiring. In fact, this marshaling of detail toward the single-minded defense of a particular ideology is a strategy that Dixon shares with Stowe. As Jane Tompkins has argued, Stowe's sentimental aesthetic is based on a similar economy of narrative detail. Tompkins demonstrates that a single scene in *Uncle Tom's Cabin* can often be expanded to give significance for the whole: "The scene I have been describing is a node within a network of allusion in which every character and event in the novel has a place. The narrative's rhetorical strength derives in part from the impression it gives of taking every kind of detail in the world into account . . . and investing those details with a purpose and a meaning which are both immediately apprehensible and finally significant" (139). The power of Stowe's aesthetic goes a long way toward explaining the lasting impact of her novel and perhaps begins to explain why Dixon was compelled to imitate it in order to contest it. The form of Stowe's novel served Dixon's purposes because he could shift its ideological orientation while exploiting the power of its narrative strategy. As Tompkins puts it, "the totalizing effect of the novel's iterative organization . . . is inseparably bound to its political purpose" (139). All in all, sentimental fiction and romance appear to have the totalizing relationship between detail and ideology in common.[17]

However, the descriptive conventions of Dixon's genre—and the racial science he has coupled with it—cannot contain the theme of mixed race completely within his ideological network. In a playful scene between Ben and Elsie in *The Clansman,* Ben seeks to reassure her of the unimportance of their political differences: "Don't waste your sweet breath talking about such things. My politics is bounded on the North by a pair of amber eyes, on the South by a dimpled little chin, on the East and West by a rosy cheek. Words do not frame its speech. Its language is a mere sign, a pressure of the lips—yet it thrills body and soul beyond words" (163). Here Ben suggests that Elsie's face *is* his politics, and in a very real sense it is; his sworn political objective is to protect features such as hers—light eyes, little chins, rosy cheeks—from the defilement of miscegenation. Yet his wishful suggestion that his politics could be identical to a face and therefore beyond language is telling. Since the translation of bodies into language in this text has proven inadequate to the message that Dixon would hope to convey, what Dixon really desires is a political message that could skip words altogether, that could escape the fact that language is a mere sign, and that could have a direct and thrilling impact on bodies and souls without translation into the "frame" of words.

Dixon wants bodies themselves, bodies that convey messages without having to stop off in words. In the end, physiognomy, as the science of reading bodies, has failed him because he could not control the play of signification when bodies are described in language. As with the passage that describes Lynch, Dixon desires descriptive closure—a description that does not transmit anything more or less than the interpretation that is embedded within it. However, it appears that this closure is not possible because the contradictions in his theory of visibility are visible in the places where the messages of his created bodies go beyond his interpretive frame.

Symptomatically, in *The Clansman* Dixon seeks to create a fantasy version of how science might read bodies, one that, unlike physiognomy, would not rely on a "translation" into language for its messages. After young Marion Lenior is raped, Dr. Cameron and his son Ben discover the identity of the rapist in a microscopic inspection of Mrs. Lenior's retina after her suicide (she was a witness to the crime). Dr. Cameron explains the process scientifically: "Psychologists hold that nothing is lost from the memory of man. Impressions remain in the brain like words written on paper in invisible ink. So I believe of images in the eye if we can trace them early enough" (312–13). Here, as with the gleam from Lynch's eyes that transmits pictures of the jungle, eyes are a conduit from the outer world to an inner one of racial identity and human thought process. In both cases, eyes provide a window into the symbolic location of the truth that both scientific inspection (in the case of Mrs. Lenior) and artistic representation (in the case of Lynch) will unfailingly identify. This gleam coming from a mind imprinted invisibly and permanently suggests a form of recording beyond writing.

However, while this metaphor/fanciful science allows for the truth of bodies to speak, the metaphor of "invisible ink" invalidates the metaphor of reading that physiognomy relies on. Furthermore, this gleam also suggests a pseudo-scientific mechanism for a kind of racial memory whose truth can only be revealed in images. The artist who paints Lynch—and who can only coin his racial identity by reference to another visual image, pictures of the jungle—and the doctor who sees images revealed by the microscope both reveal racial truth through a system of visual representation. And the fact that this novel alludes to the possibility that the truth of bodies comes across best in nonverbal situations undermines the ability of prose fiction to do the job of characterization.

The presence of an imagined science that bolsters physiognomy suggests that Dixon was worried that his science was ill-suited to an art form with an ultimately uncontrollable play of signification and interpretation. Though Dixon kept writing novels well into the twentieth century, the most perfect expression of his racial ideology was not in that form at all but rather in the 1915 film version *The Birth of a Nation.* Dixon needed a way for bodies to speak without language, and a black-and-white movie would seem to allow "color" to speak in a binary, controlled fashion. However, in a final irony, the medium of film reinscribes much of the cult of personality that Dixon's ethos of character would seek to fight. Susman argues that "the nature and form of the modern motion picture as it developed as a middle-class art form between 1910 and 1915 clearly shows its participation in the culture of personality" (282). Specifically, film places a requisite emphasis on the face and its messages, but it presents an acted self, a performance. In *The Birth of a Nation,* the black characters are really white actors in black face. This may suit Dixon's purposes to a point. If, as Michaels argues, no body can be as white as the soul embodied in a white sheet, perhaps no body can be as black as the blackness of black face. But in the end such a surface performance of blackness disembodies the visual image from the essence of the person beneath it. Film glorifies personality and performance over character, turning both whiteness and blackness into a performance.

As the mocking response to Dixon's physiognomy in the *Voice of the Negro* would suggest, Dixon's combination of historical romance and physiognomy did not go without some protest. The most sustained contemporary response to Dixon was Kelly Miller's essay "As to the Leopard's Spots: An Open Letter to Thomas Dixon," published in 1905. Miller responds directly to Dixon over his inner/outer logic: "You ask: 'Can you change the color of the Negro's skin, the kink of his hair, the bulge of his lip, or the beat of his heart, with a spelling book or a machine?' This rhetorical outburst does great credit to your literary skill;

but analysis fails to reveal in it any pregnant meaning. Since civilization is not an attribute of the color of skin, or curl of hair or curl of lip, there is no necessity for changing such physical peculiarities" (13). From this perspective, Dixon's descriptive romance is in fact meaningless when analyzed for messages other than the ones provided within descriptive closure. Apparently, questioning the relationship between body and civilization requires a different descriptive tack and, by implication, a different mode than romance.

When Gus the rapist is captured in *The Clansman*, he is taken to the Klan's hideout and "questioned" about the incident. While under hypnosis, he "[relives] the crime with fearful realism" and describes in detail the plan for the rape and the steps that led up to it. In both Dixon's novels, this is one of only a few stories told from the point of view of a black character. In some chapters loyal blacks who refuse to leave their masters become the narrative focus for a portion of a chapter, but in those instances the narration is secured by a code of behavior of loyalty as surely as the white point of view is secured by the code of Anglo-Saxon purity. Gus's narrative gives Dixon's fantasy of the type of narration that would be necessary to explore such topics—something beyond an inner/outer logic grounded by a code. And it is fearfully realistic, a mode of description willing to relinquish its hold on what it speaks to the reader.

To see how the realist authors who also tackled the subject of mixed race differentiated themselves and their chosen genres from the sentimental and romance tradition that both Dixon and Stowe employ, we must look at their self-assertive strategies and fantasies. It is particularly important to track the uses of the term *character*, and the ways character is equated with both race and the body in the process of characterization. The shift from character to personality in Dixon's fiction suggests that the very conception of the unified self was part of what Dixon was defending in his racial jeremiad. To maintain unity of character, and its direct and untroubled relationship to the features of the body, a population must keep its blood unmixed. Shifts in the concept of racial character can therefore be detected in the contrasts between genres that would defend unity of character and those that would allow it to be supplemented with less anchored and more fragmented notions of personality and performance.

3

Pudd'nhead Wilson's Phrenological Photograph

An author's introduction titled "Whisper to the Reader" begins Mark Twain's novel *Pudd'nhead Wilson.* Placed above it is a quotation from the Ben Franklinesque calendar composed by the title character, David "Pudd'nhead" Wilson: "There is no character, howsoever good and fine, but it can be destroyed by ridicule, howsoever poor and witless. Observe the ass, for instance: his character is about perfect . . . yet see what ridicule has brought him to. Instead of feeling complimented when we are called an ass, we are left in doubt" (1). From the first page of this novel, character is presented as a far from straightforward property. Though the ass has a perfect character, its perfection has been destroyed by the way it has been characterized. This aphorism, and events in the plot of the novel that clearly echo it, suggests that since character requires a translation through characterization, it can be perverted as it is made common knowledge. Twain's recognition of possible distortions in the characterization of character implicitly questions whether scientific accounts of character—the ones Thomas Dixon takes as givens—are in fact self-evident.

Wilson's aphorism also asks the reader to "observe the ass"—a kind of shorthand for "take the ass as an example." However, this word choice also raises the question of whether we can see what ridicule has obscured and through this observation detect the true character of the ass. This tension between characterization and the visible will replay itself in the events of the novel as *Pudd'nhead Wilson* presents mixed-race characters whose white skin foils the ideology of racial visibility. While scientific racism relies on the binary categories of black and white, visual inspection cannot ultimately place a light-skinned African American into that binary. By focusing on the invisible blackness of his main characters, Twain examines the very mechanism whereby scientific and cultural ideas about race and blackness are created and received and how they rely on imperfect observation imperfectly converted into characterization.

Twain's novel is constructed to test assumptions about race on two levels: plot and genre. The plot of *Pudd'nhead Wilson* is put in motion when the nearly white slave Roxy switches her child and her master's child in the cradle. The events of the novel then revolve around the contestable blackness of both Roxy and her usurping child, Tom Driscoll. Twain suggests that Roxy's performance as a slave and her child's performance as a white southern gentleman comprise what is visible to those who seek to judge their characters. The novel's plot disrupts the direct and clearly detectable relationship between racial character and physical appearance that physiognomy and scientific racism depend upon. In addition, Twain places this plot-level theme of the questionable visibility of race and racial character within a generic framework that is particularly vulnerable to its instabilities. *Pudd'nhead Wilson* is in part a satire of sentimental fiction, a prose form (like the historical romance) that relies on fixed types. The romance provides a direct and physiognomic relationship between appearance and character, suggesting that character is easy to read and determine. However, in Twain's novel this process of reading is a humorously inaccurate way to arrive at knowledge about others; just as the character of the ass cannot be read correctly, nearly all assessments of character fail. In this way, Twain builds a satire of sentimental fiction that is as much a satire of racial science. He questions the human ability to judge character from physical observation by constructing a critique of the physiognomy that underlies both sentimental and scientific characterizations.

However, as I will argue, at times the novel would seem to establish a firmer relationship between body and character. The means by which Tom's identity is finally determined by David Wilson, and by which the true heir of the house of Driscoll is restored after twenty years of slavery, raises the possibility that the body really can be read infallibly. In the last third of the novel the genre begins to shift and the satire of sentimental fiction gives way to a more straightforward detective fiction plot. As this shift occurs, character becomes easier to read, the mixed-race characters are worked back into the racial binary, and suspect and satirized physiognomy is replaced with a more or less completely reliable phrenology. The change in genre from satire of sentimental fiction to detective fiction coincides with a return to more fixed and stereotypical links between character and physical description. As a result, it appears that these genres provide different frames for reading character. As the frame shifts, so do the conventions for characterization and physical description, and thus the novel's apparent stand on racial science and visibility appears to shift along with them.

Interestingly, in Twain's remarks on written description he appears less concerned with the conventions of genre than with the direct and accurate representation of visual detail. One of Twain's repeated maxims for the merits of good descriptive writing was the notion of using the pen to "photograph." Twain used this metaphor in a January 21, 1879, letter to William Dean Howells in which he complimented the powers of description displayed in *The Lady of the Aroostook:* "It is all such truth—truth to the life; everywhere your pen falls it leaves a photograph" (qtd. in Cummings 94). The same metaphor appears in the "Whisper to the Reader" at the start of *Pudd'nhead Wilson,* although without quite the same straightforward sincerity. Since the novel ends with a bit of courtroom drama, Twain humbly warns his reader that "a person who is ignorant of legal matters is always liable to make mistakes when he tries to photograph a court scene with his pen" (1). Twain reassures his readers that his mistakes will be minimal since he subjected his courtroom chapters to "rigid and exhausting revision and correction by a trained barrister—if that is what they are called" (1). The barrister in question turns out to be an expatriate acquaintance of Twain's in Florence who studied law "part of a while" thirty-five years ago: "He was a little rusty on his law, but he rubbed up for this book, and those two or three legal chapters are right and straight, now. He told me so himself" (1–2).

Though Twain indicates that a photographic form of representation is ostensibly being attempted in the courtroom chapters of *Pudd'nhead*

Wilson, he undermines his own claims to realistic accuracy from the start. Presumably, Dixon's mode of fiction, with its closed, singular reading of physical appearance, is not realistic by Twain's standards; it relies on a strategy of representation by which physical details are arranged in ideologically motivated ways that violate the notion of using the pen to photograph. Yet as an alternative to the ideological arrangement of detail, photography too will be found wanting. Twain brings two genres with their different frames for the construction and reading of character to a climax in this "realistic" courtroom drama and in the process seemingly provides a scientific means for reading the body that will anchor their physiognomy. But, as I will argue, the ironies that result from their mutual failings suggest that mixed race may be just as disruptive to photographic realism as it is to physiognomic characterization.

Twain and Phrenology

Despite his pose as an American innocent with virtually no interest in books, Mark Twain was an intellectually curious lifelong reader. Hyatt Waggoner's account of Twain's familiarity with scientific topics, dating back to the 1930s, has been augmented by more recent studies.[1] According to Waggoner, Twain's knowledge of science, "while not profound or in any sense rigorously accurate, was nevertheless inspired by enthusiastic interest, and was, for the average layman of the day, comparatively comprehensive" (359). In particular, Waggoner notes that Twain "had a philosophically sound, if not scientifically detailed, knowledge of the main outline of anthropology. This knowledge was, in fact, one of the principal bulwarks of his deterministic philosophy" (359). While Twain's "determinism"—the tendency of his later works to present humans as mechanisms, devoid of true agency in a universe governed by set physical laws—is one of the more widely studied scientific themes in his fiction, an understanding of his interest in anthropology and other sciences of man does not by necessity lead to an examination of Darwinian materialism.[2]

In particular, some critics have noted that the pseudo-science of phrenology makes an appearance in Twain's intellectual record at fairly regular intervals throughout his life. As a nineteen-year-old he copied long passages from George Sumner Weaver's *Lectures on Mental Science According to the Philosophy of Phrenology* (1852) into a memorandum book. Twain later had phrenological exams performed on himself on at least three occasions (the last in the winter of 1900–1901). Also, in his autobiography, Twain makes reference to the midcentury heyday of phrenology, noting that when he was living in Hannibal phrenologists would make frequent visits to the town to deliver lectures and examine patients.[3] The traveling phrenologist notably appears as the Duke in *Huckleberry Finn;* one of the Duke's many scams is to lecture on the science of phrenology and provide charts of character for twenty-five cents apiece.

The version of phrenology that Twain copied into his memorandum book was an expanded application that had begun to resemble physiognomy. German Johann Gaspar Spurzheim, an influence on Weaver and other American phrenologists, had taken phrenological analysis beyond the head alone by combining a focus on the skull with the ancient theory of cardinal humors. According to that theory, bodily features such as the arrangement of countenance, body fat, and musculature corresponded to four psychological types called temperaments: lymphatic, sanguine, bilious, and nervous. As Spurzheim saw it, the phrenological examination should take in the physiological makeup of the patient to determine his or her temperament, thus grounding the reading of the skull in the whole physical context. Phrenology was taken beyond the minutiae of the skull and applied more holistically—and less exactly—to the entire body. According to Alan Gribben, "By 1847 the *American Phrenological Journal,* undisputed authority on every subject within its field, was routinely defining 'the doctrine of temperaments' as 'the physiology and general form of body and face as indicating character' " (46).[4]

Weaver, a Universalist minister who lived in St. Louis in the 1850s, was a popularist of the science who spread phrenology to backwater towns as a means of self-improvement.[5] According to Gribben, the young Twain copied Weaver's descriptions of each temperament, placing the sanguine first in his order because he saw it as his own. He even added small details to it to make it better fit his physical appearance: though Weaver explained that the sanguine is the "burning, flaming, flashing temperament" and therefore "hangs out its signs of fire in its red, blazing hair and countenance," Twain noted that it may also find expression in sandy hair like his (Gribben 49). In 1862, Twain incorporated the doctrine of temperaments into a letter to his sister to explain why he had previously predicted financial success for himself with such total and misfounded assurance: "Don't you know that people who always feel jolly, no matter where they are or what happens to them—who have the organ of Hope preposterously developed—who are endowed with an uncongealable sanguine temperament—who never feel concerned with the price of corn—and who cannot, by any possibility, discover any but the *bright* side of a picture—are *very* apt to go to extremes, and exaggerate, with 40-horse microscopic power?" (*Letters* 157). Here Twain's attitude toward phrenology is difficult to determine. It is unclear whether this gentle self-mocking is also designed to undermine faith in phrenological self-understanding. In any event, the phrenological language of organs and temperaments—whether taken seriously or not—serves as a means for self-characterization, allowing Twain to describe his character to his sister. And, as critics have documented, the concepts and language of phrenology—especially references to temperaments—are clearly present in many of Twain's subsequent literary characterizations.

Interestingly, the addition of the temperaments to phrenology undermined any superior interpretive authority it might have claimed over physiognomy. Phrenology in its original and purest sense imagined that it could read character virtually infallibly. As Randall Knoper explains, "The allure of phrenology lay in the certainty associated with the indexical. If the material surface of the body registered—as a mold would, through physical impression—the qualities of the interior, the science of phrenology could secure . . . the knowledge it promised" (100). An indexical relationship does not rely on the arbitrary relationships like those that structure language. In a linguistic system a word or sign is linked to the thing it signifies through convention but not through any natural connection. Both physiognomy and the phrenology of temperaments rely on a system that is arbitrary like language; red hair refers to a certain type of personality because it is conventionally taken to do so (or because it relies on a metaphorical relationship between the red color of fire and the heat of a fiery personality). But phrenology relies on a relationship with a more solid guarantee: the bump on the skull is a direct and physiological impression or index of the bulge of the brain below it. The relationship between the brain as character and the body as expression is natural, not symbolic.[6]

Consequently, Twain became increasingly convinced that phrenology, as it was practiced, did not avoid the structures of interpretation that make readings of character vulnerable to distortion.[7] By the time Twain wrote "The Secret History of Eddypus" (February–March 1901 and 1902), he had outgrown his boyhood fascination with phrenology as a reliable method for determining character.[8] In this story, a man who lives in the distant future finds a manuscript written a thousand years earlier by "Mark Twain the Bishop of New Jersey." The manuscript describes an episode where "Mark Twain" goes to visit phrenologists for an exam. The way the frame narrator introduces the episode matches the historical Twain's developing attitudes toward phrenology: "He ['Twain'] never explains, except figuratively, who or what the phrenologists were, and it seems probable that he was not able to classify them quite definitively; for whereas in the beginning of his third chapter he twice speaks of them as 'those unerring diviners of the human mind and the human character,' in later chapters he always refers to them briefly and without ornament as 'those damned asses' " ("Secret History" 199). For the "Mark Twain" in this story, the phrenologists who were once trusted to read character eventually become objects of derision.

In the episode itself, the character Mark Twain discovers that his head is swelling, and he wishes to learn if "this enlargement would enlarge [his] mental capacities and make a corresponding aggrandizement in [his] character" (200). He visits the phrenological offices under an assumed name and in a turban because he cannot find a hat to fit. The reading he leaves with concludes that he "probably keeps a harem," that he "worships himself," and that he is "born for a thief" (202). As he is now suspicious that the phrenologists are "guessers," he makes a second visit under his true name and dressed in his bishop's attire. This time he leaves after having been told that "others are dirt in presence of this purity," that he possesses a "divine humility," and that he is "the golden palace of truth" (203). Twain ends the episode by remarking that "phrenology is the 'science' which extracts character from clothes" (203). Apparently, phrenology does not read character from the body at all but from other visible signs that can be changed or even deliberately manipulated. Most importantly, phrenologists take externals like clothes into account in order to arrive at flattering readings that befit a patient's social status.[9]

Twain clearly became deeply suspicious of character readings. Accordingly, his fiction often fights against the way phrenological logic and language had penetrated prose genres in the last decades of the nineteenth century. As a result, Twain's skepticism toward phrenology is often a determinant of his satire. For example, phrenology and physiognomy had been adopted into the genre of travel writing. As Gribben has documented, Twain read George Combe's *Notes on the United States of North America during a Phrenological Visit in 1838–9–40* in preparation for writing his own travel narrative *Life on the Mississippi* (1883). Deleted manuscript pages for *Life on the Mississippi* praise Combe's text. However, despite Twain's praise for Combe, in his own text he takes a sarcastic tack toward the central aim of a phrenologized travel genre, namely, the determination and then representation of the character of a region and its inhabitants.

In the second main section of *Life on the Mississippi,* Twain catalogs how people begin to "change" as one moves through regions. However, he conducts the narration with self-conscious satire. He provides observations about people and behavior, but with an accompanying sarcastic commentary: "'This morning, struck into the region of full goatees.' . . . The goatee extends over a wide extent of country; and is accompanied by an iron-clad belief in Adam and the biblical history of creation, which has not suffered from the assaults of the scientists" (168). This mocking conflation of the trivial detail with the generalizing observation continues: "'At the railway stations the loafers carry both hands in their breeches; it was observable, heretofore, that one hand was sometimes out of doors,—here, never. This is an important fact in geography.' If the loafers determined the *character* of the country, it would be still more important, of course" (168, emphasis added). As these observations and their deflating commentary suggest, Twain is interested in maximizing the potential humor, but he makes a joke out of his reluctance to ascribe importance to details of appearance and gesture as they pertain to the assessment of regional character.

It is not surprising, then, that one memorable incident in *Life on the Mississippi* is concerned with creating humor out of complacent readings of physical detail. In a digression from the account of his travels on the Mississippi, Twain describes a voyage on a seafaring vessel that took him to California "in the early days" (268). On that voyage, he had formed an acquaintance with a man who was "engaging in his countrified simplicity and his beaming good nature" (268). Twain had assessed the man visually and arrived at what he felt was an informed reading: "The first time I saw this Mr. John Backus, I guessed, from his clothes and his looks, that he was a grazier or farmer from the back woods of some western State—doubtless Ohio—and afterward when he dropped into his personal history and I discovered that he *was* a cattle raiser from interior Ohio, I was so pleased with my own penetrations that I warmed to him for verifying my instinct" (268). Here Twain is the guesser who uses clothing to form an impression of a stranger. Other passengers on the boat size Backus up as well, and he becomes the target of a team of professional gamblers who eventually maneuver him into a card game where he is poised to lose thousands of dollars in gold. However, at the climactic moment, it turns out that Backus is a professional gambler who all along had been conning the other gamblers. The fact that both Twain and the other gamblers were so sure of the man's character and identity from outward signs (signs that he had obviously orchestrated) had made the con possible. Backus's story suggests that character can be performed and that visual signs can be manipulated to foil visual assessment.[10]

Pudd'nhead Wilson displays Twain's recognition that phrenology and the readings it promises are often ironically and comically inaccurate. In addition, Twain shows an awareness that physiognomic language and concepts had penetrated popular genres. In *Pudd'nhead Wilson,* Twain continues a project he began in *Life on the Mississippi:* he treads the line between fulfilling generic conventions and constructing a satire of them. In *Life on the Mississippi,* he writes a travel narrative, but becomes sarcastic when it comes to reporting on regional character—the aspect of that genre which had become phrenological. And, in *Pudd'nhead Wilson,* he writes a novel that conforms to the conventions for sentimental fiction set in the South, but he constructs a satire by pointing out the assumptions about character and visual assessment contained within that genre. Additionally, in *Pudd'nhead Wilson,* Twain comments upon and corrects existing observations of character made by southerners about themselves and about the African Americans in their midst. He thereby surveys the damage that physiognomic assessments of character can do when they are used as the basis for drawing racial and social distinctions. All in all, he turns his critique of phrenology upon a region of the country that believes in physiognomic certainty. As such, Twain uses the invisible blackness of two of his central characters to explore the limits of the pseudo-sciences of character and the dubious ways in which sentimental genres seemed to derive their narrative logic from them.

Racial Character and White Imitation

The melodramatic plot elements in *Pudd'nhead Wilson*, as some critics have pointed out, are lifted from tragic octoroon fiction. As Adrienne Bond explains, this genre had a very developed set of conventions, including "a pastoral setting; a protagonist who is legally black but who appears to be white . . . ; episodes in which characters disguise themselves as members of the opposite sex; a foil from Europe or New England (often an inventor or scientist) who is free from local superstitions; and a dramatic ending in which the villain is apprehended by a *deus ex machina*" (60). Additionally, the protagonist, a light-skinned mulatto, is usually the child of a man who is a member of the First Families of Virginia. Owing to the machinations of a character known as the southern Cavalier—a profligate and immoral aristocrat—the mulatto protagonist is sold into slavery to settle the debts of an estate.[11]

Twain's text makes use of all these conventions. Despite its exceedingly conventional and melodramatic plot line, however, *Pudd'nhead Wilson* does not play on its own melodrama. Twain has borrowed the trappings of a sentimental genre, but he submits the genre to satire. As Bond argues, Twain empties the genre of its melodrama by changing the "metaphysics" that surrounds its conventions. Specifically, "the sentimental formula involves a traditional metaphysics of hierarchies and dualities; its plot is the transcendent story of good versus evil acting itself out through fixed types. It ends with the restoration of essential order. Twain, on the other hand, uses the deterministic theories of the nineteenth century as his 'metaphysics.' Consequently the story becomes a series of actions determined by environment and chance, acted out by characters whose identities are relative and always subject to change" (60). And, I would add, Twain's reversion to the sentimental formula extends beyond plot to descriptive conventions. Since sentimental fiction is based on a strict relationship between outer appearance and inner character, the story of good types versus evil types depends on passages of physical description. The octoroon has white skin, so that white exterior becomes a sign for the superior white character inherited from aristocratic ancestors. Physical description provides messages about the character of characters and establishes the types which ground the morality of the story. Twain, however, destabilizes this element of sentimental fiction. Though Bond argues that Twain unfixes sentimental types by replacing transcendent moral fixity with materialist determinism, I believe that most of the satire of fixed types is created by the novel's questioning of the absolute visibility of the signs that signal such types and of the blood or character that the visible is supposed to guarantee. Twain's novel depicts the flawed detection of type and thereby ridicules the physiognomy that underlies the genre it satirizes.

For example, the very first scene of the novel evokes a convention of tragic octoroon sentimentality but pokes fun at the belief that visual types provide fixed messages. Like a typical tragic octoroon novel, *Pudd'nhead Wilson* begins with scenic description that evokes the pastoral: "The scene of this chronicle is the town of Dawson's Landing, on the Missouri side of the Mississippi . . . it was a snug little collection of modest one- and two-story frame dwellings whose whitewashed exteriors were almost concealed from sight by climbing tangles of rose vines, honeysuckles and morning-glories" (3). The rest of this long passage goes on to emphasize the uniformity of the visual impact of these homes and concludes with the observation that, with a cat asleep out front, a "home was complete, and its contentment and peace were made manifest to the world by this symbol, whose testimony is infallible. A home without a cat—and a well fed, well petted, and properly revered cat—may be a perfect home, perhaps, but how can it prove title?" (3). Here the description turns from the satisfaction of convention to satire. Twain makes direct reference to the fact that setting in this genre is supposed to communicate something; the setting generally serves as a symbol of the perfection of a place that will be troubled by the original sin of slavery. However, Twain foregrounds the latent message to indicate that in the community of Dawson's Landing, a "perfect" home depends on an outward sign that is read by others. Without the infallible testimony of such a symbol, perfection would not be visible and could not be proven. Thus, in the opening passage the novel mocks the narrow use of the visual to stand as symbolic evidence of some larger, moral truth.[12]

Yet while this community relies on the testimony of visual symbols, it is often unable to read them correctly. The first real action of the novel is an account of how the town of Dawson's Landing welcomes the scientific northerner David Wilson. Wilson is "a homely, freckled, sandy-haired young fellow, with an intelligent blue eye that had frankness and comradeship in it and a covert twinkle of a pleasant sort" (5). However, when Wilson remarks that he wished he owned half of a dog that was making an annoying racket so that he could kill his half, the townspeople are thrown by their inability to see his remark as a joke. Clearly this inability comes from Wilson's deadpan humor, a form of ironic humor that relies on a straight-faced delivery.[13] Accordingly, "the group searched his face with curiosity, with anxiety even, but found no light there, no expression they could read" (5). As a result, in a whispered conversation among the citizens, Wilson is dubbed a fool for wanting to perform the obviously impossible act of killing half a dog.

Since they cannot read his expression, the citizens judge Wilson's character from the evidence of the ironic joke he makes. In this way, Wilson's joke actually impedes the other characters' ability to read the clear physiognomic message in his features. Though his face declares that he is intelligent, these readers find his covert twinkle impossible to detect. His deadpan performance of seriousness is indistinguishable from a real seriousness; in a sense, his expression covers his face. As a result, when one citizen ventures to read his character—"It ain't going too far to say he is a pudd'nhead. If he ain't a pudd'nhead, I ain't no judge, that's all"—the reading becomes truth (6). The truth of the reading is ensconced in the name that it suggests: "Within a week he had lost his first name; Pudd'nhead took its place" (6). By this act of misreading, Wilson's character has been set as surely and incorrectly as the character of the ass in the novel's opening aphorism.

The satire mounts as physiognomic truth remains invisible to the community in the early chapters. For example, the white-skinned slave Roxy is presented in a manner that highlights the contradictions between her physiognomy and her status as a slave. She is presented from Wilson's point of view as he sits in his home and eavesdrops on a conversation going on under his window but out of his line of sight. Importantly, Roxy's speech is pronounced and unmistakable slave dialect. Therefore, when she is finally made visible physically the narrator highlights the stark contrast that develops: "From Roxy's manner of speech, a stranger would have expected her to be black, but she was not. Only one-sixteenth of her was black, and that sixteenth did not show" (8). The physical description that follows plays with what is actually visible:

> She was of majestic form and stature, her attitudes were imposing and statuesque, and her gestures and movements distinguished by a noble and stately grace. Her complexion was very fair, with the rosy glow of vigorous health in the cheeks, her face was full of character and expression, her eyes were brown and liquid, and she had a heavy suit of fine soft hair which was also brown, but the fact was not apparent because her head was bound about with a checkered handkerchief and the hair was concealed under it. Her face was shapely, intelligent, and comely—even beautiful. (8)

Roxy is "majestic" and "statuesque"—interesting diction implying that she approaches the standard of beauty most often aligned with the Caucasian ideal, Greek statuary. However, the way in which her hair is concealed and thus not available for visual assessment foreshadows the act of concealment that concludes this passage of description: "She had an easy independent carriage—when she was among her own caste—and a high and 'sassy' way, withal; but of course she was meek and humble enough where white people were" (8). Though Roxy's eyes are full of character, the intelligence in her face is as invisible as Wilson's. Wilson's intelligence is obscured by his deadpan performance, and Roxy's intelligence is obscured by her performance as a slave. Though her carriage speaks of independent sassiness, she very deliberately hides the messages that her superior physiognomy should transmit in order to present the expected meekness of the slave.[14]

Through these passages of description, Twain presents the logic that allows both for the plot of the novel and for its satire of sentimental fiction. If physiognomy is not reliable, if the messages that physical appearance sends are liable to be interfered with by deliberate or miscalculated performances, then the assurances of physical appearance are not enough to prevent identity from being deliberately manipulated. Specifically, the switched-baby plot works because the two babies cannot reliably be told apart by their bodies but can easily be distinguished by externals. As the narrator tells us, though Roxy's baby "had blue eyes and flaxen curls like his white comrade," nonetheless, "even the father of the white child was able to tell the children apart—little as he had commerce with them—by their clothes: for the white babe wore ruffled soft muslin and a coral necklace, while the other wore merely a coarse tow-linen shirt which barely reached to its knees, and no jewelry" (9). In a narrative supposedly co-opting the conventions of sentimental fiction, in which identity is a fixed property of the body, even for a father it is a property of clothing. As Twain's critique of phrenology insists, people who claim to read bodies really read clothes.

Interestingly, Wilson as a character is placed explicitly outside this failed logic of phrenology. Specifically, he is able to prove the intelligence the narrator had attributed to him by seeing beyond the clothing of the children. In one scene, Wilson looks at the babies and remarks to Roxy that "they're handsome little chaps. One's just as handsome as the other too" (9). Roxy's exaggerated pride in the compliment—"Bless yo' soul Misto Wilson, it's pow'ful nice o' you to say dat, caze one of 'em ain't on'y a nigger"—suggests that the mere fact of race should be enough to make the babies unequally beautiful (9).

In fact, Roxy herself is incapable of believing the compliment until she dresses her child in borrowed clothes. In the scene that sets the plot in motion, Roxy is stricken with the fear that her child could someday be sold down the river. She resolves to drown herself and her child to escape this fate but stops first to change into her finest dress so as to make a handsome corpse. Once she has dressed, she is struck with her own beauty and moved to style her previously concealed hair "like white folks" (13). This outward creation of a white image, the result of seeing her own (white) beauty in the mirror, gives her the inspiration to make her son as handsome by dressing him in the other infant's clothing. In doing so, Roxy is finally able to see her own child: "She propped the child in a chair and stood off to inspect it. Straightway her eyes began to widen with astonishment and admiration, and she clapped her hands and cried out 'Why, it do beat all—I never knowed you was so lovely. Marse Tommy ain't a bit puttier—not a single bit'" (14). The twin distorting factors of race and clothing prevent even a mother from seeing the physical beauty of her child.

The narrator, however, is extremely clear that whatever Roxy sees when she looks at her child in his slave-child's garb is purely conventional. From the start, the narrator discounts the one-drop rule, explaining that "to all intents and purposes Roxy was as white as anybody, but the one-sixteenth of her which was black out-voted the other fifteen parts and made her a negro. She was a slave, and salable as such. Her child was thirty-one parts white, and he, too, was a slave, and by a fiction of law and custom a negro" (8–9). First, the narrator mocks the language of fractions of race by humorously attributing volition to that part of Roxy that is black, as if it could be thought of as separate enough to "vote" against the other parts. In fact, using the language of voting in this context points to the resolutely undemocratic logic of the one-drop rule. Though in most things American the majority rules, in this case some laughably small fraction takes precedence. Second, the one-drop rule is divested of any biological or existential reality since it is only a "fiction" of law and custom. For racial science, the language of minute percentages is no embarrassment; Dixon boldly claims that one drop of black blood is enough to taint a generation. However, such a claim can hold only within an assumed framework of neo-Lamarckian inherited racial character. If blood carries inherited traits, then the one-drop rule has biological validity. The remark that Roxy's baby is only by fiction a Negro would seem to discount completely the notion of inherited racial character.

In fact, Twain provides environmental explanations for so-called innate racial characteristics. The narrator spends some time examining the proclivity toward petty crime that Dixon labels one of the black race's inherited traits. In *The Leopard's Spots,* the Reverend Durham claims that under slavery African Americans were kept up to honest standards, but after emancipation they once again displayed an innate tendency toward dishonesty. *Pudd'nhead Wilson,* however, makes it clear that petty thievery was far from unknown under slavery and that such behavior is actually a reasoned response to specific conditions. By the narrator's account, slaves "had an unfair show in the battle of life, and they held it no sin to take military advantage of the enemy—in a small way" (11). Theft is a response to slavery, not a justification for it. The narrator then notes that a black man who steals a chicken is "perfectly sure that in taking this trifle from the man who daily robbed him of an inestimable treasure—his liberty—he was not committing any sin that God would remember against him in the Last Great Day" (12). As Lee Clark Mitchell argues, the novel demonstrates that "not biological inheritance, but chattel slavery creates those differences that sustain racism" (301). Dixon's line of causation is reversed in Twain's treatment: the idea of racial character is revealed, as Mitchell puts it, as a "self-confirming logic, parodied in the novel as creating the very behavior it supposedly describes" (301).

Twain also raises the issue of imitative black behavior. In the scene where Roxy interrupts her tragic resolve to kill herself in order to attend to her "death-toilet," Twain appeals to both the notion of an innate Negro taste for brightly colored clothing and an innate imitativeness. Her dress is "a cheap curtain-calico thing, a conflagration of gaudy colors and fantastic figures," and when she makes up her hair "like white folks" she adds "some odds and ends of rather lurid ribbon and a spray of atrocious artificial flowers" (13). Roxy stops in her plan for suicide when she remembers a sermon where a preacher had used the example of a servant's baby switched with a queen's to explain that the rewards of election are randomly distributed acts of fate. However, the message that Roxy derives from this example is that she is justified in switching the babies because "de preacher said it his own self, en it ain't no sin, caze white folks done it. *Dey* done it—yes, *dey* done it; en not on'y jis' common white folk, nuther, but de biggest quality dey is in de whole bilin'" (14). Though Roxy is the butt of the joke for her imitation of white folks, the same explanation can be given for Roxy's behavior as the one that Twain used to argue that theft is not a sign of an unreasoned racial instinct. If it is ridiculous to deprive a man of everything and then use his petty thievery as a justification for the initial deprivation, it is equally ridiculous to prevent a slave access to education and fine things and then label his or her failure of taste and understanding as a sign that the race is incapable of civilized deportment.

Yet there is a better explanation of what Twain is up to than this extrapolated argument. *Pudd'nhead Wilson* systematically subjects the southern aristocracy to precisely the same charge that Dixon would make against African Americans. According to Twain, white southerners make themselves ridiculous by imitating a type of behavior they do not fully understand. Accordingly, the novel makes reference to sentimental fiction, especially southern Cavalier fiction, in order to construct a satire of southerners' attempts to imitate codes of chivalric behavior. As Eric Sundquist notes in *To Wake the Nations*, the 1880s and 1890s saw a revival of sentimental interest in all things southern, testifying to a "widespread need, spurred by economic and political crises, to resurrect a romantic image of the Old South" (230). Twain projects this romanticism backward onto the antebellum period in order to render its object ridiculous. For example, much humor is derived from the name Roxy gives her son, "Valet de Chambre": "Roxana had heard that phrase somewhere, the fine sound of it had pleased her ear, and as she had supposed it was a name, she loaded it onto her darling" (9). However, the name her master gives his son—"Thomas à Becket"—is remarkably similar in both cadence and pomposity. Tom's name serves as only one example of how the white aristocracy of Dawson's Landing falls guilty of Twain's famous charge of Walter Scottism: in *Life on the Mississippi* Twain spends a chapter leveling and defending his claim that southerners suffer from a tendency to revere the ways of chivalry as depicted in the "mediaeval romances" of Sir Walter Scott. As Twain claims, "The south has not yet recovered from the debilitating influence of his books. Admiration of his fantastic heroes and their grotesque 'chivalry' doings and romantic juvenilities still survives here" (285).[15]

The true cost of this debilitation is that reverence quickly gives way to imitation and inflated self-image. As Twain notes, the most obvious sign of Walter Scottism is the southern predilection for faux-gothic architecture or "imitation castles." Though such castles are in and of themselves harmless, they are the "symbol and breeder and sustainer of maudlin Middle-Age romanticism" (286). Twain offers an excerpt from the "prospectus" of a Kentucky "Female College" which takes great pride in describing its "old castles of song and story" before it launches into a bit of southern pomp: "The president is southern by birth, by rearing, by education, and by sentiment; the teachers are all southern in sentiment, and with the exception of those born in Europe were born and raised in the south. Believing the southern to be the highest type of civilization this continent has seen, the young ladies are trained according to the southern ideas of delicacy, refinement, womanhood, religion, and propriety" (286). Twain remarks, "The man who can blow so complacent a blast as that, probably blows it from a castle" (287). The chain of logic is direct: a reverence for architecture is a symptom of the perverted self-characterization that results when southerners regard themselves as the descendants of the racial groups depicted in Sir Walter Scott's romances.

Twain, of course, undercuts this characterization of the southern as the "highest type" of civilization. A footnote to this passage in *Life on the Mississippi* reprints newspaper articles detailing instances in which southerners had killed each other wantonly in farcical "duels" while the legal apparatus stood unwilling to prosecute admitted murderers. Accordingly, Twain's most cutting critique of the white aristocracy of Dawson's Landing in *Pudd'nhead Wilson* involves dueling. From the start, the town's two main citizens—Tom's uncle and guardian Judge Driscoll and his friend Pembroke Howard—are described as proud descendants of the First Families of Virginia, or FFV. They are thereby the aristocracy of Dawson's Landing: "In Missouri a recognized superiority attached to any person who hailed from Old Virginia; and this superiority was exalted to supremacy when a person of such nativity could also prove descent from the First Families" (58). As Twain explains, keeping up the traditions of the FFV involves being honorable "without stain or blemish" according to "the nicest requirements of the Virginian rule" (4). As such, one must be "an authority on the 'code,'" a code of behavior that includes dueling. For instance, people know that Howard is a gentleman because he is "always courteously ready to stand up before you in the field if any act or word of his had seemed doubtful or suspicious to you, and explain it with any weapon you might prefer, from brad-awls to artillery" (4).

In *Pudd'nhead Wilson,* Twain casts dueling as overreactive and violent bullying. Dueling works its way into the plot after Roxy's son Tom is kicked by one of the twin Italian visitors to the town.[16] When Tom sues for assault, his uncle is devastated. He sees it as shameful to appeal to the legal system for retribution when a duel is clearly called for.

As Twain notes, the code of the FFV requires that legal considerations give way before the code of honor: "Honor stood first; and the laws defined what it was and wherein it differed, in certain details, from honor as defined by church creeds and by the social laws and customs of some of the minor divisions of the globe that had got crowded out when the sacred boundaries of Virginia were staked out" (58). Twain's sarcasm deflates the worth of this code by mocking its inflated reverence for the sacred ground that sustains it. And as Sundquist notes, the reluctance of the FFV to take recourse in the law is one of the novel's finest points of satire directed at late-nineteenth-century racial policy; while in antebellum Dawson's Landing the code and law are disjunct, in the New South "the code and law were approaching identity to the extent that the code was based on racial or genealogical purity, and mob pressure dictated the legal suppression of African American political rights" (243). Moreover, while white supremacists like Dixon would argue that the defense of honor is a sign that southern Anglo-Saxons are descended from the most democratic people of the globe, Twain pits the codes of the southerner, with his love for barbaric dueling, *against* the workings of democracy. In *Pudd'nhead Wilson,* appealing to the rules of a democratic society makes one dishonorable. These gentlemen of Dawson's Landing, with their quick recourse to violence and their pompous superiority, are using their notions of a romantic and ancient code in an empty way, shallowly imitating a largely imaginary past. *Pudd'nhead Wilson* thus reverses Dixon's claim that educated blacks display a "shallow veneer of imitation culture." In this novel, white southerners are most guilty of engaging in burlesque mimicry.

Pudd'nhead Wilson throws both of the standard indicators of race in the sentimental model—bodies and blood—into question. First, the physiognomy that undergirds the visibility of race and the descriptive logic of the sentimental romance is destabilized. In this novel, the readings that physiognomy depends upon are vulnerable to the distortions of performance and external signs like clothing. Twain suggests that bodies do not transmit reliable messages about character or, more importantly, reliable messages about race. Second, the notion of an innate racial character transmitted through blood is undermined when racial traits are attributed to conditions, like slavery, or when the supposed black racial trait of imitativeness becomes a part of the characterization of the novel's white supremacists.

Blood and the Fixed Character

Pudd'nhead Wilson burlesques southern attitudes toward race and the genre that is bound to the racial pseudo-science which supports them. But despite this satire, Twain's novel contains some scenes that apparently reinforce rather than undermine neo-Lamarckian notions about blood and its relationship to racial character. Critics have often argued that these same scenes contain undermining elements and that Twain's position is clearly distinct from that of his characters. Yet while both observations are true, they do not diminish the sense that the novel begins to change and that its stand on race shifts uncomfortably. For example, though dueling provides Twain with the means to ironize his white characters' neo-Lamarckian white supremacy, the theme also allows for some troubling pronouncements on the power of blood and character. One of the sources of humor in the scene in which the Judge and Pembroke Howard are informed about Tom's failure to issue a challenge to a duel is that the two men flatly refuse to believe the report; a near-fainting Judge Driscoll cries weakly, "Say it ain't true, Pembroke, tell me it ain't true!" and Howard responds with certainty, saying, "You know it's a lie as well as I do, old friend. He is of the best blood of the Old Dominion" (59).

The novel clearly mocks absolute belief in blood because these men cling to it irrationally in the face of more direct testimony. However, the mockery has an uncomfortable feel since such assumptions about the supposed purity of Tom's blood are not exactly accurate, as the reader well knows. When the Judge wonders that one of the "blood" of his "race" has gone to court or calls Tom "the base son of a most noble father," it is possible that the novel is pointing to the deficiencies in Tom's racial character (60). Interestingly, Tom is taken to task by Roxy in a parallel scene: "You refuse' to fight a man dat kicked you, 'stid o' jumpin' at de chance. . . . Pah! it make me sick! It's de nigger in you, dat's what it is. Thirty-one parts o' you is white, en on'y one part nigger, end dat po' little one part is yo' *soul*" (70). Roxy has the same faith in blood as the two white aristocrats, and she has the requisite knowledge to account for the flaw in Tom's character.

According to these speeches, Tom's character is really just a matter of blood and therefore should be identical with the racial inheritance of his body. Yet the question of why this black racial character is not visible hits Roxy directly. She remarks to herself that though there "ain't enough nigger in him to show in his finger-nails, en dat takes mighty little—yit dey's enough to paint his soul" (70). As Roxy has adopted the sentimental white code based on an inner/outer logic, she must work through the discrepancy between the clear evidence of Tom's non-white (by her standards) behavior and his white exterior. She falls back on the visual logic of painting, but she is forced to imagine a color that paints on an invisible surface—the human soul. The color of Tom's behavior is located in his body even if the criteria of visibility cannot be met.

It is easy to argue that Roxy is the victim of the humor that develops out of this scene. First, she re-creates the flawed logic of racial partitioning that the narrator had mocked earlier when she gives a percentage of Tom the power to outvote the other portion. Then she follows this racial arithmetic with a farcical account of her son's descent that imitates the FFV's preoccupation with ancestry. She begins by wondering aloud why the blood of Tom's real father, the Colonel Burleigh Essex, had not prevented him from backing out of a duel:

> What ever has' come o' yo' Essex blood? Dat's what I can't understan'. En it ain't only jist Essex blood dat's in you, not by a long sight—'deed it ain't! My great-great-great-gran'father en yo' great-great-great-great-gran'father was ole Cap'n John Smith, de highes' blood dat Ole Virginny ever turned out; en *his* great-great-gran'mother or somers along back dah, was Pocahontas de Injun queen, en her husbun' was a nigger king outen Africa—en yit here you is, a slinkin' outen a duel and disgracin' our whole line like a orney low-down hound! Yes, it's de nigger in you! (70)

Roxy's confused genealogy mocks all faith in such lineages, and makes her a clear target for satire.

Nonetheless, despite the satire, these two scenes return the notion of racial inheritance to the center of the narrative in a way that is difficult to dismiss. The novel seems to arrive at a position that would validate

Roxy's claims—Tom is, in fact, part black, and he does fail miserably in the execution of behavior labeled white. The resulting internal inconsistency between the novel's ironic thrust and its plot construction has been debated at length by critics.[17] I would suggest that when Roxy provides a possible surface for Tom's invisible color, it indicates that the generic mode for the handling of racial subjects is shifting. Formerly, the satire of the distorting physiognomy of sentimental fiction had questioned the activity of aligning the body with fixed symbols. Yet the last third of the novel edges back toward validating race as a fixed property of the body. Though it is likely that all believers in blood in the novel are the victims of satire, and that Twain and his narrator do not endorse Roxy's claim that Tom's behavior is the result of racial inheritance, the story itself begins to slip back into an emphasis on Tom's tendencies and eventually on the racial truth that his body speaks invisibly.[18]

Understanding this symptomatic shift back toward the body requires an exploration of the novel's—and Twain's—larger conception of character and its fixed tendencies. In the early chapters when Twain undermined notions of innate black criminality and imitativeness, he also established that race and identity depend on habit and performance. For example, while Roxy was able to execute the switch because only clothes secured the relationship between bodies and names, she was able to sustain it because she separated identity from bodies. Roxy spends the night after the switch practicing treating her child like her master and her master's child like a slave: "As she progressed with her practice, she was surprised to see how steadily and surely the awe which had kept her tongue reverent and her manner humble toward her young master was transferring itself to her speech and manner toward the usurper, and how similarly handy she was becoming in transferring her motherly curtness of speech and peremptoriness of manner to the unlucky heir of the ancient house of Driscoll" (16). Roxy is surprised to find that nothing inherent to the baby who was her master determined her feeling of awe. It was a product of her own attitudes and for that reason could be transferred to another. Roxy's experience suggests that identity is established and maintained interpersonally, through the dynamic between individuals. The mode of address sustains the identity of the individual, not something intrinsic to the body.

Twenty years later, Tom experiences the profound extent to which his own identity is sustained interpersonally. When Roxy tells Tom his true racial status—part of her bid to extort money from him and exact revenge for the obnoxious way he had behaved toward her for years—he goes through a difficult adjustment:

> For days he wandered in lonely places thinking, thinking, thinking—trying to get his bearings. It was new work. If he met a friend he found that the habit of a lifetime had in some mysterious way vanished—his arm hung limp instead of involuntarily extending the hand for a shake. It was the "nigger" in him asserting its humility, and he blushed and was abashed. And the "nigger" in him was surprised when the white friend put out his hand to shake with him. (45)

Though this passage uses the same language as Roxy's explanation for Tom's racial inheritance—"it's the nigger in you"—the quotation marks signal a disruption of her logic. In this case, the "nigger" in Tom exerts influence over his behavior because he has a new understanding of himself, not because it has painted his racial soul. His previous white man's confidence was the involuntary response—the "nigger" in him is his self-censorship. In fact, Tom's new understanding leads him to re-create his mother's performance of blackness:

> He dreaded his meals; the "nigger" in him was ashamed to sit at the white folks' table, and feared discovery all the time; and once when Judge Driscoll said, "What's the matter with you?—you look as meek as a nigger," he felt as secret murderers are said to feel when the accuser says, "Thou art the man!" Tom said he was not well, and left the table. (45)

Tom's meekness is the result of his guilt, fear, and altered sense of himself, but not of his blood or the humbleness of his physiognomy, just as in Roxy's case. And as with Roxy, it is his meekness that gives him the visible appearance of blackness. The performance makes the white master see him as a "nigger." Color and even identity only appear in the dynamic between object and interpreter. When the Judge fixes upon the racial character of Tom's behavior, he is reading a performance rather than the features of Tom's body.

Though these examples suggest that cultural identities are performed and then interpreted, it is important not to assume that they add up to an argument for a completely disembodied or constructed identity. In *Pudd'nhead Wilson,* the process of reading character is often liable to be wrong or motivated by community opinion. In this sense, character is created as surely as identity can be performed to provoke such a reading. However, the fact that character, even racial character, is often misread does not invalidate the fact that it is a genuine phenomenon in Twain's universe. Though humans will err in reading character, and err in attributing real existence to their own creations, character does not become an invalid term in this novel. Twain shows uneasiness about the difficulty of reading visual data and recognizes that such readings often serve the needs of those who have the power to give their readings cultural authority. Nonetheless, his fascination with character is also a product of his frustration with the prospect of never being able to read it properly.

There is no doubt that Tom does possess a depth of character that cannot be affected by hiccups in his attitude and performance. The narrator notes that for "as much as a week" after he experienced his racial destabilization "Tom imagined that his character had undergone a pretty radical change. But that was because he did not know himself" (45). The narrator, however, does know Tom, and the truth is that Tom's character cannot be radically altered:

> The main structure of his character was not changed, and could not be changed. . . . Under the influence of a great mental and moral upheaval his character and his habits had taken on the appearance of complete change, but after a while with the subsidence of the storm both began to settle toward their former places. He dropped gradually back into his frivolous and easy-going ways, and conditions of feeling, and manner of speech, and no familiar of his could have detected anything in him that differentiated him from the weak and careless Tom of other days. (45)

Tom's character has formed lines that are too deep to erase, and it is accompanied by a set of habits that are just as fixed. Though both give an appearance of change, the visible evidence of character—his ways, his feelings, and his manner of speech—return to their previous appearances in due time.

In the first third of the novel, we are given a glimpse of how these lines of Tom's character came to be drawn. According to the narrator, Tom "was a bad baby, from the very beginning of his usurpation" (17). The passage that follows seems to suggest that Tom was encouraged to be selfish, self-gratifying, and peevish through the spoiling he received as a baby: "He was indulged in all his caprices, howsoever troublesome and exasperating they might be; he was allowed to eat anything he wanted, particularly things that would give him the stomach ache" (18). The narrator contrasts the results of Tom's spoiling and Chambers's rough treatment on both their physiognomy and their characters: "Tom got all the petting, Chambers got none. Tom got all the delicacies, Chambers got mush and milk. . . . In consequence, Tom was a sickly child and Chambers wasn't. Tom was 'fractious,' as Roxy called it, and overbearing, Chambers was meek and docile" (18–19). Though this example would seem to suggest that both bodily constitution and character are the results of how children are raised, Tom also possesses a base and unalterable "nature." The explanation the narrator gives for Tom's meanness both to his slave/boyhood companion and to his slave/mother is a "native viciousness" (20).

Twain's concept of character thus seems to include a balance between the effects of training and an innate nature. One of the chapter headings from Pudd'nhead Wilson's calendar provides relevant commentary: "Training is everything. The peach was once a bitter almond; cauliflower is nothing but cabbage with a college education" (23). It is important to note that *training* is for Twain a very flexible term.[19] It refers in some cases to the nurture one receives after birth. For example, Judge Driscoll uses the term when he privately accounts for the source of Tom's cowardice in backing out of the duel: "He is worthless and unworthy, but it is largely my fault. . . . I have indulged him to his hurt, instead of training him up severely and making a man of him" (67). The Judge admits that the blood of the FFV alone is not enough to make a man a gentleman: it requires "training up." However, the term *training* in Wilson's calendar has different connotations when taken literally. With his horticultural example, Twain is clearly playing off of training as a process of selective breeding that results in the measured transmission of innate properties. Thus, training is everything because the term can refer to all varieties of influence—to nurture *and* to inherited qualities.

The most important of all of Twain's terms associated with character is *habit.* Tom's discovery that he is black most of all affects his habits in social situations. In the examples cited above, Tom is unable to shake hands, as the "habit of a lifetime" suddenly fails him, and after the upheaval is over his habits return because his character has not been altered (45). Roxy too falls victim to the power of habit as her practicing after she switches the babies takes root:

> By the fiction created by herself, [her son] was become her master; the necessity of recognizing this relation outwardly and of perfecting herself in the forms required to express the recognition, had moved her to such diligence and faithfulness in practicing these forms that this exercise soon concreted itself into habit; it became automatic and unconscious; then a natural result followed: deceptions intended solely for others gradually grew practically into self-deception as well; the mock reverence became real reverence, the mock obsequiousness real obsequiousness. (19)

Roxy trains herself so well that the interpersonal dynamic with Tom designed to secure his identity becomes habit to her. As a result, this automatic and unconscious behavior has an effect on her identity. Her performance is so perfect that she stops experiencing it as a performance. As the narrator notes, "In her worship of [Tom] she forgot who she was and what he had been" (19).

Thus, we are left with a multiple sense of what character is and how it comes to be fixed. In some sense it is native, but it is also trained. Furthermore, the habits that attach to character are so powerful that they can disrupt identity. In Roxy's case they result in a performance of identity that becomes completely unconscious to her. *Pudd'nhead Wilson* does direct part of its satiric force against those, like the FFV, who believe that innate and inherited qualities assure their superiority. The novel also seeks to put into play the various influences that affect character in order to underline its multiple determinants. However, the play between the acquired and the innate, the pliant and the fixed, begins to shut down as the novel draws to a close. As Sundquist explains, Twain himself "reaches no satisfactory judgment about the ratio between instinct and training in the case of Tom" (255). This inconsistency is in part the result of his editing choices:

> In his original manuscript, Twain had allowed Tom to realize, when Roxy reveals to him his true identity, that the "nigger" in him was the Lamarckian result of "decades and generations of insult and outrage" whereas his "white blood" was "debased by the brutalizing effects of a long-drawn heredity of slave-owning." But such rational meditation is deleted from *Pudd'nhead Wilson,* where the pared-down focus on the hidden mark of blackness, the "nigger" in Tom, is placed before Twain's readers as a stringent test of their ability to differentiate social construction from "nature." (256)

Were the Lamarckian calculus made this clear, the source of Tom's character would require no decoding. But with the puzzle left up to the reader to decide, the construction of the novel itself suggests that Tom is born lacking. And, I would argue, the fact that the novel in some sense validates Roxy's assumptions about Tom's invisible color is symptomatic of a more subtle shift from the satire of the fixed types of sentimental fiction to a more determined relationship between body and character. Twain's understanding of the origins and influences for character may have been flexible and complicated, but generic requirements lack such flexibility.

The Detective of the Indexical Body

As critics have noted, in its final chapters *Pudd'nhead Wilson* becomes a detective story.[20] Tom murders his uncle while trying to steal money to settle his gambling debts and consequently his fluid identity of the first third of the novel is replaced by the fixed character of the "villain." Wilson steps into the foreground of the novel as he agrees to defend the twins after they have been falsely accused of Tom's crime. Once the detective genre takes shape, what had been performance is refigured as disguise; the detective figure's job is to reestablish the truth of the body by penetrating the disguise. Thus, as the detective, Wilson must find a way to read Tom's character by making use of ways that read the body which circumvent the face and thereby negate the effects of deceptive and disguising performances.

Twain was interested in detective fiction and made several attempts to write in the genre, most notably in his novel *Tom Sawyer, Detective.* According to Susan Gillman, his "forays into exploiting the contemporary market for detective fiction" were inspired by the success of the first Sherlock Holmes story to appear in the United States, *A Study in Scarlet,* published in *Beeton's Christmas Annual* in 1887 ("Sure Identifiers" 95). Interest in detective fiction was clearly reaching noticeable levels in the 1880s; one of the earlier scholars of the genre, A. E. Murch, notes that the *Saturday Review* commented on the popularity of detective fiction in 1883. Though literature concerned with crime and with the unraveling of mysterious circumstances can be given a long history, most critics agree that the genre took shape in the nineteenth century under the influence of Edgar Allan Poe. According to LeRoy Lad Panek, Poe's stories of C. Auguste Dupin—stories like "The Murders in the Rue Morgue"—established a generic pattern that would later be domesticated by Doyle and given a wide audience (10). With Doyle's domestication came the distillation of the formula: the detective story is "a tale in which the primary interest lies in the methodical discovery, by rational means, of the exact circumstances of a mysterious event or series of events . . . [and] designed to arouse the reader's curiosity by a puzzling problem which usually, though not always, concerns a crime" (Murch 11).

The detective story focuses primarily on the individual who acts as the agent of investigation and who unravels the mystery. In this sense, part of the pleasure of the genre comes from watching the genius of the detective in action as he cuts through the layers of detail that make the circumstances unclear and hones in on the true explanation. Pleasure also comes from the intellectual apparatus used to reach the truth: "Sometimes the answer to the riddle may depend upon a scientific or pseudo-scientific fact of which [the reader] was previously unaware. His enjoyment is then enriched by the acquisition of interesting scraps of information on one or another of the many scientific subjects that can be harmoniously linked with the plot of a detective story, such as chemical tests for various poisons, details of forensic medicine, [and] the systematic examination of material clues" (Murch 15). While the degree to which scientific information is "harmoniously linked" to the plot of *Pudd'nhead Wilson* is open to question, Twain found an apt way to capitalize on this particular generic convention. While writing the novel, Twain read Francis Galton's work on fingerprints with great interest. In that work, Galton demonstrates most of what has come to be common knowledge about fingerprints: their singularity allows them to serve as a method of personal identification, and they can establish the identity of the same person over the course of his or her lifetime. Twain subsequently incorporated the science of fingerprints (or, as Galton called it, "dermoglyphics") into the fabric of his plot. The science of fingerprints becomes the means by which Wilson will untangle the twin mysteries of identity and murder at the center of the novel.[21]

Wilson's services are clearly much needed. The community of Dawson's Landing has been well established as a poor judge of character, and after Tom has committed murder the community continues to exhibit its tendency to perpetuate incorrect readings. In this case, the normal mode of visual assessment is thrown off because Tom's behavior counterfeits all the expected external signs of the bereaved nephew: "Everybody was pitying Tom, he looked so quiet and sorrowful, and seemed to feel his great loss so deeply. He was playing a part, but it was not at all a part. The picture of his alleged uncle, as he had last seen him, was before him in the dark pretty frequently, when he was awake, and called again into his dreams when he was asleep" (99). Tom is not acting, but since the assumed signs of grief are indistinguishable from guilt and fear, the town still does not read him correctly. Even Mrs. Pratt, the caretaker of his uncle's house who has known Tom since childhood, reads Tom mistakenly on the basis of his behavior. His sorrowful demeanor brings her to realize, " 'as she had never done before,' she said, what a sensitive and delicate nature her darling had, and how he adored his poor uncle" (99).

Luckily, Wilson already has all the information he needs to reveal the truth behind Tom's performance. From the start of the novel, Wilson had been taking samples of people's fingerprints on glass slides and labeling them carefully with name and date.[22] In a novel where character is most often improperly read (e.g., with the misreadings of Wilson's face and Roxy's), a means appears by which one who is trained in a supposed science of the body can arrive at a correct reading. By moving the marks used for reading character from the face to the hand, the novel opens up a space for an assessment of the body that avoids the dissimulations of performance and makes the invisible visible. As Wilson later explains when he brings his fingerprint evidence into court, the fingerprint is the most reliably constant part of any person's anatomy: "These marks are his signature, his physiological autograph, so to speak, and this autograph cannot be counterfeited, nor can he disguise it or hide it away, nor can it become illegible by the wear and tear of time. This signature is not his face—age can change that beyond recognition" (108).

The series of events that leads to Tom's conviction and public exposure as an impostor depends on the movement from a false reading based on mistaken notions about character to a correct reading based on fingerprints. Yet the truth the fingerprints promise at first remains beyond Wilson's reach. Wilson too has discounted Tom, and he is desperate to find another suspect. He also must explain away the circumstantial evidence that appears to damn the twins: they were discovered standing over the body, the crime was committed with their knife, and the Judge and one twin had made public threats on each other's lives. Wilson "refused to suspect Tom; for firstly, Tom couldn't murder anybody—he hadn't character enough" (98). Here, the detective's judgment of Tom's character, based on casual assessment, is incorrect. Additionally, Wilson does not believe that Tom would murder his uncle if he was not sure that the will which named him as heir was once again intact. He concludes that "Tom could not have been aware of it, or he would have spoken of it, in his native talky unsecretive way" (98). Wilson is still stuck in the confines of physiognomic logic since he reads Tom's "native" character from rather secondhand evidence.

The main drama of the detective section of *Pudd'nhead Wilson* is thereby created by the events that lead Wilson beyond his own assumptions about character to a system of reading that does not rest on merely conventional relationships. Critical judgments of Tom's nature and character that assume and therefore preserve his innocence are flawed due to the inherent problems of physiognomy. They rely on outer signs of character that work in a metaphorical sense—Tom's physical signs of sorrow and lack of character are made equivalent to his innocence. Yet, as we know, physiognomy is unreliable because it cannot guarantee a natural relationship between sign and referent; such relationships are only conventional. The conventions of sentimental fiction are all that guarantee the inner/outer logic, and thus the genre is vulnerable to satire that exposes the potential for error in these assumed relationships.

For Wilson to prevail, physiognomy must be supplanted by the indexical relationships of phrenology, or at least by a manner of reading bodies that relies on the indexical rather than the metaphorical. In general, detective fiction rests upon just such a shift; the genre enacts a movement from unfixed relationships to fixed ones. As Lawrence Howe explains, "Detective fiction explores the indeterminacy of language in order to restore the stability of the law, to honor what the genre portrays as an inherent truthfulness of language" (501). Howe quotes D. A. Miller, arguing that the closure of detective fiction " 'consists in a depletion of the signifiers generated by the crime and accumulated in the course of inquest,' making all signs appear to lead to the inescapable solution of the mystery, as if the relation between sign and referent were fundamentally stable" (501). In *Pudd'nhead Wilson,* fingerprinting allows the detective to make the misleading signification of Tom's disguises and performances irrelevant. Wilson is thus able to pare away faulty metaphorical and physiognomic readings, leaving a single narrative line based on indexical certainty.

The turn in the case comes when Tom's hand unwittingly connects him to the crime even while he is performing his innocence. Wilson has a fingerprint on the murder weapon that does not match either of the twins, and he has eyewitnesses who saw a veiled woman leaving the Judge's house by the back door just after the crime. Wilson pours over his fingerprint collection in a vain attempt to find a woman whose finger matches the print. When Tom ventures over to Wilson's house to goad him over his impending failure, he leaves a print on one of the slides. Wilson immediately sees that the print is identical to the one on the murder weapon, and the scales of physiognomy fall from his eyes. He chides himself for his blindness: "Idiot that I was! Nothing but a girl would do me—a man in girl's clothes never occurred to me" (104). When Tom's hand reveals the truth that his performances were designed to hide, Wilson is able to see that the testimony to gender provided by clothing is only circumstantial. Wilson thus turns to fingerprints to form an alternative basis for his case that avoids interpretations of performance by reading the body rather than clothing.

On the first day of the trial the prosecution establishes that it will convict the twins on the basis of "a chain of circumstantial evidence without break or fault in it anywhere" (100). Yet circumstantial evidence is at its heart interpretive. It fits details together into a narrative chain extrapolated from selected circumstances into a speculative account of the reality of the crime. Accordingly, at the head of the chapter in which the murder trial begins, an excerpt from Wilson's calendar observes that "even the clearest and most perfect circumstantial evidence is likely to be at fault, after all, and therefore ought to be received with great caution. Take the case of any pencil, sharpened by any woman; if you have witnesses, you will find she did it with a knife; but if you take simply the aspect of the pencil, you will say she did it with her teeth" (99). A reading of the pencil that attends only to visual details merely tells a story about the circumstances that resulted in its appearance, much as a reading of Tom's performances only results in a confirmation of whatever story of Tom's character one wishes to confirm.[23]

Consequently, Wilson builds a case based on indexical signs, purged of the circumstantial and thus interpretive narrative of the prosecution's chain. He enlarges several key fingerprints from his collection, and "arrange[s] [the] results according to a plan in which a progressive order and sequence was a principal feature" (105). He then informs the court that he may not need the testimony of his witnesses because he has "other testimony,—and better" (105). As he explains, "Every human being carries with him from his cradle to his grave certain physical marks which do not change their character, and by which he can always be identified—and that without question" (108). These marks signal identity in an indexical sense rather than a conventional or interpreted one; a fingerprint's unique marks allow it to function as a direct impression of an individual's singularity. Accordingly, Wilson's progressive sequence of fingerprints provides an indexical link between crime and criminal. As Wilson notes, a fingerprint "consists of the delicate lines of corrugations with which Nature marks the insides of the hands" (108). The fingerprint is a natural sign for identity, a mark superior in every sense to other interpreted signs.

When Wilson presents his case in court, a noticeable split develops between the inhabitants of Dawson's Landing, who still rely on their flawed physiognomy, and the newly enlightened Wilson. We are given doubled readings of Tom's various reactions to the proceedings. Wilson's assumptions about the community's incorrect readings are paired with his correct ones. When Wilson announces that he will produce the person who left the fingerprint on the murder weapon, there is a sensation in the court and most people turn to Tom to see his response: "Wilson stole a glance at Tom, and said to himself, 'He is flying signals of distress, now; even people who despise him are pitying him; they think this is a hard ordeal for a young fellow who has lost his benefactor by so cruel a stroke—and they are right'" (109). Wilson sees how one might read Tom's signals incorrectly, but he also understands the correct source of Tom's distress. Once Wilson has proven that the twins' fingerprints do not match the one on the murder weapon and announces that he will produce the killer, we are once again given a false reading to accentuate its irony: "Tom's eyes were starting from their sockets—yes, it was a cruel day for the bereaved youth, everybody thought" (111).

At the climax, however, Tom's body produces one final sign that Wilson will not let Dawson's Landing misread. Wilson displays a series of enlarged fingerprints from two individuals which he explains that he had taken at intervals between infancy and adulthood. When he shows that the prints switch at about eight months, he reveals two truths simultaneously: "The murderer of your friend and mine—York Driscoll . . . sits among you. Valet de Chambre, negro and slave—falsely called Thomas à Becket Driscoll—make upon the window the finger-prints that will hang you!" (112). A chain of indexical evidence now ostensibly links Tom's body directly to the crime without having to stop off in the unfixed relationships of language and circumstantial interpretation. And this chain ends with what Wilson sees as a final sign:

> Tom turned his ashen face imploringly toward the speaker, made some impotent movements with his white lips, then slid limp and lifeless to the floor.
>
> Wilson broke the awed silence with the words—
>
> "There is no need. He has confessed." (112–13)

With Wilson's reading of Tom's bodily gesture, there is no need for the final fingerprint in the indexical chain or for Tom to even speak his own confession. His body confesses for him just as the prints left inadvertently on a glass slide, the mute testimony of his body, previously allowed Wilson to crack the case. Finally, the people of Dawson's Landing and Wilson read the same messages sent by Tom's body: he is black, and he is a murderer.

Yet, of course, Tom has *not* confessed. This bodily gesture is merely taken to be an assurance of guilt by a community that attaches a certain cultural value to the courtroom faint. In this way, Tom's faint is the most circumstantial of evidence and does not prove that he is a murderer any more than his fingerprint "proves" that he is black. Both signs are only meaningful within a semiotic system of signs and gestures. Accordingly, since the neat generic ending has been accomplished on the basis of the certainty of these signs, it is vulnerable to disruptions of its self-contained logic. Predictably, Twain provides disruption to this detective ending and to the sentimental fiction that it supplanted.

The Ironic Return of Romance

Though Wilson's victory is total, it has some strange consequences. Most significantly, it works to restore the generic logic it defeated. Wilson's case was predicated on the rejection of physiognomic truisms, yet after the trial Dawson's Landing is given back both its romance and its physiognomy. First, the townspeople have been given a lesson in the correct reading of the scientific stranger. One citizen asserts, "This is the man the likes of us have called a pudd'nhead for more than twenty years. He has resigned from that position . . . but it isn't vacant—we're elected" (114). As the townspeople are able to read Wilson's character correctly, the democratic logic of voting is put back on the side of justice. The metaphor of voting now serves as a marker for the consequences of the correct reading of character, since the public assessment of Wilson's character is finally in line with his intelligent physiognomy.

In addition, the events of the trial eliminate one of the major embarrassments to sentimental physiognomy: the dissonance between Roxy's body and her status as a slave. Though previously Roxy had to counteract her majestic bearing with a meek performance in order to be seen as a slave, she is now appropriately adjusted after being publicly exposed as the culprit behind the switch: "The spirit in her eye was quenched, her martial bearing departed with it, and the voice of her laughter ceased in the land" (114). Now Roxy looks her part and need perform her meekness no longer. And most tellingly, once the visible is again reliable, the twins are "heroes of romance . . . with rehabilitated reputations" (114). The romance has been restored by the detective plot. Now that Roxy no longer disrupts the ability of visible signs to attest to racial character and the twins are heroes again, it appears that the world of the novel can once again sustain romance.

I say "appears" because this romance is precarious. The order restored at the end of the novel is punctuated by ironies that prevent some of the fixed types of the romance from being restored. After the trial, "Tom" and "Chambers" are switched back. Yet Chambers finds that he suffers from another sort of fix: "The real heir suddenly found himself rich and free, but in a most embarrassing situation. He could neither read nor write, and his speech was the basest dialect of the negro quarter. His gait, his attitudes, his gestures, his bearing, his laugh—all were vulgar and uncouth; his manners were the manners of a slave. Money and fine clothes could not mend these defects or cover them up, they only made them the more glaring and the more pathetic" (114). The newly restored heir does not have the training to carry off his new identity, leaving a disturbing dissonance between his physical performance and his status. In fact, he seems to be incapable of covering over his own dissonances. Unlike Roxy in the novel's early chapters, Chambers cannot stage a misleading performance to cover up his own inappropriateness. Though the logic of sentimental physiognomy has been restored, Chambers's white skin and blood do not guarantee his aristocracy. Accordingly, the narrator admits that Chambers's predicament is no longer appropriate to narrate: "We cannot follow his curious fate further—that would be a long story" (114). Chambers threatens to break out of the frame of this newly restored genre because his very existence invalidates the inner/outer logic that defines it.

Twain has arrived at an expression of liminality—Chambers is thrust into a position that is no position. He is permanently suspended between two planes of existence, performing an identity that is coded as black while inhabiting a position in his community that is incompatible with that performance. He is left without a stable racial position because the force of his black performance renders him insufficiently white. In effect, Chambers becomes like one of the islands that so amused Twain in *Life on the Mississippi.* Occasionally, Twain explains, part of the Mississippi River breaks over its banks at the start of a sharp curve to cut off the distance and run straight to rejoin the course at the bottom of the curve, creating an island. However, in some cases it is impossible to give that new island a geographical designation. For example, since Mississippi's state line is defined as extending "to the channel" and Arkansas's is defined as "the middle of the river," in one instance a cutoff "threw this big island out of Arkansas, and yet not within Mississippi" because it appeared on the Mississippi side of the middle of the river but on the Arkansas side of the channel (248). As Twain explains, "a freak of the river here has sorely perplexed the laws of men and made them a vanity and a jest" (248). The island, like poor Chambers, occupies a position that thwarts a man-made binary. And just as the river has made the laws of men ridiculous, so the act of creation that produced Chambers has similarly made a vanity and a jest of the laws of men, in this case the laws of racial designation.

The closure of the detective plot—in which the indexical proof of Tom's identity creates the liminal Chambers—has once again put the fixed types of sentimental romance in jeopardy. This is the pinnacle of Twain's satire: once the fixed types have been restored, the order that results is ironic and imperfect. Yet the destabilization of genre goes deeper. The ironies of the sentimental plot in turn threaten the detective plot. The false Tom's fate renders the detective ending absurd when the creditors of his "uncle's" bankrupt estate assess him as a piece of property. They conclude that "if he had been delivered up to them in the first place, they would have sold him and he could not have murdered Judge Driscoll, therefore it was not he that had really committed the murder, the guilt lay with the erroneous inventory. Everybody saw that there was reason in this" (115). The governor pardons Tom so that he can be sold down the river, and he is divested of his status as the murderer as soon as he is black and a slave. Because of this twist, the chain of signification that had pared down to the indexical proof of Tom's guilt is not able to hold, and he is reclassified. The murder is essentially attributed to writing and not to a body at all; the "erroneous inventory" commits the crime. This outcome violates the generic imperative in detective fiction to construct a chain of fixed signs that leads to an agent who can be fingered as the criminal, and everyone sees reason in this generic violation because the fiction of an author-less murder is necessary in order to maintain the system of slavery. Thus, Chambers's liminality disrupts the sentimental conclusion, and Tom's evasion of responsibility for the murder perverts the detective plot.

So what finally is left after each of these two generic frameworks is rendered ironic and unfit for the task of containing racial paradoxes? Eric Sundquist would argue that this artistic self-destruction allows *Pudd'nhead Wilson* to enact (and perhaps allegorize) the legal travesties of the Jim Crow era: "No literary work of the late nineteenth century more accurately embodied the erosion of promised racial equality in the age of Jim Crow, not least because its own powers of representation and philosophical inquiry seem continually on the point of collapse" (225). Sundquist narrates the shortcomings of the logical gymnastics the post-Reconstruction Supreme Court had to resort to in order to strip U.S. citizens of social rights as rendered distinct from political ones and draws a comparison to Twain's own confusion: "The Court's inability to separate political from social inequality (even as it claimed to draw a clear line between them) left it caught in the same quagmire of assumptions that underlay theories of African American 'reversion' and 'degeneration,' and that reappears in Twain's garbled, unsatisfactory representation of the sources of Tom Driscoll's behavioral traits" (255). For Sundquist, the clear parallels between the novel's disjunctions and the inconsistencies in both racial science and public policy result in a larger reflection upon the capacity of novelistic fiction to do justice to racial representation: "*Pudd'nhead Wilson* comes close to being debilitated by its suffocating racial crisis, which is concurrently a crisis in artistic representation" (269).

Twain's sutured-together generic hybrid was intended to stage satire, and it does so effectively because it results in a generic and logically impossible conclusion. Though generic hybridity confuses the racial message, Sundquist would suggest, and I would agree, that the novel creates final ironies around the dictates of representation itself. Specifically, the novel undermines the photographic realism that would seem to be the alternative to generic impossibilities. Just as Twain undermines his claim to photograph the courtroom in his preface, the way in which he has used the foibles of physiognomy to burlesque the conventional racism embedded in sentimental fiction effectively disrupts the logic of the photograph as well. Though Roxy is the novel's best reader of faces and characters—she was always convinced that Wilson was not a pudd'nhead—she is fooled when she is forced to read a face presented in a static image, like a photograph. In one scene Roxy confronts Tom about the trick he has played on her, selling her down the river to pay off his debts. When Roxy describes the cruel circumstances that motivated her to escape, Tom shows his anger because he so badly wanted her out of the way: "The expression of this sentiment was fiercely written on his face, and stood thus revealed to Roxana by a white glare of lightning which turned the somber dusk of the room into dazzling day at that moment. She was pleased—pleased and grateful; for did not that expression show that her child was capable of grieving for his mother's wrongs and of feeling resentment toward her persecutors?" (86). As Tom's face is illuminated by the flash, the writing upon it is clear enough. But Roxy interprets the signs of his anger wrongly as testimony to a depth of empathy that her son is not feeling. The flash that illuminates Tom's face in a single instant has the effect of a photograph; it creates a still picture that is an exact register of the visual impact of Tom's face. But despite the exactness of the register, the photograph does not provide infallible evidence of character. Roxy's reading is an interpretation, and it is simply wrong.

The key to understanding what the novel says about the ability of representation to capture truth without distortions, generic or otherwise, may lie in *Life on the Mississippi,* where Twain also discusses the questionable reliability of photography. In an incident that seems to be a warm-up for the murder plot of *Pudd'nhead Wilson,* a chapter titled "A Thumb Print and What Came of It" contains an inset tale in which a murder is solved using a bloody thumbprint. The protagonist got the idea to use the print from an old Frenchman: "In these days we photograph the new criminal, and hang his picture in the Rogue's Gallery for future reference; but that Frenchman, in his day, used to take a print of the ball of a new prisoner's thumb and put that away for future reference. He always said that pictures were no good—future disguises could make them useless; 'The thumb's the only sure thing,' said he; 'you can't disguise that'" (237). As in *Pudd'nhead Wilson,* the face is not reliable, and a photograph of the face is too static to register possibilities of change and performance. As such, the episode in which Roxy misreads

Tom's "photograph" implies that if any form of representation is to be a proper testimony to character, it should not imitate the photograph. The realist's metaphor of photography does not provide a way to establish a mode for representation that is in the end any more reliable than physiognomy. Though the photograph seems to offer a fixed, direct relationship between representation and thing represented—a photograph is indexical inasmuch as it provides an impression made on a photographic plate—it cannot register the mutability of human character.

Life on the Mississippi demonstrates how closely related characterization and writing are for Twain. Writing apparently has the potential to characterize so correctly that it often can be more truthful than observation or visual assessment. Twain suggests that George Washington Cable is such a "masterly delineator" of southern "inner life and history" that "the untrained eye and vacant mind can inspect it and learn of it and judge of it more clearly and profitably in his books than by personal contact" (313). He also notes that despite Joel Chandler Harris's shyness there is "a strong and beautiful nature hidden behind it, as all know who have read the Uncle Remus book; and a fine genius, too, as all know by the same sign" (330). In both these cases, writing has the potential to transcend the limits of visual inspection and offers a mode of representation more reliable than any other. In this way, if physiognomy and visual assessment cannot provide a means for reading character, one must rather literally read it in a book. After all, Tom's invisible color is not visible as it paints his soul, but rather as the narrator constructs it in narrative unfolding.

Twain reports in *Life on the Mississippi* that one of the first and hardest lessons he learned about piloting steamboats is that the river cannot be learned as a series of static pictures:

> I went to work now to learn the shape of the river; and of all the eluding and ungraspable objects that ever I tried to get my mind or hands on, that was the chief. I would fasten my eyes upon a sharp, wooded point that projected far into the river some miles ahead of me, and go to laboriously photographing its shape upon my brain; and just as I was beginning to succeed to my satisfaction, we would draw up toward it and the exasperating thing would begin to melt away and fold back into the bank! (88–89)

Twain eventually discovers that he must learn the river not as a series of static visual images but as set of possibilities. As an object that looks different from different angles and in different light, the face of the river can only be read if it is understood to be mutable and a constant threat to the laws of man. And once this lesson has been learned, the river becomes narrative rather than visual:

> The face of the river, in time, became a wonderful book—a book that was a dead language to the uneducated passenger, but which told its mind to me without reserve, delivering its most cherished secrets as clearly as if it uttered them with a voice. And it was not a book to be read once and thrown aside, for it had a new story to tell every day. (94)

If the river becomes an indirect parallel for the contingencies of race that render it difficult for humans to write it into their books, it also becomes the only kind of "book" that could contain it—a book that is capable of being as mutable as its theme. *Pudd'nhead Wilson* suggests that failing this kind of narrative, the theme of race will constantly break over the banks of genres and make a mockery of attempts to contain it. Just as the courts could not draw a line between social and political rights, and mapmakers often cannot draw a clear line between states, novels will never be able to tell us where to draw the line between black and white. But since Twain never really promised to provide a photographic image of his racial theme, one is left to wonder what happens when a self-confessed realist like Howells—the man who is such an admirable prose photographer—tries to represent an invisible color.

4
Howells and Chesnutt: The Racial Uses of Genre

There is a certain elegant simplicity to Thomas Dixon's fiction. Though his novels at times lapse into barely coherent political ranting and racial jeremiad, there is a geometrical precision to their racial themes: whites with the proper political beliefs are good, and all blacks but the most loyal are evil. His fiction is also simple because, like most melodrama, it has no self-awareness. Dixon's novels are all manifest content with no metaliterary commentary on their own fictiveness. Twain's *Pudd'nhead Wilson,* in contrast, has a highly developed layering of fictional self-consciousness. Twain is interested in subjecting southern racial hypocrisies to satire, but he is also interested in mocking the southern Cavalier mode of fiction that most obviously perpetuates them. As a satire of a society *and* its chosen fiction, Twain's novel depends on a type of narration that can communicate to the reader an awareness of the fictive constructions it mocks and can communicate its political messages at the expense of its characters. If Dixon's heroes are vehicles for Dixon's politics, Twain's characters illustrate only what Twain's politics are not.

William Dean Howells in *An Imperative Duty* and Charles Chesnutt in *The House Behind the Cedars* take a different tack from Dixon in their novels of passing. These fictional treatments of race by so-called realist authors provide more artistic depth than Dixon's flat racial melodrama. Like Twain, both authors are interested in how a fiction of law and custom supports the racial logic of the one-drop rule, and so both their novels explore the social pressures faced by a black woman who can pass as white. Howells and Chesnutt are also interested in how the fictiveness of the one-drop rule is connected to reading and the social uses of fiction in a more literal sense. Their characters discuss and even manipulate the fictions that work to establish racial truths, and, in consequence, both novels contain a metaliterary discussion of how fiction creates and manipulates racial identities.

Chesnutt, an African-American novelist who himself could have passed for white, frequently used his writing to address the problems of the color line and the paradoxes of birth and ancestry it creates. For example, each story in his collection *The Wife of His Youth* (1899) turns upon an irony of the fiction of color and caste. As Eric Sundquist notes in *To Wake the Nations,* Chesnutt has often been slighted by critics because he wrote only on racial subjects.[1] In contrast, *An Imperative Duty* represents Howells's only attempt at a sustained treatment of the problems of race. Nonetheless, since both authors are commonly identified as part of a literary trend away from the conventions of Dixon's fiction, it is interesting to see how both work with an identifiable theme—passing—that was commonly treated by the most sentimental of sentimental novels. I would argue that it is their meta-level discussion of the relationships between constructed notions of race and literary conventions that represents the least sentimental feature of their aesthetics because these discussions allow them to comment on the role that sentimental expectations play in race issues.

Though it is clear that Howells and Chesnutt had what we would now see as more constructed senses of race than Dixon, it is important to note that as men of the nineteenth century both authors nonetheless believed in innate, inherited differences between white and black. To a large degree they accepted the doctrine of the superiority of Anglo-Saxon civilization. Both, however, were able to acknowledge the amalgamated nature of the U.S. population without Dixon's racial hysteria. Neither novelist argued that the mulatto is a degenerate and the harbinger of future racial degradation. Rather, the case of the white-skinned black character allowed Howells and Chesnutt to explore the mutability of racial character and the possibility that such "new people"—as Chesnutt called them—might represent some less dire set of racial consequences.

A recognition of the mutability of racial character leads each author to an exploration of the connections between fiction and race. As I will argue, both novels suggest that if not color but a social fiction makes the white-skinned black person black, then a manipulation of fictional expectations can serve to change the way identity is perceived and constructed. For example, Howells presents a northern doctor who is able to see the mixed-race heroine's character in such a way that he rejects the white supremacist's condemnation of the racial taint; this doctor argues that black blood can be a positive influence on inherited "white" racial tendencies. He is thus able to convince the heroine that she need not follow the model of the novel of passing and renounce him. Rather, she can create her own ending for her "story," one that is presumably realistic rather than sentimental. Chesnutt's novel also suggests that in the absence of visible blackness, the mixed-race character's racial identity and character can be fixed by a self-fashioning story that he or she tells. Chesnutt's mixed-race characters accordingly try to incorporate the conventions of the racialized southern romance into the story of themselves in order to privilege their white southern blood.

As the novelists play out the consequences of these fictional manipulations of identity, they both also demonstrate that racial fictions often play out along generic lines. Howells's novel ends with marriage and thus evokes comedy, while Chesnutt's ends with his heroine's death and takes on a tragic cast. As I will argue, the mechanism for the resolution of the plot of each novel appears to rest on the consequences of the scientific characterizations made by the male figure who forms a romantic attachment to the mixed-race heroine. Both novelists use their heroes as stand-ins for scientific/social understandings of racial character. Thus, both novels provide an awareness that when characterization calls upon racial science, rhetorical constructions can determine genre or at least create the conditions which tend toward certain generic forms of closure.

Chesnutt's use of death and Howells's use of marriage suggest that the key difference between the two novelists lies in how they arrive at such opposite forms of generic closure. As I will demonstrate, Howells is invested in the power of mixed-racial tendencies and the reality of cross-strain marriage—and thus the comic ending that makes such marriages representable—because it promotes his own theories of the values of literary realism. Ironically, however, he cannot imagine black/white miscegenation in the United States. Chesnutt can imagine such a thing, as is clear from his nonfiction, but he does not allow for interracial marriage in his novel. Chesnutt demonstrates that the white romantic story that his heroine uses to construct her white identity is not anchored (as southerners assume) by racial memory transmitted by blood but rather by the operation of white social power. When Chesnutt's heroine cannot wield this power because of her gender, the genre shifts to tragedy.

The fact that both authors cannot allow their novels to end with a mixed-race marriage in the United States suggests that their realism takes into account the laws that govern social interaction. Both novels end with a kind of erasure: Howells's hero and heroine marry, but they leave the United States to live in Italy, and Chesnutt's heroine dies. Because both novels reject sentimental structures for characterization, they call attention to the way that character is a product of the assumptions behind the narrative viewpoint brought to bear on it. The fact that genre is entangled with characterization in both novels suggests that genre has become a subject of realist fiction rather than a constraint upon it. But the fact that neither novel resolves the sentimental dilemma of the tragic mulatto and her white lover without an erasure implies that while one realist achievement lies in the less codified representation of character, the realist novel cannot present plot-level conclusions that do not accord with actual social possibilities.

Howells and Comic Temperament

Howells was a frequent contributor to the literary debates of his day. From his writings on literature we know that he was an avowed opponent of sentimental fiction and the historical romance. While Harriet Beecher Stowe argued in her introduction to *Uncle Tom's Cabin* that her fiction represented an advance over previous characterizations and therefore implied that sentimental fiction as she wrote it was a progressive force, Howells, as I argued in chapter 1, reversed the argument. He used evolutionary language to champion realistic fiction over other literary forms, since he believed that realism was the truly progressive genre and represented an advance or development in human civilization. Since realism transcended formalized and conventional depiction, it escaped from superstition and misguided social restrictions. As Kenneth Warren explains, Howells believed that "civilization comes through literature, specifically realistic literature. What one reads shapes one's tastes and determines the degree to which one is civilized" (77).

For this reason, Howells's fiction is often metaliterary: when commentary on other fiction is a plot point, the literary battle becomes quite explicit. Accordingly, the novels that best illustrate Howells's departures from sentimental plotting are those in which he makes the shortcomings of sentimental fiction a theme. For example, in *The Rise of Silas Lapham* (1885), Howells presents a love triangle that resembles one which his characters have encountered in a sentimental novel titled *Tears, Idle Tears.* In the sentimental novel, a female character renounces her lover on point of honor to another woman who had loved him first. However, in Howells's supposedly realistic rewriting of this sentimental scenario, characters faced with the same love triangle adhere to an "economy of pain" in which renunciation is no longer equated with honor: the lovers marry so that only the odd woman out is made miserable, thus reducing the net pain. The comic closure of marriage is a realistic solution in that it avoids melodramatic self-renunciation and defies sentimental expectations. *The Rise of Silas Lapham* also uses metafictive themes to advance Howells's argument about art and civilization. One character notes that he has "occasionally met young girls who were so brutally, insolently, willfully indifferent to the arts which make civilisation that they ought to have been clothed in the skins of wild beasts and gone about barefoot with clubs over their shoulders" (103). As Warren notes, this passage signals that while "many members of middle-class nineteenth-century America were only too willing to identify savagery and barbarism with ethnic immigrants and blacks, Howellsian realism made a concerted effort to unfix the barbaric from ethnic identification and set it floating throughout the social body" (77).[2] The true test of civilization in *Lapham,* one could argue, involves the ways its characters—female characters in particular—respond to the sentimental fiction they read.

Not surprisingly, when Howells attempted to write his own realistic version of the novel of passing he placed his characters in situations that would allow them to undermine or reject conventions from the sentimental tradition. *An Imperative Duty* turns very much on the point of renunciation. An orphaned young woman named Rhoda Aldgate is passing as white without her knowledge. The audience is given this information by her aunt as she confides in a young doctor named Edward Olney. Rhoda is about to receive a proposal from a white minister, and the aunt concludes that she must tell her niece the truth. She does so, but dies of an accidental overdose of a sleeping draught directly after the emotional scene. Rhoda breaks off all contact with the white minister. Meanwhile, Olney ponders the implications of the situation and after a respectful amount of time proposes to Rhoda despite her racial ancestry. Rhoda feels that it is her duty to serve her race and tries to refuse. However, at the doctor's prompting, she accepts his proposal and his offer to take her to live in Italy as a white woman. The fact that the mixed-race woman marries her white lover avoids the sentimental expectations of sacrifice and renunciation that Howells mocked in *The Rise of Silas Lapham.*

However, in this novel the pressure on the heroine to renounce her lover rests on more than a simple generic expectation that a true heroine will bravely renounce her own happiness if there is some impediment to her romantic attachment. Rather, renunciation in the novel of passing derives from strong prohibitions against mixed marriages. Howells is thus playing against sentimental fiction on two fronts. To defeat sentimental plotting, the heroine cannot successfully renounce her lover. But since that social prohibition against miscegenation is based on fears about inherited racial traits and character, Howells must recast the nature of racial inheritance—establish a new kind of racial character—in order for his novel to end in marriage. And in order to redraw racial character, he must carefully and pointedly characterize the heroine of his novel of passing. Put bluntly, in order to reject the sentimental plot line, Howells has to reject both sentimental characterization and pseudo-scientific ideas about racial character. Both ends are served by the novel's studiously unsentimental hero.

Howells highlights his hero's perspective as a scientifically minded observer and his unsentimental vision of racial character. As the novel opens, Olney, who has been living in Italy, spends the afternoon observing the people of Boston and speculating on matters of race and type. The narrator notes that his observations come "after an absence so long that it made everything once so familiar bewilderingly strange." He first views the "poorer class" and tries to puzzle out the paradox of why they have an "English look" when the poor he saw in Liverpool looked "American." He concludes that there must be a "common type among people who work with their hands for a living . . . the proletarian type" (137). The young women who to him look pale and crooked are made so, he believes, by "an effect of physical delicacy from their hard work and hard conditions" (138). Olney then reflects further, after "looking at them scientifically," and concludes that with better conditions the proletariat female may give birth to "a race as hale and handsome as the elder American race," but that she represents a painful transition from "Old World to New" (137). The scientific Olney is thus able to discount the inflexible logic of distinct and unchanging national types. He sees a similarity between the peoples of various nations who are subjected to similar conditions, and concludes that the physical appearance of one generation does not absolutely determine the appearance of the next.

Yet when Olney examines African Americans from the perspective of one defamiliarized, he reaches different conclusions. He discovers that, owing to a recent influx from the South, there are more blacks in Boston than when he left. He decides, however, that he "would not have known the new arrivals by anything in their looks or bearing. Their environment had made as little impression on the older inhabitants, or the natives, as Time itself makes upon persons of their race, and Olney fancied that Boston did not characterize their manner, as it does that of almost every other sort of aliens" (140). Apparently, African Americans do not change as a result of new conditions. Unlike the Irish working girls, they show no signs of physical or behavioral shifts and therefore have not been "characterized" by Boston.

Accordingly, Olney's characterization of African Americans proceeds in language that suggests timelessness, uniformity, and a character modified only by conscious imitation:

> They all alike seemed shining with good-nature and good-will, and the desire of peace on earth. Their barbaric taste in color, when it flamed out in a crimson necktie or a scarlet jersey . . . was invariably delightful to him; but he had to admit that their younger people were often dressed with an innate feeling for style. . . . They [African-American men] carried on flirtations of the eye with the young girls they met, or when they

> were walking with them they paid them a court which was far above the behavior of the common young white fellows with the girls of their class in refinement and delicacy. The negroes, if they wished to imitate the manners of our race, wished to imitate the manners of the best among us; they wished to be like ladies and gentlemen. (140–41)

In part, the passage attempts to attach new, positive associations to old, recognizable racial characteristics. For example, Olney labels the often stereotyped racial predilection for colorful clothing "barbaric" but is pleased by it and suggests that it is coupled with an innate sense of style. Also, he implies that the gentle character and loving "good will" attributed to loyal blacks under slavery will create the conditions for wider social acceptance of African Americans after emancipation. From his fresh perspective, Olney sees that blacks are capable of courtly behavior; the chivalric attitude of black men toward black women suggests that the race is by no means incapable of behaving in the romantic mode of ladies and gentlemen as they adopt the courtly manners of socially superior whites. Nonetheless, this behavior is only imitation; every other characteristic Olney mentions is unchanging and innate.

Olney is thus set up explicitly as an observer of type. His ostensibly fresh and unusual observations of blacks are meant to establish a revisionist account of racial character. Though the characterization of African Americans provided from his perspective lists rather typical racial characteristics, these characterizations are described in positive, approving terms. Olney is presented as an authority on what value the unchanging and innate features of black racial character can be said to possess and thus serves as a vehicle for the novel's racial themes. In fact, Howells has made Olney a man of science specifically because his scientific readings of character are meant to stand in contrast to more casual and ineffective efforts. *An Imperative Duty* sets up a contrast between scientific interest in human faces and character and the potential danger that unscientific sentimentalizing of character poses if it is directed at fiction rather than reality.[3]

In particular, Rhoda's aunt Mrs. Meredith uses precisely the wrong sort of vision of character trained upon the wrong medium. Olney had previously made the acquaintance of Rhoda and her aunt in Italy, and at the time of this meeting he had been

> immersed in a long and serious analysis of *Romola* with the aunt, who appeared to have a conscience of prodigious magnifying force, cultivated to the least degree by a constant training upon the ethical problems of fiction. She brought its powerful lenses to bear upon the most intimate particles of Tito's character; his bad qualities seemed to give her almost as much satisfaction as if they had been her own. (147)[4]

When his characters enter into the character of fictional characters, Howells suggests that they sentimentalize in a negative sense.[5] Here Olney faults Mrs. Meredith for having developed a suspect system of ethic vision and for examining George Eliot's creation of Tito down to its most trivial "particles." Olney has even been able to determine Mrs. Meredith's character by way of her close attention to fictional characters:

> So much impression of her character had been left from their different meetings in Florence that he had already theorized her as one of those women, commoner amongst us than any other people, perhaps, to whom life, in spite of all experience, remains a sealed book, and who are always trying to unlock its mysteries with the keys furnished them by fiction. They judge the world by these novels they have read, and their acquaintance in the flesh by characters in stories, instead of judging these by the real people they have met, and more or less lived with. (158)

Mrs. Meredith's problem is akin to that of the author of sentimental fiction: she uses fiction as a way to produce a representation of life rather than use her own experience as a way to judge the fidelity of fictional representation. Her "character" is to judge the character of characters and use this judgment to guide her in a life to which she seems to have no direct access. Mrs. Meredith thus serves a double purpose. The narrator's comments on her reading habits allow for metanarrative criticism of sentimental modes of characterization and character evaluation. Also, she acts as a foil to Olney, who does not filter his observations through fiction and thus appears to be a better and more scientific judge of character.

Since Olney is the device through which we are to get an accurate and scientific vision of character, the narrator first describes Rhoda from

Olney's point of view as he remembers their first meeting: "He recalled the particulars of her beauty; her slender height, her rich complexion of olive, with a sort of under-stain of red, and the inky blackness of her eyes and hair. Her face was of almost classic perfection, and the hair, crinkling away to either temple, grew low upon the forehead, as the hair does in the Clytie head. In profile the mouth was firmly accented, with a deep cut outlining the full lower lip, and a fine jut forward of the delicate chin" (147). In Rhoda's features there is a tension between the racially exotic and the classically perfect. Her inky black eyes and her full lips are racial markers. Yet, as with the African Americans in the park, Howells is careful to give each racialized characteristic a positive revaluation. Each mark of "blackness" is paired with an adjective with positive connotations that reclaims and legitimizes that feature for a woman of quality. Her complexion is rich and olive (rather than "yellow"—the adjective that white supremacists often used). Her mouth is "firmly" accented and her chin has a "fine" jut, making her facial angle, which Olney significantly recalls in profile, an erotic and aristocratic characteristic rather than an atavistic prognation. Overall, Rhoda's head is classically perfect and reminds Olney of Greek statuary. While the descriptive language in this passage flaunts potential racial markers rather than attempting to render them invisible, the passage also insists that Rhoda's face is as visually pleasing as the archetype for Anglo beauty, Greek sculpture.

Olney provides a reading of Rhoda's character to accompany the description as he scans his memory of Rhoda's face for signs of ancestral inheritance: "He recalled his sense of her wearing this family face, with its somewhat tragic beauty, over a personality that was at once gentle and gay. The mask, he felt, was inherited, but the character seemed to be of Miss Aldgate's own invention, and expressed itself in the sunny sparkle of her looks, that ran over with a willingness to please and to be pleased, and to consist in effect of a succession of flashing, childlike smiles" (147). Olney finds evidence of Rhoda's heritage in her face. According to Olney, Rhoda wears an outer family mask over a sunny and childlike character. Rhoda's character, in its basic good-natured, lighthearted gaiety, interestingly recalls the description of blacks which Olney gave earlier. This masked but somehow detectable inner spirit seems Rhoda's "own invention" to the as yet unenlightened Olney. But once Rhoda's racial identity is revealed, Olney concludes that her child-like character is inherited from her one partially black parent. Rhoda's invisible blackness is thus visible both in the jut of her lip and in her character as expressed by her succession of sunny smiles, but her face is also masked much like Dixon's sphinx-like mulattoes.

In this way, Howells places a mask over his heroine's character and then provides two readers of character who must learn to see underneath it. Specifically, the different ways in which Olney and Mrs. Meredith read the character beneath the mask create the tension that underlies the rest of the novel. And with this metanarrative of character comes also a metaliterary debate over how the facts of character should direct the narrative unfolding of Rhoda's life. In a scene that occurs before Rhoda's secret has been revealed, Mrs. Meredith and Olney discuss *Romola* once again. Mrs. Meredith says that she finds the double-dealing Tito's character "enviable" in that he is able to sleep at night even with a guilty conscience. When Olney responds lightly, Mrs. Meredith becomes heated and anxious. Olney assumes that she has worked a transference between her evaluations of Tito's and Rhoda's characters, inwardly admitting that Rhoda's character is "so apparently free of all personal responsibility. . . . It might be that Mrs. Meredith had lost sleep in revolving the problems of Mrs. Aldgate's character and the chances of her being equal to the duties that had left so little of Mrs. Meredith" (150). Ironically, though Olney is still ignorant of what Mrs. Meredith conceals, he is absolutely correct. Mrs. Meredith is concerned with the racial implications of Rhoda's lighthearted irresponsibility and with the likelihood that she might well have to choose whether to reveal her racial background to her future husband.

Mrs. Meredith's view of Rhoda's character has direct consequences for narrative closure. She believes that the secret blood cannot stay hidden. It will result in an atavistic reversion in Rhoda's children, and it is all too visible in her very makeup: "It might come back in a hundred ways. I can hear it in her voice at times—it's a *black* voice! I can see it in her looks! I can feel it in her character—so easy, so irresponsible, so fond of what is soft and pleasant! . . . She cannot forecast consequences; she's a creature of the present hour; she's like them *all*! I think that in some occult, dreadful way she feels her affinity with them, and that's the reason she's so attracted by them, so fond of them. It's her race *calling* her!"

(171). Mrs. Meredith reads Rhoda's character and concludes that her childlike spiritedness is inherited from black racial stock as a racial characteristic. But most importantly, Mrs. Meredith believes that this racial visibility necessitates that Rhoda not marry any man who does not know the truth. This reading of the visibility of racial character creates her opposition to Rhoda's impending engagement and marriage. Mrs. Meredith's insistence on the consequences of the racial visibility of Rhoda's character implies that a marriage plot is an impossibility.

However, Olney offers a different interpretation of the consequences of Rhoda's character and a different shape for the plot. When Rhoda enters the room directly after Mrs. Meredith's above remarks, she begins to describe a black waiter in the hotel whom she has found amusing. She blurts out, "He's so sweet! I should like to *own* him, and keep him as long as he lived. Isn't it a shame that we can't *buy* them, Dr. Olney, as we used to do?" (172). When Rhoda leaves again, Mrs. Meredith claims that her reading has been justified and that the race instinct is asserting itself in Rhoda's attraction to African Americans. Dr. Olney responds that it may as well be that it was "the other-race instinct asserting itself" (172). He reads Rhoda's remarks as evidence that the fifteen-sixteenths of Rhoda which are descended from white southern slave owners have resulted in a racial instinct toward viewing African Americans as chattel. At this point, the narrator notes that Dr. Olney has found some "hope" in his last observation which he then imparts to Mrs. Meredith. However, that conversation is only alluded to and not represented. The novel lapses into silence on the subject of Olney's new vision of Rhoda's character because the main source of suspense has become how the scientific Olney will find a way to reread it and restore the marriage plot.

In the not-so-incidental discussions of race at the beginning of the novel, Howells has already given Olney's scientific stand on miscegenation: "I've been more and more struck with the fact that sooner or later our race must absorb the colored race; and I believe that it will obliterate not only its color, but its qualities. The tame man, the civilized man, is stronger than the wild man; and I believe that in those cases within any one race where there are very strong ancestral proclivities on one side especially toward evil, they will die out before the good tendencies on the other side, for much the same reason, that is, because vice is savage and virtue is civilized" (161). Howells's Olney appears to condone miscegenation because he believes that the superior qualities of the white race will dilute and eradicate the influences of inferior races.[6] Yet Olney also leaves open the possibility that the evil parts of both races will be erased through mutual change, implying that even the Anglo-Saxon has room for improvement. Olney's belief in the workings of racial evolution provides hope for Rhoda's character. Making the novel end in marriage is at least in part a matter of seeing Rhoda's mixture of characters and temperaments scientifically enough to make her marriage to a white man evolutionarily sound—and narratively possible.

Olney is clearly the man who can achieve this form of scientific vision, though it alone is not enough. For example, when Olney first learns of Rhoda's secret he feels his scientific vision slipping. After experiencing disgust (which Howells calls a "race instinct"), Olney feels compromised by having been confided in: "His feeling was unscientific; but he could not at once detach himself from the purely social relation which he had hitherto held toward Miss Aldgate. The professional view which he was invited to take seemed to have lost all dignity, to be impertinent, cruel, squalid, and, to involve the abdication of certain sentiments, conventions which he was unwilling to part with, at least in her case. Sensibilities which ought not to have survived his scientific training and ambition were wounded to rebellion in him" (165). Olney's unscientific reaction, in which he finds he cannot take a scientific view of Rhoda without abandoning certain feelings for her, must be accommodated. He must learn how to see Rhoda's racial situation scientifically while at the same time not abdicating certain social and narrative "conventions" which tend toward the novelistic trappings of romantic love. If Olney can find a way to preserve his social feelings for Rhoda, he can construct a story line—based on his scientific vision of the prospects of miscegenation—that will allow him to love her.[7]

The waiting period that Olney endures after Mrs. Meredith dies and Rhoda has sought to isolate herself from all acquaintances is filled up by Olney's search through available generic conventions to find one that will contain both his scientific vision of racial character and his emotional feelings for Rhoda. First, he imagines "a scene in which Rhoda owned her love for him, and for his sake and her own, consented to throw convention to the winds, and to unite her fate with his in [marriage]" (206). However, at this point Olney labels this flouting of "convention" as "preposterous melodrama." The challenge is for him to come to regard that potential scene as the very opposite of sentimental melodrama. Olney then imagines a series of interviews with Rhoda and "construct[s] futures varying in character from the gayest happiness to the gloom of the darkest tragedy, lit by the one high star of self-renunciation. Olney got almost as much satisfaction out of the renunciation as out of the fruition of his hopes" (219). He is still locked in a way of thinking that makes him see all possible narrative unfoldings as sentimental: his happiness and engagement to Rhoda would be melodrama; her self-sacrifice and renunciation of their love would be a tragedy that would be satisfying because it fulfills sentimental expectations. Even the most scientific critic of fiction can find satisfaction in fantasies of sentimental self-sacrifice.

When Olney has made up his mind to propose, he knows that he must work with Rhoda's sentimental generic expectations in the same way that he worked with his own. Not surprisingly, Rhoda responds to his proposal with a melodramatic staged confession:

> She sprang to her feet and gasped hoarsely out, "I am a negress!"
>
> Something in her tragedy affected Olney comically; perhaps the belief that she had often rehearsed these words as answer to his demand. He smiled. "Well, not a very black one. Besides, what of it, if I love you?"
>
> "What of it?" she echoed. "But don't you know? You mustn't!"
>
> The simpleness of the words made him laugh outright; these she had not rehearsed. She had dramatized his instant renunciation of her when he knew the fatal truth. (227)

Olney's strategy is to confound Rhoda's generic expectations and thus shift the scene from tragedy to comedy. He finds comedy in the fact that Rhoda had actually practiced a response to his proposal based on her "dramatizations." And her predictions for his response to her confession are based on the sentimental tradition of tragic octoroon fiction, where the suitor often responds with disgust to the confession of the racial stain. As a result of Olney's failure to play his generic part, however, the entire scene must shift registers:

> As a tragedy the whole affair had fallen to ruin. It could be reconstructed, if at all, only upon an octave much below the operatic pitch. It must be treated in no lurid twilight gloom, but in plain, simple, matter-of-fact noonday.
>
> "I can't let you," she began, in a vain effort to catch up some fragments of her meditated melodrama about her. (227)

Olney has destroyed the generic conventions that would make tragedy inevitable and self-sacrifice necessary. Whereas Mrs. Meredith had been the senex—the figure in classical comedy who stands in opposition to the marriage that will eventually result in closure—Rhoda has herself become the force that prevents the comic marriage. She does so because she has expectations based on fictional models where the character must renounce her lover in self-sacrifice.

At this point, Howells explicitly links generic modes of fiction with racial character. Specifically, Rhoda feels compelled to act the part of the sentimental heroine because she has a hereditary disposition to make the self-sacrifice that closes off sentimental fiction. She has inherited Puritan "dutiology" from her white ancestors, and Olney sees that these inherited factors drive her to sacrifice her own happiness:

> He knew that in her hours of despondency there was that war between her temperament and her character which is the fruitful cause of misery in the world, where all strains are now so crossed and intertangled that there is no definite and unbroken direction any more in any of us. In her, the confusion was only a little greater than in most others, and if Olney ever had any regret it was that the sunny-natured antetypes [*sic*] of her mother's race had not endowed her with more of the heaven-born cheerfulness with which it meets contumely and injustice. His struggle was with that hypochondria of the soul into which the Puritanism of her father's race had sickened in her, and which so often seems to satisfy its crazy claim upon conscience by enforcing some aimless act of self-sacrifice. (149)

The happy character that is explicitly the birthright of the black race is once again set in contrast to the other component of Rhoda's personality, her Puritan temperament. However, Olney does not give the white temperament priority over the black character. Indeed, he views the white Puritanism as a form of pathology, a contagion which creates and then feeds a tendency to react to situations with the excessiveness and irrationality of a hypochondriac.[8] Olney thus suggests that aspects of black inherited character actually temper and neutralize the inherited puritanical belief in fatalistic determinism.

Olney's decision to marry Rhoda is logically consistent with his racial theories, since he does not place Rhoda's visible black characteristics in a necessarily inferior place to her white ones. Though Olney clearly believes that the white race is the superior one, he is willing to let the positive qualities of another racial strain ameliorate some of its less desirable tendencies. His viewpoint would perhaps be different if Rhoda were proportionally more black, but she is the daughter of an octoroon and is hardly endowed with a significant amount of black blood. Amalgamation is the most attractive option, at least in this case, given what Olney has told us about the process of miscegenation. Though racially determined characteristics remain distinct and the presence of both can be detected—as they are in Rhoda's internal war—the power of the minority blood over the majority can sometimes bring favorable results.

Furthermore, when the narrator notes that there is "no definite and unbroken direction any more in any of us," he in effect suggests that we are all mulattoes torn between the multiple inherited impulses of our varied stocks. In a larger sense, then, the marriage of different types provides a way to work toward an optimal balance between temperaments. If the Puritan type has become enfeebled by an excessive worship of duty, it is best to cross it with more easygoing racial tendencies so that in time the good and virtuous tendencies will win out over the negative. In this novel, therefore, marriage represents the possibility of racial progress on the level of the human race as a composite. As Jane Marston notes in the context of another of Howells's novels, "If synthesis may be assumed to issue from thesis and antithesis . . . marriage represents not closure but advancement" (237). Though the marriage of Olney and Rhoda creates comic closure, it also represents race progress in the Hegelian sense of perfection to be found in the future.

Furthermore, since marriage is made possible when the genre turns from a sentimental tragedy of renunciation to a comedy of racial progress, Howells's comic ending represents a literary evolution as well.

Within the novel, characters reject conventional narrative lines and construct a more realistic form of narrative closure. In doing so, they make possible a marriage that is necessary for racial progress. Literary evolution is thus rather directly associated with racial evolution. If those with Puritan temperaments are drawn to duty and sacrifice, they must also be drawn to fiction that dramatizes questions of conscience and obligation through sacrifice and self-renunciation, as Mrs. Meredith is drawn to Eliot's *Romola.* But *An Imperative Duty* implies that miscegenation will result in a racially balanced population with a drastically reduced affinity for such sentimental fiction. In this sense, the novel imagines the creation of an audience for itself. Howells's realism goes beyond the education of its audience; it sets up a literary example of how it might eugenically engineer it.

But this audience is apparently not to be created in the United States. The overt plot-level racial message is undermined by the banishment of Rhoda and Olney to Italy. The racial synthesis that this marriage represents is removed, and the American reading public will not be infused with the blood that will best cure its lapses in literary taste.[9] However, despite Howells's reluctance to endorse miscegenation in the United States, he has already established a racial need for a new kind of fiction. If, as Howells claims, we are all mixtures of different types of inherited tendencies, and if like Rhoda we therefore suffer from self-division as a result, then the new realistic fiction must find a way to represent this new form of character. Sentimental fiction presented character as unified and singular because it assumed that racial types were singular and unmixed, but realism must find a way to represent a character that is multiple and self-alienated. Howells has in effect suggested that a theme for realistic fiction is the multiple and self-divided nature of consciousness. Even if a white-black character cannot be contained by the marriage plot and thus punctures plotting, the representation of mixed character has taken over the center of the novelist's set of concerns.

Chesnutt and Tragic Liminality

Charles Chesnutt's views on the nature of racial identity are readily available in his published nonfiction. A three-part series of articles in the *Boston Evening Transcript* in 1900 (the same year *The House Behind the Cedars* was published) outlines Chesnutt's support for recent arguments that would complicate the relationship between race and bodily features: "Scientific research has swept away many hoary anthropological fallacies. It has been demonstrated that the shape or size of the head has little to do with the civilization or average intelligence of a race. . . . Even color, upon which the social structure of the United States is so largely based, has been proved no test of race" (96). In rejecting the fallacious logic of racial phrenology and the hegemony of color, Chesnutt denied that racial populations can be sharply divided or clearly distinguished. In fact, he noted that the notion of the purity of Caucasian racial types has been exploded since the "conception of a pure Aryan, Indo-European race has been abandoned in scientific circles, and the secret of the progress of Europe has been found in racial heterogeneity rather than in racial purity" (96). Chesnutt attacked the theories of the existence of pure, superior Germanic or Anglo-Saxon "tribes," suggesting that the notion of a pure white population is a suspect one.

Chesnutt's purpose in arguing for the fundamentally amalgamated nature of racial types is to reduce resistance to his overall thesis in the series. Specifically, he predicted that interbreeding between whites, Native Americans, and blacks would eventually result in a "future American" composite of all racial populations inhabiting North America. Chesnutt reminded his audience that they most likely already accepted that the perfection of the American type would be "brought about by a combination of all the best qualities of the European races, and the elimination, by some strange alchemy, of all their undesirable traits" (96). Chesnutt thus reprised Olney's argument that Europeans will come to be "characterized" by the United States and that through intermarriage crossed strains will result in fitter types. However, Chesnutt laid heavy and direct emphasis on the point that Howells's novel presented only as a special case; Chesnutt's alchemy of amalgamation necessarily included African Americans.

Yet, interestingly, while Howells allows his mixed-race heroine to marry a white man, Chesnutt foils his novel's proposed mixed marriage. In *An Imperative Duty* blackness is visible in inherited racial temperaments and characteristics—even in the case of a woman who is fifteen-sixteenths white. Therefore, the object in the way of the marriage is a set of scientific concerns about atavism and racial instincts. Since Olney is a man of science, he can work the recharacterization necessary to make the marriage viable. In contrast, Chesnutt demonstrates that the obstacles in the way of mixed marriage are not scientific at all. He believes that the racial character of a person physically indistinguishable from white cannot be distinguished from white either. Throughout his novel the mulatto protagonists cannot be read as black, since both their bodies and the character they project are white. In fact, Chesnutt echoed Twain in the third article in his *Boston Evening Transcript* series when he stated that "it is only a social fiction, indeed, which makes of a person seven-eighths white a Negro; he is really much more a white man" (106).

Thus, since Chesnutt turns scientific concerns into versions of social fictions, the impediment to the marriage becomes itself a function of those fictions. Chesnutt's mixed-race characters, in the absence of anything that he would call black, manipulate the social fictions of race to become white. They use southern narratives of beauty and love to achieve marriages that will establish them in white social positions. In this way, racial identity becomes the result of relationships, and white social power becomes identical with social positioning within those relationships. But in his choice of tragedy for his novel's ending, Chesnutt betrays an understanding that the narrative tools which construct identity depend on power systems that lie beyond the passing character's control. The tragedy of *The House Behind the Cedars* results because Chesnutt cannot conscientiously create a hero like Olney. Chesnutt's white lover has total control over the genres of social fiction and works Olney's trick in reverse: he uses the language of scientific racism to recharacterize a white woman and to make her ineligible for the marriage that would make her socially white. A lack of control over the genres of identity results in a tragic outcome for the novel's heroine.

The House Behind the Cedars tells the story of John Warwick and his sister Rena, the children of a quadroon mother and a wealthy white man. In early adulthood, John left his mother and sister in Patesville, North Carolina, to pursue a law career and to pass in South Carolina (where by law he is a white man). At the beginning of the novel, a recently widowed John returns home after an absence of ten years to convince his sister to leave their mother and move to his home. Once there, Rena will help care for his son and enjoy the privileges of passing. Rena hesitates but then complies. Once there, she falls in love with an aristocratic man named George Tryon. On the advice of her brother, she accepts Tryon's proposal, although in order to protect John's status in his community she decides not to tell her future husband her secret. When Tryon accidentally discovers the truth and breaks off the engagement, Rena bitterly renounces passing and goes to teach at a black school. In a climactic, desperate attempt to avoid both Tryon (who has come to find her, perhaps to make her his mistress) and a lecherous mixed-race man who is now pursuing her (euphemistically and literally), she runs off into a swamp. She is rescued by a black man from her hometown who has loved her since childhood, but it is too late. She suffers from exposure and dies in her childhood home behind the cedars.

This plot is clearly quite melodramatic. And as in all his fiction, Chesnutt skillfully uses melodramatic plotting to highlight racial injustices. As Eric Sundquist notes, "Like a great deal of the literature of miscegenation and passing, Chesnutt's color line stories (which he once described as 'sermons') are dominated by melodrama, and their fundamental trope is irony" (397). Since the plot is packed with coincidental reunions and recognitions, Chesnutt can play up the ironies of what is actually recognized. For example, the most pervasive irony of the novel is that both Rena and John are routinely assumed to be white by casual observers. The novel opens as John returns to Patesville after his ten-year absence, and the way he and his sister are introduced emphasizes this irony. John is "tall, dark, with straight, black, lustrous hair, and very clean-cut, high-bred features," and despite his darkness, the superiority of his features lead the white clerk at the hotel to conclude that he must be a wealthy white businessman (2). When John leaves the hotel he finds himself following an attractive young woman. He assumes that she is white and only later realizes that she is his sister.

Thus the novel uses the physiognomy of race to render the one-drop rule virtually meaningless. The two mulatto protagonists are incapable of being read as anything but white and superior; moreover, they are read as signs of white racial perfection. For example, once Rena has come to live with John in South Carolina, he observes with pride the ease with which she has adapted to the life of a wealthy white woman: "Her graceful movements, the quiet elegance with which she wore even the simplest gown, the easy authoritativeness with which she directed the servants, were to him proofs of superior quality" (65). Rena appears to be at ease with authority and privilege even without being born in it; John takes her elegance as a sign of the "superior qualities" inherited from their white ancestry. In the same way, the white aristocrat Tryon is particularly resolute in his belief that Rena displays signs of white racial inheritance. When John hints to Tryon that he and his sister do not come from an old or distinguished family, Tryon responds that he needs no family connections to prove Rena's worth, as "she carries the stamp of her descent on her face and in her heart" (84). Tryon's contemplations of Rena cannot detect anything but the "fine aureole of superiority [that] surrounded her." He concludes that "she represented in her adorable person and her pure heart the finest flower of the finest race that God had ever made" (98).

In addition to mocking the observational powers of white supremacists, Chesnutt's novel directly refutes discussions of the black race in scientific literature. Characters read articles and pamphlets asserting monolithic and singular accounts of racial character and abilities and respond to them in varying ways. Tryon idly picks up a medical journal in a doctor's waiting room and reads an article on the "perennial race problem" that repeats a familiar formula: "Owing to a special tendency of the negro blood, however diluted, to revert to the African type, any future amalgamation of the white and black races . . . would therefore be an ethnological impossibility; for the smallest trace of negro blood would inevitably drag down the superior race to the level of the inferior" (106). While Tryon certainly would agree, John and Rena refute such arguments since their small traces of black blood are undetectable in body or character. Tryon's own judgments of Rena's face and heart make arguments about the properties of small amounts of blood ridiculous.

Clearly, Chesnutt places the physical assessments of his mixed-race characters in direct and ironic juxtaposition with the pronouncements of scientific racism. In an inset narrative that gives background to the novel's events, a young John approaches an attorney named Judge Straight seeking legal training. The judge sits in his office "reading a pamphlet,—presenting an elaborate pro-slavery argument, based on the hopeless intellectual inferiority of the negro, and the physical and moral degradation of mulattoes, who combined the worst qualities of their two ancestral races,—when a barefooted boy walked into the office"

(164). The boy—John—announces that he wants to be a lawyer. The judge is intrigued by his forwardness and replies, "I can't imagine who you are. It's plain that you are a lad of good blood, and yet I don't know whose son you could be" (165). Though the judge is hesitant to help John once he learns of his true status, he sees another young boy outside his office and makes a comparison "in connection with the book he had been reading" between the boy, whom he knows to be the son of parents "whose blood was presumably of the purest strain," and John: "The boy was sallow, with amorphous features, thin shanks, and stooping shoulders. The youth standing in the judge's office, on the contrary, was straight, shapely, and well-grown. His eye was clear. . . . He was no darker than many a white boy bronzed by the southern sun; his hair and eyes were black, and his features of the high-bred, clean-cut order that marks the patrician type the world over" (167). The judge takes John's physical superiority as the justification for helping him: "Again he looked in vain for any sign of negro blood. The least earmark would have turned the scale, but he could not find it" (171). The judge weighs John's physical appearance in order to reach his opinion on his racial character. Consequently, he is forced by the lack of any visible racial marks to accept John's ambitions and, implicitly, to reject scientific racism's claims for the categorical inferiority of the Negro in general and the mulatto in particular.

In fact, the judge comes to a different understanding of what determines the identity of mixed-race individuals when he takes up a law book and discovers that in South Carolina a person of seven-eighths white ancestry is legally white. It becomes clear to the judge that law and custom operate substantially in the establishment of race and, by extension, racial character. Legal strictures allow the judge to see John's position in terms of social constructions rather than scientific formulae. Thus, when the judge agrees to take John on as an office boy he indicates a new understanding of how John can construct his own position: "If you are willing to come into my office, sweep it, keep my books dusted, and stay here when I am out, I do not care. To the rest of the town you will be my servant, and still a negro. If you choose to read my books when no one is about and be white in your own private opinion I have no objection" (173). The judge discounts the importance of the trace of blood and suggests that John's relationship to books is the defining quality of his self-positioning: as a black boy John dusts the books, but as a white boy he reads them.

The novel thus suggests that relationships to iconic markers can serve as the determining components of social identity and self-conception. In fact, for the siblings, blackness appears to exist on the external and symbolic level, figured by a system of relationships to people and to objects. When John follows Rena on the street, he understands her position as a black woman only as he examines her manners toward others, especially her kindness to an old black woman and a black child. Her sympathy for people of color, or her lack of repulsion by them, is the quality most inconsistent with her white exterior and is her most telltale racial marker. Once John and Rena have been reunited with their mother, the contrast that develops between their speech and her thick, phonetically rendered accent makes it clear that the siblings are of mixed ancestry.[10] Whereas John and Rena could pass as white, their mother is racially marked by speech. Accordingly, when Rena decides to pass she must "conform her speech, her manners, and in a measure her modes of thought, to those of the people around her" (74). This adjustment in external behavior, especially speech, is sufficient to erase Rena's blackness.

Chesnutt's protagonists' black identities are not a set of inherited tendencies that need to be viewed scientifically and accommodated for in race progress. But since identities are established by a set of relationships, John and Rena need to replace their relationships with black individuals with ones that will establish them in white social circles. Importantly, the protagonists create new social identities through shifts in the stories they tell about themselves; Chesnutt illustrates that social positioning can be created by narrative positioning. For example, the euphemism for the racial stain that John and Rena hide is "the old story." As John says to his mother and Rena upon his initial return, "I haven't felt under any obligation to spoil things by raking up old stories that are best forgotten" (18). When he talks about his life since he had left, "his story had for the women the charm of an escape from captivity, with all the thrill of a pirate's tale" (21). In leaving his old story behind, John inserts himself into a new one. And as he becomes a character in an escape narrative, he implicitly becomes a new person, distinct from the one depicted in the old story.

When John makes it clear that he is interested in taking Rena back with him, he indicates that it will be necessary to insert her into a new story as well. He remarks, "Of course she will have no chance here, where our story is known. The war has wrought great changes . . . but it hasn't wiped *that* out. Nothing but death can remove that stain, if it does not follow us even to the grave. Here she must forever be—nobody! With me she might have got out into the world; with her beauty she might have made a good marriage" (36). In order for Rena to be somebody, she must find an audience that is not already familiar with her old story. As John makes clear, it is the knowledge of the story, the inescapable presence of a narrative of origins—rather than anything physically observable—that maintains the "stain." Rena can remove the stain and make herself a story that ends in a good marriage if she follows her brother into his escape narrative and abandons her old story.

Of course, Rena's new story must come from a genre that has the requisite racial associations.[11] John himself used the romance so beloved of the prewar South in his self-making: "From Bulwer's novel, he had read the story of Warwick the Kingmaker, and upon leaving home had chosen it for his own. He was a new man, but he had the blood of an old race, and he would select for his own one of its worthy names" (29–30). Here John shows that he knows the mythical associations assumed to exist between romantic genres and the "old blood" of the white race. Rena too uses the white racial associations of this genre to write herself into the new story that will make her white. First, she must choose a new name. She picks "Rowena" from Sir Walter Scott's *Ivanhoe,* a choice dictated by white southerners' reverence for romance fiction, and a fortuitous one since Rena's society debut in Clarence, South Carolina, takes place at a Scott-influenced "tournament" of horseback riding and fancy sword work: "The influence of Walter Scott was strong upon the old South. . . . During the month preceding the Clarence tournament, the local bookseller had closed out his entire stock of 'Ivanhoe,' consisting of five copies, and had taken orders for seven copies more. The tournament scene in this popular novel furnished the model after which these bloodless imitations of the ancient passages-at-arms were conducted, with such variations as were required to adapt them to a different age and civilization" (45–46). At the tournament, Rena's handkerchief is taken by Tryon as a token, and John is pleased at the way in which

"Rowena" has become narratively positioned: "The incident is quite in accord with the customs of chivalry. If George were but masked and you were veiled, we should have a romantic situation,—you the mysterious damsel in distress, he the unknown champion" (52).

When Tryon wins the tournament and declares Rena "the Queen of Love and Beauty," she becomes the very symbolic center of the entire romantic construction. She is the most noteworthy of the Scott-themed ladies (as one man remarks of Rena, "There are six Rebeccas and eight Rowenas of my own acquaintance in the grand stand, but she throws them all in the shade"), and she is crowned as the archetype of all that white racial pride exists to protect. As Dixon demonstrates, reverence for the romantic narrative of Anglo-Saxon physical perfection rests on a belief in the transcendent beauty of white women. However, as Chesnutt notes, the connection between the white race and romance is not what the South would like to think it is: "The South before the war was essentially feudal, and Scott's novels of chivalry appealed forcefully to the feudal heart" (45). Though southerners believe that they are the inheritors of Scott's romance because they are the descendants of the race from which Scott's genius sprung, Chesnutt recognizes that the resemblance between the operation of power under slavery and the feudal system represented in Scott's medieval romances actually creates the link. Thus, white power, not white racial memory, connects the romance to southern whites. By implication, the blood in John's veins does not guarantee his connection to Bulwer, but the power he wields as a white man sustains it.

Once Rena is engaged to Tryon, the tension in the novel rests on the question of how well she maintains the romantic story line. As long as she is an Anglo-Saxon princess, her story will end in marriage to her dashing suitor. Tryon himself sees their romance in such terms: "To win this beautiful girl for his wife would be a worthy task. He had crowned her Queen of Love and Beauty; since then she had ascended the throne of his heart. He would make her queen of his home and mistress of his life" (70). But Rena knows what can disrupt this romantic narrative. She fears "he would discover her secret and withdraw. . . . [I]t was too good to be true. The Prince would never try on the glass slipper" (71). Despite the fact that Rena's physiognomy labels her the embodiment of Anglo-Saxon racial perfection, the real test is her tenuous connection to the

Anglo-Saxon racial narrative. If her old story were known, the romance would dissipate and marriage would be impossible.

As with the debates between the lovers in *An Imperative Duty*, Chesnutt's novel lapses into explicit discussion and concern over possible endings for its own plot. Rena resists the marriage plot because she senses that a happy ending may be incompatible with her old story: "Rena's shrinking from the irrevocable step of marriage was due to a simple and yet complex cause. Stated baldly, it was the consciousness of her secret . . . [and] the secret that oppressed her took on a more serious aspect, with tragic possibilities" (74). Rena believes that tragedy is a more likely ending than marriage, even though the only context she has comes from stories of the transcendent power of love: "She had read some of the novels in the bookcase in her mother's hall, and others at boarding school. She had read that love was a conqueror, that neither life nor death, nor creed nor caste, could stay his triumphant course" (75). Even so, Rena suspects that race as an axis of difference cannot be overlooked in the context of her love story.

John, however, believes that Rena can establish a marriage plot by rewriting the expected terms of the narrative of interracial love. First, John accuses her of taking a "tragic view of life." He argues that marriage is a "contract" for the future and that it does not require the revelation of all past events: "We are under no moral obligation to inflict upon others the history of our past. . . . Still less are we bound to bring out from this secret chamber the dusty record of our ancestry" (79). John equates their black relations with the old story they have abandoned. And by giving the story of their racial ancestry the materiality of an old manuscript, John is better able to dismiss it as irrelevant to Rena's happiness. John also works a shift in the language of self-sacrifice that governs the novel of passing. While the heroine is normally expected to renounce her lover to serve her race, John suggests that Rena's true sacrifice is to give up her desire to tell Tryon the truth in order to protect John and his child. Rena is profoundly affected by this argument since "it had never before occurred to her to regard silence in the light of self-sacrifice. It had seemed a sort of sin; her brother's argument made of it a virtue" (82). This new light allows Rena to abandon her tragic view and helps her give in to the white fairy tale.

Yet Chesnutt demonstrates that it is not Rena's view that matters.

Though she looks the part and actively works to write for herself the story that erases old stories and relationships, the power over narratives of identity ultimately lies elsewhere. It is white social authority that governs how genres and characterization are deployed in the everyday manipulation of identity. For example, after Tryon has learned Rena's secret and broken off their engagement, he begins his own narrative speculations. He begins to believe that he can rewrite Rena back into fairy-tale whiteness: "He had heard sad stories of white children, born out of wedlock, abandoned by sinful parents to the care and adoption of colored women. . . . He was in a state of mind where any sort of fairy tale would have seemed reasonable" (205). After some deliberation, he decides that in all possible narratives of reconciliation, Rena's blackness is irrelevant to the fact of his whiteness: "If he should discover—the chance was one in a thousand—that she was white; or if he should find it too hard too leave her—ah well! he was a white man, one of a race born to command. He would make her white; no one beyond the old town would ever know the difference" (205). Rena cannot make herself white, but Tryon believes he can.

Yet Tryon's resolve to use his white power cannot last after he loses his ability to see Rena as a white beauty. At one point when she has returned to her former life, Tryon secretly drives up to Rena's house and sees her dancing with a black man. This vision of her in a black context is enough to shock Tryon out of his complacent thoughts about the narrative malleability of Rena's racial identity:

> How had he been so blind as not to have read long ago the character of this wretched girl who had bewitched him? To-night his eyes had been opened—he had seen her with the mask thrown off, a true daughter of a race in which the sensuous enjoyment of the moment took precedence of taste or sentiment or any of the higher emotions. Her few months of boarding-school, her brief association with white people, had evidently been a mere veneer over the underlying negro, and their effects had slipped away as soon as the intercourse has ceased. With the monkey-like imitativeness of the negro she had copied the manners of white people while she lived among them, and had dropped them with equal facility when they ceased to serve a purpose. (223)

Tryon inserts Rena into the discourse of scientific racism and Dixonesque white supremacy. Where he had previously seen her face as the embodiment of white racial perfection, her face is now a "mask" that can be thrown off. After reading Rena's character without the "veneer," Tryon sees his desire to rewrite Rena's story as "the outcome of a sickly sentimentality to which he recognized now, in the light of reflection, that he was entirely too prone" (224). All thoughts of Rena are "banished from the realm of sentiment to that of reason" (234). Scientific racism provides a more reasonable characterization of a "black" Rena, and the other vision of her belongs to the sickly sentimentalism of an abandoned genre.

Strangely enough, though Tryon forms a new characterization of Rena, nothing affects how he sees John. After the initial breakup, Tryon writes a letter to John in which he explains that he "shall never be able to think of [John] as other than a white man" (153). Rena herself begins to understand that as a woman she cannot maintain the power to control her story. She tells John, "A man may make a new place for himself—a woman is born and bound to hers" (181). The crucial difference seems to be that as a woman she is too vulnerable to how she is seen; Rena's identity depends more on the mind-set of the apprehender than the features of the apprehended. For example, once Tryon calls off the engagement, he begins to have dreams in which Rena "by some hellish magic" is "slowly transformed into a hideous black hag." In other words, he actually reverses the stereotype of the beautiful mulatto as each of the elements of her physical appearance transform themselves: "With agonized eyes he watched her beautiful tresses become mere wisps of coarse wool, wrapped round with dingy cotton strings; he saw her clear eyes grow bloodshot, her ivory teeth turn into unwholesome fangs" (147). The white man's vision is at the center of the generic characterizations of Rena's body.

Rena also knows that since Tryon can now only see her as a black woman, her reputation is threatened by his white power. Before the novel ends, Tryon's passion for Rena once again gets the better of him and he seeks contact with her. He writes her asking for a meeting, but she responds that they could not meet without scandal: "As a white man, this might not mean a great deal to you; as a woman, shut out already by my color from much that is desirable, my good name remains my most valuable possession" (258). Because of Rena's gender, her racial identity depends on the mind-set and attitudes of others. Therefore, she is in a vulnerable, ill-defined space. The novel's final scene, in which Rena is pursued by Tryon on one path and a black man on another, is a metaphor for the twin vulnerabilities of her position: "In one [path] she recognized the face of George Tryon, flushed with anticipation. . . . Advancing confidently along the other path she saw the face of Jeff Wain, drawn, as she imagined in her anguish, with evil passions that would stop at nothing" (271). When she rejects both men and both paths and sets off into the uncharted swamp, she succumbs both to the powerlessness of her gender position and the liminality of her racial identity.

Interestingly, when Rena is displaced from her white life, the metaphor that describes her liminal position is drawn from the dynamics of language acquisition: "It was much as though one, having acquired the vernacular of his native country, had lived in a foreign land long enough to lose the language of his child-hood without acquiring fully that of his adopted country. Miss Rowena Warwick could never again become the Rena Walden who had left the house behind the cedars no more than a year and a half before" (213). This metaphoric construction implicitly suggests that the time she has spent in her adopted racial group has rendered her incapable of resuming her place in her previous one. Her names have been transformed into empty signifiers: "Rowena" has no significance for her old social group, but "Rena" can no longer contain the person she has become. She ends up in an ambiguous, doubled state of linguistic identification that echoes the emphasis on her liminal racial state. She is functionally literate in the cultural languages of two separate racial categories and is aware of her biological claims on both, yet social custom forces her to identify herself with the one that perhaps less suits her and which affords her little social opportunity.

Thus, though Chesnutt clearly demonstrates that Rena is as fit in an evolutionary sense as any white woman to marry Tryon, he does not end the novel with that happy circumstance. As Eric Sundquist has explained, marriage as a form of reconciliation and healing in fiction had some particular connotations during this period which Chesnutt drew upon: "In an age dominated by literary accounts of sectional reunion symbolized by North-South romantic alliances, Chesnutt's stories of reunion were typically dedicated to the postbellum reunification of scattered or racially divided black families. Marriage was a sign of communal healing, just as it remained, in the color line plots, a sign of continuing racism" (300). Clearly, Dixon's *The Clansman* offers an example of the former literary trend, since the marriages at the end of the novel bring northern and southern families together in mutual recognition of the tenets of white supremacy. And as Sundquist notes, the reunion of racially divided black families through marriage, as Chesnutt depicts it, is at heart a recognition that the color line continues to enforce racist notions of who is fit to marry whom. In *The House Behind the Cedars*, the failure of Rena and Tryon's romance clearly demonstrates the strong grip of racial thinking and prohibitions.

Yet I would argue that Chesnutt thwarts the marriage primarily for more specific artistic reasons. The tragic ending is the final and most powerful gesture in Chesnutt's larger battle with negative characterizations of mulatto character. The scene in which Tryon discovers the truth of Rena's ancestry (and which sets in motion the events that end with her death) comes about because Rena learns that her mother is ill and insists on going to see her. Tryon happens to be in Rena's hometown during her visit and is aghast when Rena is pointed out to him on the street as an exceptionally good looking mulatto woman. But the coincidence is not the point; this narrative event is not designed to call attention to the plot, but rather to characterization. As the narrator remarks of the siblings, "Had they possessed the sneaking, cringing, treacherous character traditionally ascribed to people of mixed blood—the character which the blessed institutions of a free slave-holding republic had been well adapted to foster among them; had they been selfish enough to sacrifice to their ambition the mother who gave them birth, society would have been placated or humbugged, and the voyage of their life might of been one of unbroken smoothness" (128). For people who pass, maintaining a white story requires that everything from the old one, including living relatives, be relegated to the status of dead manuscripts. If the siblings possessed the character ascribed to them by scientific racism, they would have been able to pass without tragedy because they would have had no trouble sacrificing old relations. This novel's tragic ending, though sentimentally conventional and appropriate, is employed as a means toward a representation of mixed-race character.

Rena's failure to pass successfully itself refutes scientific characterizations, and the fact that the narrative ends in tragedy is a sign for the true range of virtue of the mulatto character. Chesnutt achieves his goal for recharacterization by aligning the genre of tragedy with his vision of racial character.

Circumstantial Photography and the Mind Behind the Mask

In his criticism, Howells pointed out the inadequacies of the sentimental mode of representation. He called for fiction that depicted the everyday details and circumstances of life rather than just fulfilling convention. However, such an aesthetic left him open to the charge that his realism was not art because it did not present things artistically. Some critics claimed that realism gave a mere picture of reality valued for its fidelity in representation rather than any aesthetic qualities. One of the best examples of such an attack comes from a reviewer with the initials "R. P." writing in the *Catholic World* in 1885:

> Two men study some object in nature, say a plant. One of them will drink in with his eye all its visible beauty. . . . He seizes a brush and with a few bold strokes reproduces all these traits upon a canvas. That is Art. The other observer plucks up the plant by the roots and brings it home to his herbarium. There he makes minute and careful diagrams of it, probably with the aid of a camera. . . . That is Science; and therein lies the difference between the novel writing of, say Nathaniel Hawthorne and novel-writing as Mr. Howells pursues it. (Cady and Cady 42–43)

The reference to the camera is telling. The reviewer seeks to align scientific vision, the cold fidelity of representation of the camera, and the literary realists in order to disparage the aims and techniques of realistic representation. In fact, the critic has diagnosed the source of Howells's reputed disdain for art:

> He regards novel writing as a science and not as art. This is, perhaps, a natural outcome of what Mr. Spencer would call heredity and environment. The Puritan mind is scientific, analytical. It is too severe and cold

> and suspicious to fuse into the constructive enthusiasm of art. . . . Thus it is curious to note how the Puritan mind in Mr. Howells, finding itself by a freak of circumstance, working at an art, takes it strongly in its hands and transforms it into a science, and a science intended to have a useful application. (Cady and Cady 42)

This formulation fits rather oddly with Howells's discussion of the Puritan temperament in *An Imperative Duty.* Whereas Howells would align Puritanism with sentimental fiction, the reviewer aligns Puritanism with realism and mechanistic photography. Ironically, Howells is accused of the very thing that he seeks to eliminate from his heroine's racial stock. His battle over the characterization of puritanical tendencies suggests that one of realism's tasks was to give white Americans a fresh view of white racial tendencies.[12]

Misunderstandings of the representational aims of realism are not surprising. According to critic Ralph Bogardus, Howells's attitude toward photography in his writing is ambiguous. On the one hand, Howells is drawn to photography because it presents a mode of representation that appears to be free from the kind of sentimentalizing or idealizing that he finds fault with in sentimental fiction. On the other hand, he often asserts that the camera cannot do justice to visual scenes because it only produces a surface impression. As Bogardus explains, Howells felt that "the mere heaping up of facts—the capturing of surface details—was insufficient to make realist art" (237). Therefore, realism could favorably be compared to photography, but it must do more than simply photograph in order to do justice to its subject.

In a sense, the paradox of the powers and limitations of photographic representation mirrors the problem created by the white-skinned, mixed-race character. Specifically, from Howells's perspective, a photograph would not be sufficient to capture the supposed blackness of such a character because it would only capture the surface impression of whiteness. Racial character, inasmuch as it is assumed to be signaled by innate characteristics (many of them matters of behavior and attitude), cannot reliably be photographed. And according to Geoffrey D. Smith, Howells had a behaviorist approach to character: he worked from the assumption that "little can be known of characters (or people) except what one observes of their relationships, dialogue, and action over a period of time" (84). He argues that this behaviorism results in an understanding of characterization whereby character is not intuited or even seen, but is rather observed over a duration of time.

In *An Imperative Duty,* what Howells calls Rhoda's black racial character could not be photographed. Though her face has racial markers, her character is not visible through them. Rather, it is visible through exactly the dimension that the camera cannot record—the way one expression melts into another in a matter of moments. Rhoda's character is visible as her tragic Puritan mask gives way to a series of childlike smiles. It is the flow and contrast that creates her composite character, and the single frozen moment that a photograph creates could not do justice to a face in motion. In fact, Olney's recollection of Rhoda emphasizes the inadequacy of the frozen image. He provides a static portrait of her face, but the second reading of her expressions provides the real information about Rhoda's character. In this way, Howells's fiction suggests that mixed-race characters need to be presented through an artistic mode that does not rely solely on an analogy with photography. Howells is interested in race in an artistic/medical sense—as a diagnosis that Olney gives of the moving image of Rhoda's multilayered character.

Chesnutt's novel also aligns the realistic apprehension of character with professional expertise. The most insightful professional in *The House Behind the Cedars* is not a doctor, as in Howells's novel, but a lawyer.[13] The lawyer's perspective is after all appropriate for a novel more interested in legal constructions than in scientific ones. Identifying the connections between race and the legal system was a pervasive concern for Chesnutt, who himself was legally trained. For example, a short story from Chesnutt's collection *A Wife of His Youth* (1899) titled "A Web of Circumstance" details the case of a black man named Ben Davis who is falsely accused and convicted of stealing a white man's whip. During Davis's trial, the lawyer for the prosecution gives a speech with echoes of Twain. He declares that although he has no witnesses who will swear that Davis is the thief, he has "a chain of circumstantial evidence which is stronger even than the testimony of eyewitnesses. Men might lie, but circumstances cannot" (298). His case will therefore rest on circumstantial determinations of Davis's character: "We expect to show that the defendant is a man of dangerous character" (298). Accordingly, the narrator notes, the prosecution's rebuttal case was also "entirely on the point of character" (303).

The construction of Davis's guilt is based upon a determination of black racial character, especially an innate criminality in a legal setting. Much emphasis is placed on the interpretation of Davis's behavior when the police discovered the whip hidden in his blacksmith's shop. A witness declares he was "brazen" in protesting his innocence until the whip was found, at which point he began to show signs of fear and nervousness (301). When Davis's lawyer suggests, while cross-examining the witness, that "what [he] took for brazen impudence might have been but the evidence of conscious innocence," the constable replies that "niggers" always protest their innocence (301–2). These attempts to evoke notions of character are successful; when the jury returns a guilty verdict, the judge explains to Davis that he "can only regard [his] crime as the result of a tendency to offenses of this nature, a tendency which is only too common among [his] people; a tendency that is a menace to civilization" (311).

Though the story clearly implies that such assumptions about character are false and misleading, the account of the trial betrays an ambiguous stand on the validity of a physiognomic logic of racial character. The real guilty party, Davis's assistant Tom, is at the back of the courtroom, and the narrator describes his expression at the moment of the verdict: "If the face is the mirror of the soul, then this man's soul, taken off its guard in this moment of excitement, was full of lust and envy and all evil passions" (304). As with Dixon's physiognomy, the real guilty party's face signals his evil soul distinctly. However, the narrator's "if" also leaves some doubt, a hesitance that emerges in the description of Davis's face when he hears his sentence:

> There was a flash of despair, and then nothing but a stony blank, behind which he masked his real feelings, whatever they were.
>
> Human character is a compound of tendencies inherited and habits acquired. In the anxiety, the fear of disgrace, spoke the nineteenth century civilization with which Ben Davis had been more or less closely in touch during twenty years of slavery and fifteen years of freedom. In the

> stolidity with which he received this sentence for a crime which he had not committed, spoke who knows what trait of inherited savagery? For stoicism is a savage virtue. (313)

The narrator lapses into a puzzling mix of confident pronouncement and speculative silence on the subject of racial character. Though Davis's shame can be attributed to the acquired teachings of nineteenth-century "civilization," the narrator is more coy in his exploration of the influence of innate black and, therefore, savage traits. Yet even if the narrator is being ironic in his assessment of the virtues of savagery, Chesnutt nonetheless implies that Davis's character is divided. And in this compound of inherited tendencies and acquired habits, he is, just like Howells's Rhoda, under the influence of multiple racial determinants.

However, Chesnutt has placed a limit on his narrator's ability to know his own representation. The narrator cannot or will not provide an authoritative account of the sources of his character's divided emotional response. I would argue that the writers who followed Chesnutt and Howells sought to break this silence about what goes on behind the mask of the black character. While Howells's fiction argues that American characters experience divided consciousness by definition, and thus suggests that fiction must find a way to represent this division, Chesnutt's story betrays a reluctance to treat internal division designed to highlight the general cultural reluctance to grant black individuals any kind of psychic depth. "A Web of Circumstance" asserts that the exterior view is inherently inconclusive evidence of character, since the nature of racial character cannot be settled on the basis of Ben Davis's face. But for the sake of irony, Chesnutt is willing to let the third-person narrator's omniscience break down rather than approach the representational dilemma of his character's division. The absence of Ben Davis's own voice at this point in the narration is ironic given that his stolidity is not speaking clearly, and Chesnutt refuses to validate the specious speculations of his nineteenth-century audience.

Howells and Chesnutt come up against the limits of representation when they take on the subject of racial character. Howells's fiction, like Twain's, suggests that once the binary of race is unsettled, most modes of representation—like sentimental fiction and photography, for example—will fail to be effective and self-contained. In fact, it is possible to see the endings of both Howells's and Chesnutt's novels as gestures against the neat closure that a strict adherence to genre demands. Howells's marriage is hardly classically comic—it does not produce a happy note of social closure—and it does not end all questions of characterization. In fact, the novel continues on past the marriage to note that once in Italy, Rhoda is often at a loss for how to characterize herself and feels guilty over the fact that she must allow her American friends to assume that she is Italian. In turn, though Chesnutt's tragedy has the feel of closure and generic appropriateness, it is more accurately a form of characterization rather than a generic formula. In sentimental fiction, characterization is largely dictated by generic conventions, but in both these novels that line of connection is disrupted. Both novels suggest that once characterization is used in reverse—*by the characters*—the generic moorings are lost and the resulting conclusion will not be secure. Since these realistic writers manipulate genre rather than being constrained by it, these novels do not have the set relationships between genre and characterization that ensure a familiar and tidy narrative close.

When genre shifts from a framework to a theme, an author has more latitude to explore characterization. Twain, Howells, and Chesnutt all use this freedom to explore the reactions of a protagonist to his or her own racial ambiguity. In all three novels, the representation of the mixed-race character is richly attended to, suggesting that the internal division of character—what Dixon's fiction resists—is of central narrative interest. Chesnutt's short story suggests that the aporia facing fiction at the turn of the century had become the representation of the internal division of the mixed-race character. But as Chesnutt's third-person narrator lapses into silence on the subject, perhaps first-person narration is necessary to give the view from behind the mixed-race character's stoic mask.

5

Character and Black Art in *The Autobiography of an Ex-Coloured Man*

After a number of years serving as U.S. consul to Venezuela and later Nicaragua, James Weldon Johnson returned to New York, where he had previously been making a living writing popular songs for Broadway musical productions. He found a position as an editor at the black newspaper the *New York Age,* and in 1914 he began writing a weekly column called "Views and Reviews."[1] Johnson had written most of his novel *The Autobiography of an Ex-Coloured Man* while he was abroad, and it was published anonymously in 1912. The novel purports to be the memoir of a black man who crosses over the color line and passes for white, marrying a white woman. Johnson was interested in having the reading public take his novel for a real autobiography—a "human document," as he termed it—and since Johnson was well known in the black community he left his name off the manuscript.[2]

Once in New York, Johnson continued to develop many of the themes and topics he had touched on in the novel in his newspaper columns. For example, on January 7, 1915, he relayed the case of Mrs. Little, a resident of Detroit who was being sued for divorce by her white husband on the grounds that she had black blood in her veins. Scientists had been baffled in their attempts to prove or to refute her husband's claim conclusively until—according to a dispatch from Detroit sent to the *New York Sun*—a test had finally been found which was "considered to be infallible by Southern planters":

> Mrs. Little, according to Dr. Arthur Windsor, a prominent Ontario physician, to-day passed a test which he claims beyond a doubt proves the woman has no Negro blood in her veins. It is a test which Dr. Windsor on many occasions in his thirteen years practice in Southern States made to determine racial ancestors of persons brought to him. It is obtained by a pressure of a finger on the tip of the subject's nose where there is what is known as the alar cartilage. In the colored race this cartilage is blunt and solid, while in whites it is separated so that two distinct formations can be felt. Mrs. Little's nose, according to this test, is of Caucasian formation. (*SW* 1: 155)

Johnson follows this report with what seems like inevitable commentary: "Although the racial identity of the writer has never been questioned, we, nevertheless, on reading these words involuntarily pressed a finger on the tip of our nose, and lo and behold! the two distinct formations of cartilage were plainly felt. Poor Mrs. Little!" (*SW* 1: 155). This column, like Johnson's novel, shows an interest in disrupting complacent ideas about the detection of black or white racial identity. The column explicitly subjects both scientific notions of race and southern mythologies of physical racial determination to ridicule. Johnson concludes his column by implicating the reader: "Of course by now you have pressed the tip of your own nose." As Johnson implies, such discussions encourage an attention to the body on the part of all who encounter them.

Classically speaking, the novel of passing shares the obsessive focus on the surface of the body demonstrated in this incident. Its plot and events revolve around the physical appearance and features of the passing character. Yet Johnson is interested in having his readers take their fingers off their noses, so to speak. In *The Autobiography,* Johnson uses the first person in order to take the body from the center of the narration. Of course, first-person narration was vital to nineteenth-century African-American essays, political oratory, and slave narratives. But Johnson was the first African American to write a novel in the first person, and, as I will argue, first-person fictional narrative marks a significant shift in the way racial character and mixed race are presented.

Johnson also fights against the way the novel of passing is constrained by certain generic modes and endings. As Howells and Chesnutt demonstrate, the novel of passing's prospects for closure are limited. The plot can lead to marriage and thus be comic, or, more usually, the conventional renunciation leads to tragedy. In *The Autobiography*, Johnson in effect suggests that *all* popular representations of black characters are limited to these same two modes. As he notes, there are really only two acceptable genres: a comic one whereby the black figure is made a buffoon, and a tragic one whereby his or her social mistreatment is rendered pathetic. But, as I will demonstrate, Johnson uses the fictional autobiography in order to move beyond these generic limitations.

The narrator shows a keen interest in characterization; as he narrates his travels through the United States and Europe he gives an almost sociological account of the habits and behaviors of the people he encounters. However, when it comes to African Americans, the narrator is interested in constructing multiple sets of characterizations. He fights against the imperative to represent the race collectively, as if a single characterization would serve for the entire population. Rather, the narrator turns the formula for character around, suggesting that the only sense in which black character is collective is in the transcendent racial soul expressed in black art. In short, the characterizations of African Americans in popular art are misleading, while black art itself is genuinely representative of racial character.

The narrator's opinions on black art and its powers echo much of the preface to Johnson's anthology *The Book of American Negro Poetry* (first published in 1922 and then revised in 1931). In fact, parts of the preface to Johnson's anthology were developed from materials that first appeared in *The Autobiography*.[3] Johnson also explored the transcendent connections between characterization and fiction in the *New York Age*. In an editorial titled "Inside Measurement," Johnson discusses various available "tests" for measuring the "progress of the American Negro" (*SW* 1: 260). He rejects statistical studies of population and increased wealth because they are "outside" measurements. Like the test of Mrs. Little's nose, they take their reading of racial status from an exterior and therefore inferior position. He proposes a far better form of measurement in an editorial titled "When Is a Race Great?":

> Although there is no single recipe to be followed for making a race great, there is a single standard by which the greatness of a race can be mea-

> sured. The greatness of a race may be measured by the literature it has produced.
>
> To substantiate this assertion there is first of all the uncontrovertible [*sic*] fact that every race or people which is acknowledged as great has produced a literature which is great in more or less direct proportion to the acknowledged greatness of that race or people. (*SW* 1: 267–68)

Texts written by African Americans in and of themselves serve as evidence of racial character. As African-American literature demonstrates greatness, Johnson argues, so the race demonstrates its progress and racial worth.

As I will argue, the fictional autobiography accords well with the impulse to connect character to literature in a direct fashion. Primarily, it allows for the racial character of African Americans to be enacted rather than represented. The narrator's consciousness pervades the narrative, so while his body is absent, his character is all-present. Rather than describing a black character, the narrator demonstrates it. Clear models for this kind of characterization exist in the African-American literary tradition. Johnson draws upon Frederick Douglass's autobiographical writings, and even more directly evokes Booker T. Washington's *Up From Slavery.* As the plot of *The Autobiography* unfolds, the narrator eventually takes upon himself the task of creating art that will enact the worth of black racial character in the larger and more immediate sense.

However, toward the end of the novel the narrator witnesses a lynching by fire and shortly thereafter decides to pass, abandoning his artistic goals to write classical music based on melodies taken from the spirituals. Because the narrator fails to follow through on his racial mission to demonstrate black artistic genius—a goal that Johnson would endorse—it is also logical to posit some ironic distance between the author and the narrator.[4] But, perhaps more importantly, the fact that Johnson's narrator is not an entirely "representative" black man, in that he relinquishes his black identity, suggests that he is not the perfect enactment of character. Furthermore, as I will argue, the fact that he fails to achieve this artistic enactment of black character also questions whether such characterization is possible or desirable. In the end, the failure of the narrator's own goals for artistic racial representativeness complicates the picture of Johnson's theories of the value of black art.

Character, Characterization, and Books

The Autobiography of an Ex-Coloured Man begins with a preface ostensibly written by the book's publisher, Sherman, French & Company. But the preface is a nearly exact transcription of Johnson's recommended wording and sentiments.[5] The preface carefully lays out how Johnson's representation of black life will differ from that of previous books:

> Special pleas have already been made for and against the Negro in hundreds of books, but in these books either his virtues or his vices have been exaggerated. This is because writers, in nearly every instance, have treated the colored American as a whole; each has taken some one group of the race to prove his case. Not before has a composite and proportionate presentation of the entire race, embracing all of its various groups and elements, showing their relations with each other and to the whites, been made. (xxxiii)

According to Johnson, books on black Americans tend to describe the race as a singular whole with an all-inclusive account of racial character. In contrast, his book will engage in an accurate form of racial characterization and will correct the exaggerated accounts of virtues and vices found in other books.

The preface outlines the conditions necessary for such a representation and also gives an indirect statement of the value of first-person narration:

> It is very likely that the Negroes of the United States have a fairly correct idea of what the white people of the country think of them, for that opinion has for a long time been and is still being constantly stated; but they are themselves more or less a sphinx to the whites. It is curiously interesting and even vitally important to know what are the thoughts of ten millions of them concerning the people among whom they live. In these pages it is as though a veil had been drawn aside: the reader is given a view of the inner life of the Negro in America, is initiated into the "freemasonry," as it were, of the race. (xxxiii–xxxiv)

In this passage the metaphor of the sphinx reappears, with an echo of the masked face of Chesnutt's falsely accused blacksmith in the story

"A Web of Circumstance." In both of these fictional examples, the face of the black character is unreadable to whites and to the third-person narrator who would seek to describe the meaning of that face to an assumed white reader. But rather than leave the masked face of an African American as a textual aporia that refuses all interpretation, Johnson asserts that his book—with its first-person narration—will give the reader a glimpse of the inner life behind it.

This move behind the mask is accomplished with the rhetoric and concepts of W. E. B. Du Bois; specifically, the mask over the face of the sphinx becomes a *veil* that can be drawn aside. As Du Bois suggests in his famous formulation of double-consciousness in *The Souls of Black Folk* (1903), African Americans are separated from white America by a veil.[6] While a mask is created by impassive flesh and the failure of a face to serve as an index to the consciousness below it, the veil is a result of the perspective from which narration proceeds. Johnson implies that the veil can be pulled aside when narration comes from within the consciousness of the first-person narrator. In addition, the preface asserts that "in this book the reader is given a glimpse behind the scenes of this race-drama which is being here enacted,—he is taken upon an elevation where he can catch a bird's eye view" (xxxiv). The narrator pushes aside the veil through a spatial transcendence that gives the narration a privileged point of view.

The novel begins with a detailed account of how the narrator was able to arrive at this perspective and how he gained his position within the "freemasonry" of the race. Not insignificantly, the narrator spends his early childhood under the impression that he is white. In a key scene, the narrator is separated from the white students and grouped with the black students. This event brings awareness to the narrator, and in the pages that follow he explains how he developed a changed sense of his own status. Specifically, he arrives at an understanding of the difference between himself and his white classmates through extrapolation: "I myself would not have so clearly understood this difference had it not been for the presence of the other colored children at school; I had learned what their status was, and now I learned that theirs was mine" (15). His position has shifted, so the perspective from which he observes life changes as well: "From that time on I looked out through other eyes" (14). Since the novel draws out the time between the narrator's recognition of his racial position and his full understanding of its implications, it emphasizes the narrator's experiences with perspective. In short, he experiences what the preface describes: he finds aspects of black experience difficult to know, and he cannot understand the race drama in full.

The narrator eventually encounters a book with exemplary and proportional characterization written from a bird's-eye view that pulls the veil aside: "One day I drew from the circulating library a book that cleared the whole mystery . . . a book that gave me my first perspective of the life I was entering; that book was *Uncle Tom's Cabin*" (28). Once again Stowe's novel is a master text in the battle over the representation of race relations and racial character. But where Dixon had sought to correct the characterizations of *Uncle Tom's Cabin,* Johnson's narrator defends Stowe's vision:

> This work of Harriet Beecher Stowe has been the object of much unfavorable criticism. It has been assailed, not only as fiction of the most imaginative sort, but as being a direct misrepresentation. . . . Its critics would brush it aside with the remark that there never was a Negro as good as Uncle Tom, nor a slave-holder as bad as Legree. For my part, I was never an admirer of Uncle Tom, nor his type of goodness; but I believe there were lots of old Negroes as foolishly good as he. . . . I do not think it takes any great stretch of the imagination to believe there was a fairly large class of slave-holders typified in Legree. And we must also remember that the author depicted a number of worthless if not vicious Negroes, and a slave-holder who was as much of a Christian and a gentleman as it was possible for one in his position to be. (29)

Stowe's characterizations are at the center of the controversy over her novel, but for the narrator they ring true. Because of its transcendent perspective, this fictional representation is able to help the narrator see himself: "I do not think that it is claiming too much to say that *Uncle Tom's Cabin* was a fair and truthful panorama of slavery; however that may be, it opened my eyes as to who and what I was and what my country considered me; in fact, it gave me my bearing" (29). The narrator thus acquires a component of black identity as identified by Du Bois—a sense of how one is considered by white Americans—directly from a fictional text.

In fact, the narrator defends Stowe's characterizations because they implicitly accord with the criteria described in the preface. As the narrator noted, previous representations of African Americans had given disproportionate characterizations because they had let one element of the race stand for the whole. However, Stowe's depictions of vices and virtues are composite. She presents the full spectrum of both white and black behavior, from vicious to Christian. Thus she provides a panorama of slavery, implicitly providing a textual representation of the bird's-eye view of racial questions.

Nonetheless, the narrator explains that his understanding of life from books was inadequate, remarking that a life of reading often renders people "unfitted for the practical struggles of life" (32). Reading is the means by which the narrator achieves his understanding of himself in racial terms, but it results in an unpractical relationship to the world. For this reason he decides to go South to find a more immediate understanding of blackness. After an aborted attempt to attend Atlanta University, the narrator takes up residence in Jacksonville, Florida: "I became acquainted with the best class of colored people in Jacksonville. This was really my entrance into the race. It was my initiation into which I have termed the freemasonry of the race. I had formulated a theory of what it was to be colored; now I was getting the practice" (54). The language of the preface returns to mark the moment at which the narrator feels he has achieved the position from which correct characterizations proceed. Reading gave him the panoramic understanding of blackness necessary for transcendent narrative positioning. But his experiences in Jacksonville allowed him to take a position behind the veil and within the freemasonry of black life. As such, he feels ready to enact the structures he had previously described. He meets the standards for narration as established by the preface. He is ready to draw composite, proportionate, and truthful characterizations while pushing aside the veil.

The Genres of Black Art

The narrator fights hard to take his place within the vocabulary of narrative positioning and win the right to characterize. Therefore, it is important to look at how his attempts at characterization proceed. In the second half of *The Autobiography,* the narrator takes a trip to Europe with a wealthy white patron who pays him for his companionship and for playing the piano. The narrator eventually finds that he misses America, specifically black America. He decides that he will put his musical talents to work in a way that will reflect well upon his race: he seizes upon the idea of writing classical music based on the themes of African-American spirituals. In this respect he hopes to make it clear not only that the themes of the spirituals are great music but that they are an authentically American form of expression on which an original body of national music can be based. In order to carry out this objective, the narrator returns to the United States and begins to travel in the southern states looking for material.

Interestingly, despite the narrator's avowed interest in description and characterization, when he reaches the South he uncharacteristically refuses to characterize. Though his experiences among the rural black people of the South showed him much that was interesting, he asserts that "there was a great deal which does not require description at my hands" (122). As he explains, "Log cabins and plantations and dialect-speaking 'darkies' are perhaps better known in American literature than any other single picture of our national life" (122). In fact, these familiar characterizations have a negative impact:

> Indeed, they form an ideal and exclusive literary concept of the American Negro to such an extent that it is almost impossible to get the reading public to recognize him in any other setting; so I shall endeavor to avoid giving the reader any already overworked and hackneyed descriptions. This generally accepted literary ideal of the American Negro constitutes what is really an obstacle in the way of the thoughtful and progressive element of the race. His character has been established as a happy-go-lucky, laughing, shuffling, banjo-picking being, and the reading public has not yet been prevailed upon to take him seriously. (122–23)

As the narrator makes clear, such characterizations in American literature are limiting traditions, impeding efforts for better and more accurate characterization.

Moreover, the typical characterization of the plantation darky has conditioned the white reading public. The uniformity of comic characterization has made it impossible for white audiences to find other kinds of fictive portrayals palpable: "A novel dealing with colored people who lived in respectable homes amidst a fair degree of culture and who naturally acted 'just like white folks' would be taken in a comic-opera sense" (123). Comic characterization demands comic depiction. And since audiences are conditioned to expect comedy, any other genre of portrayal would be assumed to be comic even if not so intended. As a result, characterizing the rising black middle class is next to impossible in fiction because audiences would take it as comic satire. Interestingly, the narrator extrapolates from this essentially artistic problem to the problems of his race more generally but still retains the limits of genre as his metaphorical framework: "In this respect the Negro is much in the position of a great comedian who gives up the lighter roles to play tragedy. No matter how well he may portray the deeper passions, the public is loath to give him up in his old character; they even conspire to make him a failure in serious work, in order to force him back into comedy" (123). The narrator depicts the dilemma of the representation of African-American character—and by extension the problem facing the social acceptance of black people—in terms of a generic difference. Comedy, he claims, is the normal mode for representation, so black individuals are likewise limited to this register of emotion by the expectations of white Americans. In fact, white America determines the social role of African Americans, since it is loath to give up its old characters.

All in all, depictions of blacks drawn from sources other than the plantation tradition are blocked by white generic expectations, and the possibilities for new characterizations are sharply curtailed. Yet the narrator is not completely disheartened by this apparent impediment. Current characterizations may be narrow, but "this very fact constitutes the opportunity of the future Negro novelist and poet to give the country something new and unknown, in depicting the life, the ambitions, the struggles, and the passions of those of their race who are striving to break the narrow limits of traditions. A beginning has already been made in the remarkable book by Dr. Du Bois, *The Souls of Black Folk*" (123). Here the narrator affirms what the preface has established: it is necessary for new books on the subject of race to break with old representations of blackness and black people. And just as Johnson used Du Bois's language to describe the position from which fresh characterizations will proceed, he now cites Du Bois's book as an example of the new tradition of black literature he desires. *The Souls of Black Folk* straddles the borders between autobiography, sociology, philosophy, and political history. By implication, in order to break away from old traditions—limiting comic genres and hackneyed characterization—it will be necessary for African-American novelists to write genre-bending texts like Du Bois's.

With this series of observations on the nature of literary characterization and the proper goals for black novelists, *The Autobiography* again becomes self-conscious. Johnson's text describes the artistic aims that it seeks to meet. Though the narrator cites Du Bois's text as the primary example of the new black tradition which he calls for, Johnson's text also provides an example of genre-bending writing by an African American. *The Autobiography* seeks to break with previous modes for characterization of blacks, and it does so by violating the tradition of the novel of passing. Like *Souls,* Johnson's text is a hybrid form, crossing the novel of passing with both fictional autobiography and sociological/characterological analysis.

Yet for all that is untraditional about these two texts, both *The Autobiography* and Du Bois's *Souls* borrow in an important sense from a preexisting tradition in black American letters. As critics have noted, Johnson's other main source or model for *The Autobiography* was Booker T. Washington's autobiography *Up From Slavery* (1901).[7] Johnson emulates the form if not the factual content of the personal narrative. He has chosen, as Du Bois did before him, to evoke this tradition through first-person narration. As William Andrews has argued, the nineteenth-century slave narrative took its narrative form and force in part from the notion of "romantic individualism" (78). In such narratives the ex-slave described his or her movement from the objective status of the slave to the freedman's position of full subjectivity. First-person narration is thereby necessary because it demonstrates the power of the subject of the narrative to create a word-picture of self-mastery. Accordingly, Andrews argues that classic slave narratives like Frederick Douglass's pay particular attention to the achievement of literacy because it "is considered the ultimate form of power in the antebellum slave narrative." Specifically, "language is assumed to signify the subject and hence to ratify the slave narrator's humanity as well as his authority" (80).

Most significantly for Johnson, however, the equation of language with subjectivity achieves the separation of the surface of the body from the features of character. In narrative modes that rely on a phrenological or physiognomic logic of character, the physical description of characters by the third-person narrator is conflated with the depiction of character. Either physical features stand as emblems of aspects of character, or the third-person narrator provides a reading of those features in order to achieve characterization. However, in *The Autobiography* the relationship between physical description and characterization is broken. The character of the first-person narrator pervades the narrative account. Characterization is thus performed and enacted on every page, while physical description is largely absent. The reader of *The Autobiography* gets the "inside view"—to use Johnson's phrase—of character because he or she is taken within the veil of consciousness by the narrative point of view.

In fact, *The Autobiography* stages a contrast between generic modes that rely on physical characterization and those that do not. The places where the narrator describes himself (and others) seem to evoke a descriptive mode that is incompatible with the rest of the text's objectivity, highlighting the differences between them. For example, on the day the narrator discovers he is black he examines himself in the mirror. Though he had often heard remarks about his physical beauty, only the day he achieved this racial awareness did he "[become] conscious of it and [recognize] it" (11). As with the story of Mrs. Little, the question of ambiguous race rather naturally must lead to an inspection of the body: "I noticed the ivory whiteness of my skin, the beauty of my mouth, the size and liquid darkness of my eyes, and how the long, black lashes that fringed and shaded them produced an effect that was strangely fascinating even to me. I noticed the softness and glossiness of my dark hair that fell in waves over my temples, making my forehead appear whiter than it really was" (11). Because of the first-person perspective, the passage of description has to be staged through the mechanism of a mirror. But even at a remove, this self-description recalls the sentimental language of the novel of passing and the characteristic description of the surpassing beauty of the tragic mulatto. As Robert Fleming has argued, passages in *The Autobiography* which deal with the narrator's feelings or reactions are "characterized by a neoromantic style, by sentimental and rather inflated diction" (87). He claims that the narrator "views himself in romantic terms, as a tragic hero" (87). Thus, at the moment when the first-person narrator views himself from the position of a third-person narrator, the novel slips into a tragic and inflated style in order to describe the surface of the body. Yet this little pocket of sentimentalism stands in contrast to a narrative whole that is largely detached and sociological.

There is evidence that Johnson had considered treating the theme of mixed race in wholly sentimental terms at earlier points in his artistic development. As Joseph Skerrett has demonstrated, some of the undercurrents or minor themes of *The Autobiography* are prefigured in notes for stories that Johnson jotted down during his college days. For example, a story called "The Sins of the Fathers" would have staged unwitting incest between a white woman and her father's mixed-race bastard son. In fact, this story idea has a shadowy echo in *The Autobiography* when the narrator attends a performance of the opera *Faust* and is captivated by a young woman seated next to him. She is "so young, so fair, so ethereal" that the narrator becomes "distinctly conscious of her beauty" and cannot fight the impulse to observe her circumspectly (89): "I occasionally stole a glance at her, and each time I did so my heart leaped into my throat. Once I glanced beyond to the gentleman who sat next to her. My glance immediately turned into a stare. Yet, there he was, unmistakably, my father! looking hardly a day older than when I had seen him some ten years before. What a strange coincidence!" (98). Once again, close attention to bodies and the assumption of the trappings of a tragic mulatto plot line leads the prose of *The Autobiography* to lapse into melodrama. And at the narrator's realization that this beautiful woman is his sister, he slips into uncharacteristically inflated diction: "All the springs of affection in my heart, stopped since my mother's death, burst out in fresh and terrible torrents, and I could have fallen at her feet and worshipped her" (98). The narrator fights back the impulse to shout out to the audience, "Here, here in your very midst, is a tragedy, a real tragedy!" (98). The narrative attention to physical beauty is accompanied by the metadramatic suggestion that were this episode to form the artistic center of a work, the mode would be tragedy.

Yet this episode does not figure at all centrally in the events of *The Autobiography.* Fleming argues that the narrator's tendency to see his own life in terms of tragic genres is a point of irony. Whether this can be proven conclusively or not, Johnson chose to touch upon the tragic mulatto genre with its descriptive emphases and then to marginalize it.[8] I would argue that Johnson marginalizes the tragic mode for much the same reasons that he criticizes plantation comedy. Specifically, plantation comedy relies for its generic effects on predictable physical characterization. As Johnson observes, the laughing faces and shuffling physical presence of "dialect-speaking 'darkies'" are constitutive of the comedic genre in which they appear and signal how the audience is to respond to the work as a whole. In similar fashion, as *The Autobiography* demonstrates, the ethereal beauty of the mulatto hero and heroine is a constitutive feature of tragic octoroon fiction. When the text becomes preoccupied with physical beauty, it lapses into passages that evoke that genre.

The best illustration of the limits on racial character in traditional genres comes in the final section of the novel. Once the narrator resolves to pass, his account begins to flirt more directly with the conventions for the novel of passing. The episodes and tensions of this section create a clear contrast with the sociological characterizations of the rest of the novel. But most particularly, the last section of the novel suggests that when the narrator passes he moves from a position where he can critique the generic limitations on black experience to one where he is forced to live within them. In the early section of the novel set in Harlem, the narrator expresses sympathy for black artists because they are restricted so firmly in their range of roles. He observes that "no manager could imagine that audiences would pay to see Negro performers in any other role than that of Mississippi River roustabouts" and that black performers could only discuss with hopeful expectation the time "when they would compel the public to recognize that they could do something more than grin and cut pigeon-wings" (77). The narrator mentions one particular performer who was frustrated by the lack of opportunity to play tragedy. The narrator comments on the irony, noting, "Here was a man who made people laugh at the size of his mouth, while he carried in his heart a burning ambition to be a tragedian; and so after all he did play a part in a tragedy" (77). The actor seeks to move beyond comedy, yet his physical appearance is the basis of his comic appeal. His very body provokes his white (and perhaps black) audiences into laughter. He is trapped within the comic genre that his body dictates. As a result, the tragedy he plays is the tragedy of genre itself.

The failed tragedian becomes a parallel for the narrator once he passes, as passing reinserts the narrator into the limits of genre. The narrator explicitly acknowledges that he must become an actor himself and play the part of a white man. Initially he is struck by the comic implications of his role-playing: "The anomaly of my social position often appealed strongly to my sense of humor . . . I laughed heartily over what struck me as the capital joke I was playing" (144). Yet when the narrator meets and falls in love with a white woman, he finds that what he "had regarded as a joke" gradually transformed into "the most serious question" of his life (144). Thus the narrator plays comedy while his situation—and the physical logic of his white skin—dictates that he be involved in a larger form of ironic tragedy.

The narrator is restricted to the tragedy of the tragic mulatto (the same tragedy that Howells's Rhoda avoided through a generic shift back to comedy and which Chesnutt's Rena could not avoid) because his performance is vulnerable to a scrutiny of his body:

> Up to this time I had assumed and played my rôle as a white man with a certain degree of nonchalance, a carelessness as to the outcome, which made the whole thing more amusing to me than serious; but I now ceased to regard "being a white man" as a sort of practical joke. My acting had called for mere external effects. Now I began to doubt my ability to play the part. I watched her to see if she was scrutinizing me, to see if she was looking for anything in me which made me differ from the other men she knew. (145–46)

When the narrator becomes conscious of the necessity to bring his life into line with some form of generic closure—such as marriage—he becomes less confident in the performativity of race and more willing to concede that racial character might really be detectable. The novel of passing is often a physiognomic genre, and the narrator is conscious of the possibility that his racial character will show itself despite external effects designed to hide it.

All in all, the narrator is caught between the generic poles from which he had previously expressed a desire to escape. When he passes successfully he is living a great comedy, a comedy where his white skin and white life are a point of irony given his racial background. And when he falls in love his life becomes a tragedy that replicates the troubled romances of the tragic mulatto genre. In addition, in the tragic mode his body becomes a part of the generic focus. In the scene where the narrator tells his ladylove that he is black, he finds that he is acutely aware of his own body: "Under the strange light in her eyes I felt that I was growing black and thick-featured and crimp-haired" (149). In this way the final section of *The Autobiography* swings between generic poles. The narrator is turned into an actor who is stuck between two genres: he finds that he either must stage an ironic comedy or fall into "mulatto" tragedy. His life as a white man is ruled by a generic logic of the body.

However, Johnson does not have his narrator and his novel come to a stereotypically tragic end. After some soul-searching the white woman decides that she is willing to keep the narrator's secret, and the two marry and have children. In a single paragraph, we learn that she dies a few years later and that the narrator has since devoted his life to his children and to keeping the "brand" of race "from being placed upon them" (153). Thus, though the ending of the novel contains tragic circumstances, the typical melodramatic renunciation does not prevent the marriage. Rather, the end of the novel presents a mixed-race character who has been able to make choices with relative freedom but who is left with one resounding symbolic regret. The narrator indicates in the final pages that the real tragedy of his life is the fact that he gave up his musical ambitions. In his love for the white woman his "artistic temperament" experienced an awakening, yet the music that he wrote was "in a more or less Chopinesque style" and fell short entirely of the ambitions that he had held for his art (147). When he gave up his blackness to be a middle-class white man, he gave up the opportunity to represent his race through music. The narrator has been subsumed within generic limits and thus has given up the power that would have allowed him to be the consummate characterizer; music would have provided a means for the entire race to escape from the same generic restraints.

Art as Characterization

In the early chapters the narrator points directly to the source of his skill as a characterizer: "The novelty of my position caused me to observe and consider things which, I think, entirely escaped the young men I associated with" (54). The narrator uses his position as a white-skinned black man who has experienced the formation of a black consciousness to make narration more clear-sighted. As such, *The Autobiography* contains occasional long, analytical passages which present the narrator's observations about race and other related topics. For example, in Europe the narrator indulges in a comparison between the English and French "races" based on their capital cities: "How these two cities typify the peoples who built them! Even the sound of their names expresses a certain racial difference. Paris is the concrete expression of the gaiety, regard for symmetry, love of art, and, I might well add, of the morality of the French people. London stands for the conservatism, the solidarity, the utilitarianism, and, I might well add, the hypocrisy of the Anglo-Saxon" (100). The narrator uses his position to allow him to make unexpected observations about racial characteristics. In this case he seeks to reverse previous characterizations which would attribute a greater morality to the Anglo-Saxon.

But in general the narrator's main areas of interest are, not surprisingly, the black and white races. The first and most elaborate passage of characterization in the novel proceeds from the narrator's experiences in the black community in Jacksonville and represents the attempts the preface had forecast to break the black race down into its component groups. The narrator claims there are three distinct "classes" of southern black people, classes that can be identified by their tendency to keep to themselves. First is the desperate class generally comprised of "ex-convicts, bar-room loafers, or workers in turpentine camps" who "cherish a sullen hatred for all white men" (56). According to the narrator, such individuals often dominate public debates about the race as a whole, even though their numbers are few. But he adds that "this class represents the black people of the South far below their normal physical and moral condition. . . . And it is not at all a hopeless class; for these men are but the creatures of conditions, as much so as the slum and criminal elements of all the great cities of the world are creatures of conditions" (56). Though these black people "conform to the requirements of civilization much as a trained lion . . . goes through his stunts under the crack of the trainer's whip," the animal image is apparently illustrative rather than indicative of a racial theory. He suggests that these characteristics are not racial or evolutionary but the result of the universal effects of impoverished circumstances.

The second class the narrator describes consists of those blacks who are connected to whites through domestic service, such as waiters, cooks, and servants: "These may be generally characterized as simple, kind-hearted, and faithful; not overfine in their moral deductions, but intensely religious, and relatively—such matters can be judged only relatively—about as honest and wholesome in their lives as any other grade of society" (57). This class forms the main line of connection between whites and blacks, and, according to the narrator, there is little friction between them. Finally, the last class is made up of independent workmen and the wealthy and/or educated. These people have little contact with whites and live in their own social world.

This third class interests Johnson's narrator the most, and he explains at length that they are generally well disposed toward white people, but feel discrimination more keenly because it fails to recognize their financial and social accomplishments. Furthermore, when these accomplishments are recognized by white observers, whites assume that "colored people who have education and money, who wear good clothes and live in comfortable houses, are 'putting on airs' . . . or are, at best, going through a sort of monkey-like imitation" (58). Johnson's narrator resists the implication that those with black skin who attain the trappings of civilization are only displaying racial imitativeness: "It seems that the whites have not yet been able to realize and understand that these people in striving to better their physical and social surroundings . . . are simply obeying an impulse which is common to human nature the whole world over" (58).

In these passages of characterization, Johnson's narrator discounts the power and influence of race and emphasizes the effects of class. He asserts that the behavior of each of his classes is appropriate for the financial and social conditions of all humans with similar circumstances. Up to this point, the narrator has been careful not to create links across the classes that would be considered black characteristics. The lengthy discussion of middle-class black society in Jacksonville ends with a description of the balls that the narrator attended there and with a remark that summarizes the overall point of the passages that had proceeded it: "When one has seen something of the world and human nature, one must conclude, after all, that between people in like stations of life there is very little difference the world over" (62).

Yet the very next sentence signals an abrupt shift in characterizing strategy: "It was at one of these balls that I first saw the cake-walk" (62). From that point on, the narrator engages in the more transcendent characterization that he had previously resisted. His discussion of the cakewalk and other black arts provides the basis for a unified vision of black racial character: "There are a great many colored people who are ashamed of the cake-walk, but I think they ought to be proud of it. It is my opinion that the colored people of this country have done four things which refute the oft-advanced theory that they are an absolutely inferior race, which demonstrate that they have originality and artistic conception, and, what is more, the power of creating that which can influence and appeal universally" (63). These things are the cakewalk, ragtime music, folk songs, and folktales, and all four stand as demonstrations of racial worth because they display both originality and universal appeal. As the narrator argues, it is clear that black art is original since the inventors of ragtime music were "guided by natural musical instinct and talent," whereas white ragtime musicians are "imitators and adulterators" (73). In fact, the narrator argues, the originality of ragtime is best illustrated by its popularity: "One thing cannot be denied; it is music which possesses at least one strong element of greatness: it appeals universally; not only the American, but the English, the French, and even the German people delight in it. In fact, there is not a corner of the civilized world in which it is not known, and this proves its originality; for if it was an imitation, the people of Europe, anyhow, would not have found it a novelty" (73). Ragtime is original because it is imitated by white artists, and because its appeal demonstrates its novelty. All in all, the quality of a race's art is a sign for its racial worth.[9]

In this discussion of black art, Johnson speaks directly through his narrator. Like Howells, Johnson was familiar with Taine's argument that the character of a race is displayed in the literature and art that it produces.[10] In an editorial in the *New York Age* published on January 13, 1916, Johnson repeats nearly the same discussion of the cakewalk and ragtime as appears in *The Autobiography* and elaborates on his claim that black art is a particularly good expression of the worth of black racial character. In this version of his argument he singles out black music, folk stories, and dances as three art forms worthy of attention: "These three achievements are the greatest proof which the race has yet brought against the common charge of inferiority, because they are not the work of one or two gifted individuals but of the race as a whole. They are a demonstration that the Negro is a creator, a creator of that which has the power of universal appeal. They show that from his own inner consciousness the Negro can evolve that which will move and influence the world. And that is proof of inherent power" (*SW* 1: 287). Here the sign of racial power comes from within black "inner consciousness"—the same place from which the narrative point of view of *The Autobiography* emanates. But the artistic power of these communal art forms is even more clearly a *racial* characteristic because their manifested greatness cannot be attributed to a single person. Though Johnson's examples of black art may be low forms—popular dances and music rather than high art—they express the consciousness and power of the black racial character in direct and convincing fashion because they are collective in a transcendent sense.

Johnson raises the issue of black art in his novel and in his editorials because it had not been adequately recognized as a solid refutation of scientific pronouncements of black racial inferiority. In fact, in a commencement address to the Hampton Institute[11] in 1923, he asserted that artistic demonstrations have a better chance of defeating the body of racist argument devoted to proving black inferiority than direct counter-argument: "We might argue in the abstract that the Negro possesses intellect, that he has high ideals, that his soul is sensitive to the most delicate nuances of spiritual reactions, and yet not convince those with whom we argue. But the production of sublime music, of moving poetry, of noble literature, is that which was to be demonstrated. There is no argument about it" (*SW* 2: 59). Accordingly, in *The Autobiography* Johnson sets up an incident to illustrate his claim that argument is not effective against the logic that supports racist conclusions. In one lengthy episode, the narrator takes advantage of his white skin and rides in the white car of a Jim Crow train. There he witnesses a conversation about the race question that evolves into a debate between a northerner and a southerner on the question of black equality. Although the southerner is out-argued, he concludes with a kind of nullification: "You might convince me that you're right, but you'll never convince me that

I'm wrong. . . . We don't believe that the nigger is or ever will be the equal of the white man, and we ain't going to treat him as an equal; I'll be damned if we will" (120). The narrator is discouraged by the southerner's obstinacy, until he realizes that it suggests that the real crux of the race problem is not the condition of blacks but rather the mental attitude of whites, "and a mental attitude, especially one not based on truth, can be changed more easily than actual conditions" (120).

In this way the narrator reaches much the same point Thomas Nelson Page reaches in *The Old South.* Page argues that the race problem is created by a difference in how northerners and southerners view blacks. Johnson's narrator similarly concludes that the problem is one of how the black population of the United States is characterized, and asserts that the South insists on an incorrect characterization: "The burden of the question is not that the whites are struggling to save ten million despondent and moribund people from sinking into a hopeless slough of ignorance, poverty, and barbarity in their very midst, but that they are unwilling to open certain doors of opportunity and to accord certain treatment to ten million aspiring, education and property acquiring people" (121). The narrator expresses almost verbatim the position that Page had attributed to George Washington Cable—that the race question is at its heart the problem of the South's denying equal opportunity to deserving humans. And just as Dixon's fiction was designed to provide fictional characterizations that would support the southerner's assertion that the black race was slipping into barbarism, Johnson's fiction is designed to support the opposite characterization. The motivation for the narrator's concern with the proportional aspect of characterization becomes more apparent, given his belief in the vital need to argue for the existence of those blacks who aspire, seeking education and property. Since these aspirations are explicitly not the result of racial imitativeness, *The Autobiography* is positioned to have some material affect on how the race question is approached by those who are touched by its characterizations.

Yet, though the narrator reaches a rather positive conclusion about the power of characterization, he also faces the limits that are placed on that power. First of all, the narrator shares his insight into why it is so important for the white southerner to maintain this negative characterization of African Americans. The conclusion the narrator reaches is similar to what Twain suggests in *Life on the Mississippi:* the view that white southerners have of their whiteness is linked to their characterization of all non-white others. Put bluntly, their characterization of blacks is designed to protect their characterization of themselves: "When the white race assumes as a hypothesis that it is the main object of creation and that all things else are merely subsidiary to its well-being," the narrator argues, "sophism, subterfuge, perversion of conscience, arrogance, injustice, oppression, cruelty, sacrifice of human blood, all are required to maintain the position, and its dealings with other races become indeed a problem" (122).[12]

Much as Twain and Chesnutt do, Johnson's narrator concludes that the South has to remain mired in a largely illusory romantic past in order to maintain its self-conception, and that this aura of the past is best understood through the effects of the fictional genres which it evokes:

> The Southern whites are in many respects a great people. Looked at from a certain point of view they are picturesque. If one will put oneself in a romantic frame of mind, one can admire their notions of chivalry and bravery and justice. In this same frame of mind an intelligent man can go to the theatre and applaud the impossible hero, who with his single sword slays everybody in the play except the equally impossible heroine. So can an ordinary peace-loving citizen sit by a comfortable fire and read with enjoyment of the bloody deeds of pirates and the fierce brutality of Vikings. This is the way in which we gratify the old, underlying animal instincts and passions; but we should shudder with horror at the mere idea of such practices being realities in this day of enlightened and humanized thought. The Southern whites are not quite living in the present age; many of their general ideas hark back to a former century, some of them to the Dark Ages. In the light of other days they are sometimes magnificent. Today they are often cruel and ludicrous. (138)

The narrator argues, much as Howells does in his criticism of historical romance, that people find their animal instincts and passions stirred by romance fiction. But by implication, modern humans require a significantly more evolved form of literature. The narrator of *The Autobiogra-*

phy suggests that the South is stunted by its reverence for outdated fictional genres and Dark Ages chivalry and has failed to achieve modern humanity.

Thus Johnson's excursions on the state of white southern art are designed to support and illustrate the relationship between racial character and fiction. In short, just as black art shows racial worth, white southern art shows racial degeneracy. Accordingly, Johnson often refers to H. L. Mencken's observations on the literary failings of southern writers in his essays and addresses. Johnson cited a long passage from Mencken in a speech delivered in 1923:

> "It is, indeed, amazing to contemplate so vast a vacuity. One thinks of the interstellar spaces, of the colossal reaches of the now mythical ether . . . for all its size and all its wealth and all the 'progress' it babbles of, [the South] is almost as sterile, artistically, intellectually, culturally, as the Sahara Desert. . . . It would be impossible in all history to match so complete a drying up of a civilization. In all that section there is not a single poet, not a serious historian, not a credible composer, not a critic good or bad, not a dramatist dead or alive." (*SW* 2: 49)

In *The Autobiography*—as in his nonfiction—Johnson attributes any lack that may be accorded to the white man of the South to the fact that "most of his mental efforts run through one narrow channel" (55). It is Johnson's opinion that as a result of an overriding obsession with the race question and the supreme effort required to keep the black race down, the white South's institutions are "impassably limited" (55).[13] Yet the most significant form of limitation, for both Mencken and Johnson, is the artistic one; since art reflects the health and greatness of a race, this artistic vacuum is the most telling.

Accordingly, in his reviews in the *New York Age* Johnson was careful to praise southern writers who broke free from the limitations that seemed to hamper southern fiction. In a review written in 1922 of two books written by southern white men, Johnson instructs his readers to note "how far in advance" the two books are "of the traditional fiction about the races that has come out of the South" (*SW* 1: 278).[14] He concludes by observing that both men are "Southern white writers who have broken entirely from the old traditional school of Southern fiction and have striven to present the truth about race conditions in the South" (278). As such, both men have broken away from the artistic limitations of the southern self-conception that are a direct impediment to the truth about racial characterizations.

The task of black art is clear. It must combat the explicitly literary perspective that the white South employs to view its superiority. And in turn, it must help to provide truthful conceptions of black character. Johnson views art as a vehicle for characterization, and as a characterization of the genius of the race in and of itself. Thus, it is apparent that black art must display the worth of black racial character in order to disrupt the racial status quo as it is perpetuated in southern artistic and political formulations.

Music and Tuskegee Realism

Based on Johnson's statements about black art in his address to the Hampton Institute, it is clear that he believed art could change opinions about the racial abilities and character of African Americans. Black art is effective not only because it changes the traditions for the description of racial character, but because it *is* racial character. Since the goal is to prove that black people are capable of intellectual achievement, black art is fundamentally—in Johnson's words—"that which was to be demonstrated." Black art does not merely describe or argue for black character; it manifests black character in a far more immediate sense. According to Johnson, the race is best characterized by its ability to create moving art, and art in turn is racial character enacted.

In particular, Johnson argued that music had a profoundly transcendent power. In the preface to the *Books of American Negro Spirituals*, he explained that the spirituals can move white audiences: "For more than a half century [the spirituals] have touched and stirred the hearts of people and effected a softening down of some of the hard edges of prejudice against the Negro. Measured by length of years, they have wrought more in sociology than in art. Indeed, within the past decade and especially within the past two or three years they have been, perhaps, the main force in breaking down the immemorial stereotype that the Negro in America is nothing more than a beggar at the gate of the nation, waiting to be thrown the crumbs of civilization" (395). Black music provokes a profound emotional response from its listeners of all races, but most notably from American whites. Because of this particular affective power, music is the "main force" breaking down stereotypes; by implication, it does a better job than the direct rewriting of stereotypes in fiction because it can control the response that it desires (unlike fiction, which is often misread). In fact, Johnson suggests that music, in its power to manifest the black racial spirit, has reworked scientific understandings of racial character and acts as an alternative racial sociology.

Furthermore, black music is a more effective form of representation because it is not limited, as written art is, to certain genres. For example, in *The Autobiography* the narrator becomes inspired to bring the genius of the black race to white audiences when he sees that the racial character of black music can be divided from the genre or form that would seem to contain it. In a key scene, the narrator plays ragtime music for a roomful of German musicians. The narrator's key innovation had previously been to take the themes of Western classical music and turn them into ragtime—his ragtime version of Mendelssohn's "Wedding March" was particularly popular in New York. Yet when he plays an authentic ragtime tune, a German musician jumps to the piano. The narrator explains that the man "taking the theme of [the] ragtime, played it through first in straight chords; then varied and developed it through every known musical form" (103). The narrator realizes that the themes of black music—its racial soul—are not linked in any fundamental way to the musical body that contains them. In effect, the narrator has discovered a way to free character from the body it is assumed to inhabit. When he sees that the themes of black music can be translated into different forms, he realizes that the sorrows and hopes of black experience can be expressed in musical forms that white audiences will appreciate and respond to. Just as the black body is a limit on the artistic expression of black racial character because it determines white expectations and responses, the forms of black art restrict the transmission of its themes. But black themes worked into classical forms could express racial character without the attendant vision of the black body that previously had constrained their reception.

It is not surprising, then, that the narrator renounces his musical ambitions (and his race) when he is forced to reconnect blackness to the black body. The narrator, when he has nearly collected enough material to begin composing, spends the night in a small town. There he observes the lynching by fire of a black man and is drawn to a close evaluation of the victim: "There he stood, a man only in form and stature, every sign of degeneracy stamped upon his countenance. His eyes were dull and vacant, indicating not a single ray of thought. Evidently the realization of his fearful fate had robbed him of whatever reasoning power he had ever possessed" (136). In this scene the narrator reenacts the third-person narration of the supposed black criminal—much like the descriptions of Dixon's Gus, Twain's Tom, and Chesnutt's Dan. He replicates the dehumanizing language that attempts to read the countenance of the accused. The narrator's language recalls the now familiar image of the animal impassiveness of the black face and its failure to indicate thought. The narrator feels strangely compelled to observe the face of the victim and the corporeality of the bodily agony that results from the lynching: "He squirmed, he writhed, strained at his chains, then gave out cries and groans that I shall always hear. The cries and groans were choked off by the fire and smoke; but his eyes, bulging from their sockets, rolled from side to side, appealing in vain for help. . . . I was fixed to the spot where I stood, powerless to take my eyes from what I did not want to see" (136). The narrator is struck with the full force of the image of what white violence can do to the body of a black person. The narrator's response is a curious mixture of disgust, shame, and self-consciousness. He first feels a doubled sense of shame as both a black man and as an American: "A great wave of humiliation and shame swept over me. Shame that I belonged to a race that could be so dealt with; and shame for my country" (137).

Consequently, the narrator's decision to pass can also be accounted for in terms of double-consciousness. The ultimate reason he gives for this act is his powerful conviction that he can no longer stand to be identified as black: "It was not discouragement or fear or search for a larger field of action and opportunity that was driving me out of the Negro race. I knew that it was shame, unbearable shame. Shame at being identified with a people that could with impunity be treated worse than animals. For certainly the law would restrain and punish the malicious burning alive of animals" (139). Initially, the lynching causes the narrator to feel shame both as a black man who could be so treated, and as an

American whose nation could allow such a thing to happen. Nonetheless, he has been given tangible evidence of that fact that the black race is seen from a white perspective as less than animal, and he cannot bear to be seen in those terms. Therefore, he resolves to erase the invisible mark of his race, to fall back on his visible whiteness. As Johnson's theory of art suggests, in order to be a black artist one has to be willing to be the vehicle for and embodiment of racial character. However, the narrator cannot acquiesce to this demand once he has come to understand the white perspective on the inhumanity of the black body. The narrator had to achieve the black man's perspective in order to be the narrator of this account. But when he takes on the position of the third-person narrator he finds that this perspective cannot hold. The narrator's inherent instability in Du Bois's framework—as a white man who has only learned to see himself as black and who has chosen to be a part of the freemasonry of the race—makes it difficult for him to remain in the proper narrative position. He will no longer allow himself to be seen as a black man.[15]

In this way, the narrator abandons his plans to be a musician and fails in his project of racial representation because he cannot bear the burden of being actively representative of his people. Thus the task of *representation* blurs into the notion of *representativeness.* In the final pages, the narrator turns to a discussion of his motives for giving an account of his life. He uses the occasion of a benefit that he attended for the Hampton Institute to express his regrets about passing. The benefit was attended by many "great men," including Booker T. Washington. The narrator confesses that men such as Washington who publicly fight for the "cause of their race" make him feel regretful: "Beside them I feel small and selfish. I am an ordinarily successful white man who has made a little money. They are men who are making history and a race. I, too, might have taken part in a work so glorious" (154). It is not just blackness that the narrator has renounced; the novel ends with the famous remark: "I cannot repress the thought that, after all, I have chosen the lesser part, that I have sold my birthright for a mess of pottage" (154). Passing is an act that substitutes a small, local gain for a chance to be great or to contribute to a greater good: the narrator has given up the artistic aims that would have helped the race in a larger sense. The reference to Washington at this point is telling. The narrator notes that at the benefit "the greatest interest of the audience was centered in Booker T. Washington, and not because he so much surpassed the others in eloquence, but because of what he represented with so much earnestness and faith" (154). In order to take part in the project of racial uplift, one must be willing to be representative.

Yet the narrator is careful to contrast Washington's eloquence with his representativeness, subsuming the former in the latter. As William Andrews has suggested, in *Up From Slavery* Washington repeatedly demonstrates more respect for deeds and real-world actions than for the persuasiveness of words. Andrews concludes that this pattern of remarks can be translated into a theory of representation which he calls Tuskegee realism. Though he notes that this realism is only "quasi-literary," it bears upon the African-American literary tradition as it "attempts to restrict the traditional sovereignty of the black wordsmith by chaining the signifier to a preexistent signified and thus making the word merely reflective, rather than constitutive, of reality" (84). For Washington, the eloquent man uses words as a form of power, and believes that what he says can create reality. Yet Washington saw a faith in the power of words as a dangerous one for a race that needed to make material economic progress. Therefore, his realism sought to reduce language to a representative medium, whereby words were of value only insofar as they acted as vehicles for the things they represent.

When Johnson's narrator praises Washington, he downplays the effectiveness of his words—his eloquence—in order to praise that which Washington represents. In this way, Johnson turns Washington into a representative man who stands for what the race can achieve rather than a man whose words can work eloquently to argue that black achievement is possible. Clearly, Washington's realism and the narrator's praise for him evoke Johnson's own theory of representation. For Johnson, black art skips over the eloquence needed to argue for black worth; it acts as a reflection or direct representation of black racial character through its demonstration of that which was to be proven. Johnson's theory of artistic demonstration is part of an attempt to create the realistic representation of the black race, yet it goes beyond the creation of better genres and allows art to represent in a direct and fundamental way.

By the end of the novel, the music that would have been the narrator's racial gift has been supplanted by the prose manuscript account of his life. At the start, the narrator had suggested that his main impulses were a desire to confess his secret and "a sort of savage and diabolical desire to gather up all the little tragedies of [his] life, and turn them into a practical joke on society" (1). Writing this account is an act of generic transformation and an assertion of artistic control. Yet by the end of the novel it is clear that this transformation oscillates between the two generic limiting poles of black expression—comedy and tragedy. Furthermore, the narrator fails in Washington's schema to be representative. Thus, though the novel sets as its goal the recharacterization of black Americans, its central figure is blatantly not a model character. Put another way, the novel *discusses* what is necessary for black art to be generically unlimited and racially representative, but the art that the main character produces (and by extension the novel itself) fails to enact this discussion.

What does it mean that this text proposes an artistic theory of racial representativeness and then has its hero fail to execute it? One possibility, of course, is that the hero is an anti-hero and that all of his pronouncements on race and representation are to be taken ironically. Another possibility is that racial representativeness is still a positive value, but the narrator is a negative construction. However, I believe such readings can only be made by disregarding what Johnson had initially explained about his text and its goals in the preface. There he argued that representativeness is essentially fallacious because it takes a part as a sign for the whole. If that whole is a composite, as Johnson claims, then the representation cannot help but be disproportionate. In fact, as Lee Edelman explains, taking a part for the whole is a vital strategy of white supremacy. The tendency to represent by synecdoche is often used to suggest the "interchangability of blacks in the racial imaginary of America" (43). Edelman claims that synecdoche is the "master trope of racism":

> The figure of "blood," with its pseudo-biological provenance, has historically governed the discrimination of "race" through the classificatory calculus that yields such "types" as the "mulatto," "quadroon," and "octoroon." This mathematic of "blood" emerges, however, from a single racist theorem: whenever an admixture of "black blood" is at issue, one

> part determines the whole. . . . And just as any proportion of "black blood" . . . signifies, ultimately, an "essence" that is "black," so any representation of a black man or woman can stand tropologically . . . for the "essential character" of "the race" as a whole. (44)

The notion of a racial representativeness, in Washington's sense, is linked to a suspect and dangerous ideology of racial collectivity. Representativeness is predicated on the very same tropological basis as formulations of blood and racial character.

As I argue it, Johnson's misgivings about the dangers of representativeness play out in *The Autobiography.* In fact, I believe that his theories of art, and especially music, are fantasy constructions of a pure and non-suspect form of racial collectiveness. Specifically, Johnson argued that music and other popular art forms are vehicles for racial character precisely because they do not originate from a single individual. Black music and vernacular literature are the only legitimate forms of racial characterization for Johnson because they are not subjected to the individual perspectives that make characterization subjective and disproportionate. But most of all, music does not represent the race synecdochically. Rather, music is the perfect art form because it is representative of the thing to be demonstrated without having to be filtered through a single, representative character.

In *Up From Slavery,* Washington declares that his favorite genre is biography: "I like to be sure that I am reading about a real man or a real thing" (xx). Andrews notes that Washington sees biography as the logical extension of his own theory of representation. Yet it is clear that Johnson does not follow Washington in his insistence that biography reflect what is real; *The Autobiography* undermines the representative certainty of biography and autobiography. Since *The Autobiography* is a fake autobiography, it does not refer to any real person and only masquerades as realism. Andrews suggests that Johnson reworks Tuskegee realism, as his novel "does not leave unscathed many of the assumptions about realism—how to recognize it, how to read it,—that Washington held dear" (89).

Johnson's novel is thus more complicated than his own theory of art, and more complicated than Tuskegee realism. The irony that is so much a part of what Johnson has constructed (even if critics may never agree on how much it pervades the novel) takes it beyond a simple reflection model of representation and beyond the notion that characterization is representative of racial character. The narrator's failure to be representative when he chooses to pass means that the representative authority of the text as a whole is in question. *The Autobiography of an Ex-Coloured Man* thus points to the dangers of racial collectivity. It is limiting and dangerous for a single individual to be held up as an example of what all members of a race are and feel. In this way, the narrator's failings are ironic but they are also instructive—the representative man isn't.

Yet of course it is true that Johnson does not really abandon the notion of collectivity. He imagines that narrative representation can be replaced with music—music that will perfectly enact a disembodied racial collective. In a sense, Johnson's comments on music recall Dixon's bogus science in *The Clansman.* When Dixon's characters see the image of the rapist in the eye of a witness to the crime, Dixon creates the kind of science that would be needed to bolster his sagging racial physiognomy. In turn, Johnson uses music to bolster the suspect aims of racial characterization. Yet while Dixon's physiognomy could not be salvaged, Johnson deliberately sabotages his own perfect representation. While his novel describes the perfect art form, he refuses to allow his narrator to achieve it within the limiting confines of narrative presentation. The tension left at the end of the novel between written and non-written art displays Johnson's mixed feelings about racial character and the social efficacy of its correct representation.

Epilogue: Race and Representation

In a March 4, 1915, editorial in the *New York Age,* James Weldon Johnson places two newspaper dispatches into ironic juxtaposition. The first describes an incident in Atlanta in which a traveling dramatic production of *Uncle Tom's Cabin* was barred from performing until the play was changed and retitled "Old Plantation Days." According to Johnson, Legree was "transformed into a sort of benevolent patriarch" and Uncle Tom "made into a happy darky who greatly enjoyed being a slave and who ultimately died of too much good treatment." As Johnson remarks, it "was no doubt a great success and offended nobody's sensibilities" (*SW* 1: 12). Johnson contrasts this incident with the news that the film *The Birth of a Nation* had been given a viewing at the White House. For context, Johnson gives a summary of the damage caused by Thomas Dixon's various creations: " 'The Clansman' did us much injury as a book, but most of its readers were those already prejudiced against us. It did us more injury as a play, but a great deal of what it attempted to tell could not be represented on the stage. Made into a moving picture play it can do us incalculable harm. Every minute detail of the story is vividly portrayed before the eyes of the spectators" (*SW* 1: 12). Though Johnson treats the *Uncle Tom's Cabin* incident with humor, he is much more solemn about the film. Rewriting *Uncle Tom's Cabin* for a southern audience is relatively harmless because it merely panders to the expectations of a limited audience. Just like the novel *The Clansman,* it reaches mostly those whose opinions about racial issues are already formed. However, Johnson argues that a film representation is incalculably damaging for at least two reasons. A movie reaches a far greater audience and, unlike dramatic productions, is not as restricted in its representations. For example, in the film, "a big, degraded looking Negro is shown chasing a little golden-haired white girl for the purpose of outraging her; she, to escape him, goes to her death by hurling herself over a cliff. Can you imagine the effect of such a scene upon the millions who seldom read a book, who seldom witness a drama, but who constantly go to the 'movies'?" (*SW* 1: 12). While the play version of *The Clansman* had to be circumspect in its depiction of sex crimes, the movie is far less constrained. Furthermore, Johnson suggests that the visual representation of such circumstances has a more powerful effect on a greater number of people than a book or play ever could.

Johnson's suspicions about the forces unleashed when written art is transformed into film perhaps stem from his own experience. In 1913, following his return to Jacksonville from Latin America, he tried his hand at writing screenplays. He and his wife sold three scripts, of which at least one was filmed. The script that was filmed, as Eugene Levy explains in his biography of Johnson, was a "'darky comedy' entitled *Aunt Mandy's Chicken Dinner.* Johnson's script had a stereotyped 'mammy' and her 'pickaninnies' in the customary ludicrous situations" (150). According to Levy, the script "probably seemed rather innocent" to Johnson when he wrote it (150). After all, Johnson had made a career writing dialect songs for vaudeville and Broadway musical comedy, songs with titles like "I Ain't Gwinter Work No Mo'" and "Congo Love Song." Yet when Johnson and his wife saw the film version of this darky comedy, they were taken aback. As Johnson notes in his autobiography *Along This Way,* "We saw the exhibition of the first picture and were so disappointed in it that we were actually ashamed to see the others" (298). Though Johnson does not directly identify the source of his shame, Levy suggests that the film was "undoubtedly played in a broad and crude manner" (150). Apparently, the use of stereotypes in song lyrics and in movies are two different enterprises. While critics have noted that Johnson sought to control the negative impact of the racial typing in his songs, the film version of *Aunt Mandy's Chicken Dinner* brought those stereotypes to light in a disappointing manner.[1] Johnson never wrote another movie script.

Johnson's comments on the powers of film raise issues that other chapters above have also raised. What are the differences between the various forms of representation when it comes to the depiction of blackness and racial difference? More to the point, why does the depiction of racial difference seem to necessitate a discussion of artistic form? While Chesnutt and Howells discuss fiction and its genres, Dixon, Twain, and Johnson comment on forms of visual representation. In some cases this commentary proceeds even when its substance undermines important racial themes. For example, in *The Clansman* Dixon tackles the difficult task of describing Silas Lynch's invisible blackness by discussing how he had been characterized by his portrait painter. Ultimately, this passage suggests that Lynch does not *look* black, but his face somehow evokes a sense of blackness when painted. Through this reflection in a second media, the discursive Lynch is made black too. Dixon also locates Lynch's oratorical power in his personality—a surface-level, deliberate projection—rather than in the deeper psychical inheritance of character the white characters all possess. While this is not in and of itself inconsistent in the novel, this careful balance of visibility, surface messages, and the artistic power to capture them tips when the novel undergoes a translation into a visual medium. Film does not have the same capacity to make distinctions between personality and character, and therefore cannot maintain Dixon's most important distinction between black and white. All of the characters in *The Birth of a Nation* are actors, all project personality, all, in a sense, are in blackface. Despite Dixon's enthusiasm, the film undoes the novel's work to defend the culture of character and the absolute logic of racial difference it ensures.

Analogously, Twain appeals to photography in both *Pudd'nhead Wilson* and *Life on the Mississippi* in ways that cut right to the heart of what character is and how art can represent mutable subjects like race. At the start of *Pudd'nhead Wilson,* Twain playfully compares his novel's conclusion to a prose photograph of a courtroom scene. Yet the novel as a whole stages a convincing account of why photography is exactly the wrong metaphor for the power that fiction has to represent phenomena that defy easy classification. For example, Roxy cannot read Tom accurately in a single, photograph-like flash of lightning, Twain suggests, because character is not a static image: it is a complex conglomeration of habit, performance, and training. In *Life on the Mississippi,* Twain discovers that the river cannot be learned like a series of photographic images: it needs to be "read." By way of analogy, the river is a metaphor for racial difference and all that is unrepresentable in a medium that relies on surface detail. Race will always run over the banks of logic and of binary classification when attempts to circumscribe it use a form of writing that does not allow for race to be read rather than photographed. Otherwise, the static descriptive conventions of genre constrain the written representation of race, rendering certain racial scenarios more or less unrepresentable.

Thus, while race renders Dixon's artistic choices ironic unintentionally, Twain appears to deliberately coordinate the irony of his representational aporias. The extent and target of Johnson's irony are more open to question, but his book shows the same pattern: themes of mixed race evoke discussions of non-written artistic media. When Johnson's narrator reviews the artistic choices available for the correct and socially efficacious representation of blackness, he arrives at the conclusion that music can represent race, correcting the damage done by other artistic forms. The advantages of music are clear: it does not need to address the features of the body while it evokes a collective racial spirit. Yet the narrator's failure to achieve this aim seems to result from his inability to be a representative of that collective whole. Johnson perhaps means to suggest that only a truly representative man can create representative art, but the novel's resounding message of failure makes the representativeness of art a difficult and perhaps suspect goal.

It appears that the paradoxes and difficulties of representing racial difference at the turn of the century resulted in an artistic self-consciousness manifested as implicit and explicit comparisons to other artistic media. Since mixed race was so contentious an issue, and since as a phenomenon it presented such a challenge to racial thinking, it is not surprising that novelists were drawn to it as a subject and in turn made more aware of their own craft. Mixed race raises the fundamental question of what blackness and whiteness are, leading rather logically to anxiety about whether their essences have been captured and represented adequately. One imagines a novelist wondering if some other art form—especially a visual or non-written one—might have done better.

As the examples above suggest, the respective representational powers of written art, music, photography, and film hinge on the distinction between providing a surface representation and capturing the inner qualities or essences that do not show on the surface. But in addition to this rather straightforward line of artistic questioning, mixed race also stimulates explorations of more abstract subjects: the written art/non-written art debate is merely an entry point into a nexus of other conceptual considerations which this book has touched on. Specifically, discussions of surface versus inner representation link to higher-level discussions of representational art as a layer of mediation between the viewer and reality. As some authors discussed here have suggested, photography is ostensibly a less mediated art form than writing. While photography provides an *indexical* impression of the thing represented, written description must translate the visual through language. And since the relationship between words and their referents is arbitrary and conventional, written description introduces a layer of *metaphor* and indirection into the artistic process.

As both Sander Gilman and William Andrews have demonstrated, this power of artistic mediation can be ideologically charged. Gilman argues that artistic representation primarily relies on the icon or *representation* which metaphorically turns the depiction of individuals into a class. While mimetic *presentation* might preserve singularity, representation translates through a level of mediating synthesis which provides the typing necessary for social repression. In similar fashion, Andrews explains that some nineteenth-century thinkers believed that restrictions on the mediating powers of language could have positive ideological effects. For example, Booker T. Washington's Tuskegee realism sought to chain the signifier to the signified and make words reflective, rather than constitutive, of reality. Therefore, his realism sought to reduce language to a representative medium, whereby words were of value only inasmuch as they acted as vehicles for the things they represent. As Andrews argues, should one succeed in controlling the metaphorical power of language, making it more indexical, empty rhetoric could no longer achieve political consequences. In this way, the artistic contrast between surface impression and artistic representation can be recast as a question of the mediating power of language to represent rather than present, and the social consequences of representation itself.

The abstract tension between two modes of artistic depiction—a photographic capture of a surface impression versus a translation through language into writing—leads rather naturally to a discussion of the political uses of art and the nature of language as a constitutive force. Yet this artistic question also connects with supposedly *scientific* formulations. When Taine sought to establish the differences between the primitive psychologies of the different races, he fell back on a distinction between minds that form connections "figuratively" and minds that work "algebraically." As he explained it, the figurative mind relies on arbitrary connections between sign and signifier, while the algebraic mind uses direct connections between word and thing, as with Chinese characters. Since figurative thought reflected a supposedly higher level of mental and artistic development, Taine ranked human populations (and by extension culture and literature) using what he saw as a scientific distinction between types of mental activity. Yet that scientific distinction parallels and depends upon an artistic one: Taine's figurative/algebraic distinction clearly replicates the distinction between metaphorical and indexical representation.

Of course, the most obvious example of the conceptual overlap between artistic questions and scientific ones—and one that appears quite centrally in the novels discussed previously—is the distinction between the pseudo-sciences of phrenology and physiognomy. Phrenology looks for an indexical impression of character on the skull, while physiognomy looks for its metaphorical signs on the body. Obviously, this determining difference plays out in the same terms as the distinctions between representational and presentational art. Since character supposedly is located in the organs of the brain, the surface of the skull presents the brain rather than representing it and phrenology is an indexical science rather than a metaphorical one. To paraphrase James Weldon Johnson's remark about the best racial art, the skull *is* the thing that is to be read. In contrast, since the proponents of physiognomic readings can only claim that the features of the face and body are metaphorically linked to aspects of character, this metaphorical signification recalls the mediation of representational art. And it is here that the crux of the racial question comes into play: if the body is an index to the racial mind within, black and white bodies are clear evidence of incontrovertible racial differences, and an indexical form of art is entirely adequate for the representation of that difference. But if the body is not an index to the racial mind—if a black person can have a perfectly white body—then racial difference must be read from the body in ways that only a linguistically mediated art form can provide.

What do the repeated structures in all these formulations suggest? Fundamentally, I would argue that the representation of race and mixed race offers an entry point into the conceptual relationships that underlie the very mechanisms of signification. In case after case, when the representational challenges of mixed race as formulated in this period are expressed in the abstract, they parallel the dynamic of signifier and signified. Racial thinkers posed many crucial questions: Is the body a sign for the mind? Is the body a sign for evolutionary development? Is race the body? Does the body always display racial difference? And each one of the questions takes as a starting point the relationship between container and contained, messenger and message, representation and thing represented. These conceptual parallels suggest that the subject of race and racial difference is conditioned by our understanding of the relationship between meaning and its formal vehicle. Or, more specifically, the representation of race as we understand it cannot be extricated from the formal and figurative properties of language. As Lee Edelman has argued, the scientific account of race as a matter of blood and inheritance is created by the logic of synecdoche, the figure that also governs the logic of artistic representativeness. The dynamics of language create the lines of connection between the bodily basis of race and its artistic representation and thus set the parameters for how we conceive of it.

Logically, then, attempts to represent race, especially in written language, will reproduce racist assumptions by necessity. If representation is really iconic, as Gilman suggests, art cannot help but evoke the synecdochical logic of part for whole. In turn, representational synecdoche recalls the notion of blood—of an inheritable essence that creates the logic of a racial whole. We are locked in a series of binary ways of thinking about race which language itself reinforces for us. Art perhaps has become race: we experience race through physical description and characterization because that is how we conceptualize it. But even more, the abstractions and conventions that govern our understanding of the relationships between skin and character, and between the racial individual and the racial whole, limit our ability to imagine any other account of racial difference. If we cannot help but take representation as representative, all depictions reinforce a logic of racial character.

Insofar as language is inescapable, these conclusions seem foregone. But more than anything else, I hope this book demonstrates that binaries, and the language used to describe them, belong to history. A century ago, the nature/nurture binary did not mean what it means now. What we today formulate as two clear and distinct models of racial identity—what you inherit versus what you learn—was previously a single model: others inheriting what you have learned. Most people assume that racial thinkers in the nineteenth century were on one side of the fence (the nature side) and that anthropology of the twentieth century has brought racial thinking over to the other side. Though this account is not entirely wrong, it is entirely misleading.

In order to escape from synecdoche, from metaphors of blood, and from metaphorical and collectivist racist thinking, we perhaps need to reformulate the nature/nurture binary once again. As long as academic understandings of race start from the premise that humans have no evolutionary past, and that the only way to talk about race is as a cultural phenomenon, we cannot create a new vocabulary for race. We are stuck imagining race as a message placed (by whatever means) into a formal vehicle. But a more nuanced and scientifically responsible understanding of race may, for instance, provide the means to see genotypic, phenotypic, and cultural connections between populations that do not align with the usual racial boundary lines. We may then also see human behavior as a subtle concert between genes, body, and culture that makes the nature/nurture binary look simplistic and limiting. At this point, perhaps, we may finally be able to judge one another by the content of our character.

Notes

Introduction

1. Jane Tompkins's *Sensational Designs* (1985) stands as a key critical text in the effort to expand the American canon. And recent critical attention given to Sutton Griggs, Albion Tourgée, and Charles Chesnutt attests to a pervasive interest in literature that addresses racial questions. Griggs was an African-American novelist whose *Overshadowed* (1900) and *The Hindered Hand* (1905) have only recently been given sustained critical notice. Tourgée was the lawyer for the defense in *Plessy v. Fergusson* and wrote several novels dealing with race and race relations. Chesnutt is better known than the other two largely because of the surge of critical interest in his fiction in the last ten years.

2. Wiegman, in turn, has pointed to a critical fascination with the visible that reaches beyond passing and mixed race. She lists, among others, *Modernity and the Hegemony of Vision* (1993), edited by David Michael Levin; *Vision and Textuality* (1995), edited by Bill Readings and Stephen Melville; and John Ellis's *Visible Fictions* (1982).

3. In this study the notion of race does elide with the notion of blackness. In other words, though a study of the representation of race in American literature could quite naturally include other groups such as Native Americans and Latinos, I have chosen the more narrow focus that limits race to the black/white dynamic. As a result, I do not claim to present an exhaustive picture of thinking of race, but one that does respond to the narrowness of the period. Eric Sundquist's *To Wake the Nations* has many points of contact with the argument in this book, and thus I cite his similar statement: "The presence of black literature and culture in America, through the nineteenth and on into the early twentieth century, is far more pronounced than that of other ethnic minorities. If this book is neither a complete history nor an inclusive multicultural account. . . . [I do] rep-

resent the major issues that have framed the problem of race as it may be seen from the perspective of African American slavery and its aftermath, notably in the post-Reconstruction decades" (8).

4. See the discussion of Daniel Brinton's characterology in chapter 1.

5. One of the larger patterns of my analysis involves the give-and-take between works with Confederate sympathies and those with explicit critiques of southern mythology. In a loose sense, this pattern is paired with another that places texts by black and white authors alongside one another. For the value of this sort of analysis I once again cite Sundquist's explanation: "My argument moves back and forth—alternates so to speak—between black and white texts in order to suggest that neither perspective is by itself adequate to account for the ongoing crisis over race in American cultural and political life, just as neither black nor white authorship guarantees any sort of univocal vision or moral advantage" (7).

6. Another important source for the early stages of this project was James Kinney's *Amalgamation! Race, Sex, and Rhetoric in the Nineteenth-Century American Novel* (1985). Alongside his perceptive rhetorical analysis, Kinney provides an exhaustive survey of mixed-race characters and themes of miscegenation in American fiction.

1. Scientific Racism, Character, and American Fiction

1. In *The Color Line: A Brief on Behalf of the Unborn* (1905), southerner William Benjamin Smith declared that "*in the South* the color line must be drawn firmly, unflinchingly—without deviation or interruption of any kind whatsoever" (5, emphasis in source). A more concise and familiar example of the equation of the race problem with the color line comes from *The Souls of Black Folk* (1903), where W. E. B. Du Bois wrote that "the problem of the twentieth century is the problem of the color-line" (13). Though Smith and Du Bois would have disagreed about the validity and necessity of the color line, both agree that it is at the center of the race issue.

2. See Charles Lofgren's *The Plessy Case: A Legal-Historical Interpretation* (1987), chapter 5, for a valuable overview of racial science in the nineteenth century.

3. See Gould's *The Mismeasure of Man* (1981), which submits much of the racial science of the period to close scrutiny.

4. For more on the American School, see Lofgren 99–101. See also chapters 2 and 3 of Gould's *The Mismeasure of Man.*

5. The end of the pre-Darwinian era is generally marked by the death of Louis Agassiz—the last prominent American scientist to reject evolution. See Lofgren 101.

6. See Stocking's essay "Lamarckianism in American Science" in *Race, Culture, and Evolution.*

7. Morgan's *Ancient Society* is excerpted in Bohannan and Glazer's *High Points in Anthropology* (2nd ed.), though I'm sure the editors would agree that the racist implications of culture-evolution represent more of a low point.

8. George Louis Leclerc, Count de Buffon, was a respected natural historian of the

mid- to late eighteenth century. He advanced the theory that all living organisms had become smaller on the continent of North America.

9. See Gould, *The Mismeasure of Man,* chapter 2.

10. Other contributors to this forum included John T. Morgan, Frederick Douglass, and Joel Chandler Harris.

11. See Williamson, *New People* 95.

12. See Williamson, *New People* 97–98.

13. Stocking notes: "'Culture,' in its anthropological sense, provided a functionally equivalent substitute for the older idea of 'race temperament.' It explained all the same phenomena, but it did so in strictly non-biological terms, and indeed its full efficacy as an explanatory concept depended upon the rejection of the inheritance of acquired characters" (265).

14. From Orson S. Fowler, *Phrenological Chart* (1836). Excerpt reprinted in Davies, *Phrenology* 177–82.

15. See *A Phrenological Dictionary of Nineteenth-Century Americans,* in which Madeleine B. Stern compiles phrenological sketches of famous persons from the pages of the *American Phrenological Journal.*

16. Nelson naturally acknowledges the complexities of this strategy: "It is not coincidence, of course, that Cooper, Simms, and Bird all declare a commitment to a realistic depiction of 'Indians' and apply their romantic urges to compatriots in cause and country. Of course the breakdown between romance and realism is not so simple as even this formulation would indicate: we might also note that their Indians are probably less realistic in all than their more complicated and 'romanticized' Anglo characters" (39).

17. See Kinney, *Amalgamation!* 39–40.

18. Though I am interested in discussing the contrast between the Cavalier and his slaves, Friedman stresses the contrasts between the refined Cavalier with his well-run plantation and the neurotic, materialistic Yankee. In this way, the plantation tradition also sought to defend the South against northern criticism that it was economically backwards. Yet whether one stresses the differences between northerners and southerners or between whites and blacks, it is clear that this genre works by juxtaposing representative characters.

19. Kinney cites Joseph Holt Ingraham's *The Quadroone* (1841) as an early example of a novel-length work that uses the tragic mulatto conventions.

20. Kinney notes that *The Slave* is the first fictive slave narrative and, even more notably, the first anti-slavery novel. It therefore was the first novel to use the theme of miscegenation as part of a direct attack on the institution of slavery.

21. Carter explains the progress of Howells's thinking on Taine's theory of literature. Howells reviewed the *History of English Literature* for the *Atlantic Monthly* in 1872, calling Taine's ideas "brilliant" but calling for caution in their rigid application. But after he read a review of *Middlemarch* that quoted Taine extensively, he shifted to a rather more outspoken adoption.

22. As Pizer notes, in an 1886 "Editor's Study" piece Howells praised Perry and Hutcheson Macaulay Posnett for their "application of scientific principles to literature"

and their "conscious perception of principles which others have been feeling more or less blindly, and which are really animating and shaping the whole future of criticism" (qtd. in Pizer 96).

23. Kenneth Warren, in chapter 3 of *Black and White Strangers: Race and American Literary Realism* (1993), provides a nuanced look at the uses of characterization in the literary battles between sentimentalism and realism, addressing many of the authors and texts that I do in this book. He is especially perceptive on the point made here, that sentimental characterization could be deployed in defense of radically different political positions: "Available without its liberal humanist 'content,' sentimentalism's literary apparatus could then be harnessed to any cause that could speak persuasively of its disfranchisement and of having been unjustly despoiled by a stronger force. Sentimentalism, which scholars have credited with 'the creation of the negro for the popular mind' in ways that made emancipation possible, can also be said to have contributed to undermining the political and social gains made by black Americans during the post–Civil War period" (92).

2. Thomas Dixon and the Rhetorical Mulatto

1. Whereas the references to classical art could be seen as an attempt to give Lynch the Greek (or in this case Roman) features scientifically considered superior, Dixon makes it clear that his "chiseled" lips and "head of a Caesar" produce only pictures of the jungle.

2. The papers that address the other issues—education, lynching, religion—also recast all racial questions in terms of the representation of racial character. For example, whether to educate African Americans depends on their natural capability to be educated and how they respond by heredity to certain types of education.

3. See E. Stanley Godbold, Jr., "A Battleground Revisited." In addition to Dixon, four other southern novelists of note used this period as a setting: Thomas Nelson Page, Ellen Glasgow, Joel Chandler Harris, and John S. Wise, the son of a governor of Virginia.

4. See Bloomfield, "Dixon's *The Leopard's Spots*" 388. At Johns Hopkins Dixon met fellow student Woodrow Wilson, and that friendship would years later lead to a private showing of *The Birth of a Nation* (the D. W. Griffith film based on *The Leopard's Spots* and *The Clansman*) at the White House.

5. Joel Williamson argues in *The Crucible of Race* that *The Leopard's Spots* is a political document in the sense that it provides the closest thing to a "codification of the Radical dogma" espoused by the racial regressionists of the period (140).

6. Dixon apparently wrote quite a bit of the story of his own character into Charlie Gaston. According to Cook, Dixon won such a medal when he was a student at Wake Forest, under identical circumstances to the ones depicted in the novel. Dixon also referred to the events that led up to his winning the medal in a sermon titled "Man and Fate" as part of his argument that man has control over the formation of his own character. Williamson, who draws on Cook for his analysis in *Crucible,* elaborates extensively

on the points of similarity between the novel and Dixon's biography. As he claims, "*The Leopard's Spots* is Thomas Dixon" (160).

7. Stowe describes Tom's reaction to Legree's hideousness: "From the moment that Tom saw him approaching, he felt an immediate and revolting horror at him, that increased as he came near. He was evidently, though short, of gigantic strength. His round, bullet-head, large, light-grey eyes, with their shaggy, sandy eyebrows, and stiff, wiry, sunburnt hair, were rather unprepossessing items, it is to be confessed; his large, coarse mouth was distended with tobacco, the juice of which, from time to time he ejected from him with great decision and explosive force; his hands were immensely large, hairy, sunburnt, freckled, and very dirty, and garnished with long nails, in a very foul condition" (358).

8. Robert Ingersoll was a well-known speaker on religious subjects, and the published collections of his lectures were widely read. He subjected both religion and superstition to rationalist critique.

9. Bloomfield summarizes Dixon's theories of race and of character. He claims that the racial opinions expressed in Dixon's sermons between 1887 and 1899 are presented largely unchanged in his fiction.

10. This line clearly echoes Frederick Douglass's ringing declaration in the *Narrative* (1845) that "you have seen how a man was made a slave; you shall see how a slave was made a man" (107). Interestingly, Douglass conflates physical signs and strength of character in his account of how he was made a brute: "Mr. Covey succeeded in breaking me. I was broken in body, soul, and spirit. My natural elasticity was crushed, my intellect languished, the disposition to read departed, the cheerful spark that lingered about my eye died; the dark night of slavery closed in upon me; and behold a man transformed into a brute!" (105).

11. Michaels explains: "The state supreme court that approved the notorious Mississippi Plan explicitly acknowledged the illegality of racial discrimination: 'Restrained by the Federal Constitution from discriminating against the negro race,' the court wrote, 'the convention discriminates against its characteristics.' And the Federal Supreme Court could find no fault with this color-blind racism, ruling that . . . the 'peculiarities of habit, of temperament and of character' that distinguished blacks from whites were acceptable targets of legislation in a way that skin color was not" (191).

12. Dixon introduces the setting for his novel by noting that "it was settled by the Scotch folk who came . . . in the great migrations which gave America three hundred thousand people of Covenanter martyr blood, the largest and most important addition to our population, larger in numbers than either the Puritans of New England or the so-called Cavaliers of Virginia and Eastern Carolina; and far more important than either, in the growth of American nationality" (187).

13. Stoneman is also explicitly a type from the criminal anthropology of Italian physiognomist Caesar Lombroso. Criminal anthropologists saw ape-like morphology in human faces and bodies as signs of evolutionary regression. Evolutionary retardation then was used to explain criminal—i.e., savage or precivilized—behavior.

14. Williamson comments on this phenomenon in *New People:* "By about 1900 it was possible in the South for one who was biologically purely white to become behaviorally black. Blackness had become not a matter of visibility, not even, ironically, of the one-drop rule. It had passed on to become a matter of inner morality and outward behavior. People biologically black in any degree could not openly aspire to whiteness; but whites could easily descend into blackness if they failed in morality. Thus there was created in the white mind a new curious kind of mulatto—a mulatto who was in fact genetically white but morally black" (108).

15. This description of romance conventions is drawn from Derek Pearsall's account in *The Canterbury Tales.* In turn, Pearsall draws on Eric Auerbach's discussion of the romance in *Mimesis.*

16. Carolyn Karcher discusses Cooper's novels of contact between whites and Native Americans: "Like its prototype, the historical novel developed by Sir Walter Scott, the American version of this genre celebrated the triumph of a technologically advanced civilization over a tribal society. Unlike Scott, however, . . . American authors belonged to the conquering race, which constituted their sole audience. Their mission was not to reconcile the victor with the vanquished, much less to offer a healing vision of the two groups' eventual amalgamation under the victors' hegemony" (xv). Dixon's transposition of the genre to the Civil War and Reconstruction necessitates that it be expanded to include reconciliation, at least between whites.

17. In fact, Dixon and Stowe both employ the mode of the jeremiad. As Tompkins explains, the jeremiad in early American discourse "strives to persuade its listeners to a providential view of human history which serves, among other things, to maintain the Puritan theocracy in power" (140). While Stowe employs the form to represent abolitionist interests in a Christian context, Dixon employs it to persuade his readers to take a view of human history that maintains the power and rights of southern white supremacists.

3. *Pudd'nhead Wilson's* Phrenological Photograph

1. See Henry Nash Smith's foreword to Alan Gribben's *Mark Twain's Library* and Gribben's introduction "Howells's 'Most Unliterary' Friend." Gribben's annotated catalog reconstruction of Twain's library runs two volumes and lists nearly five thousand titles that the Twain family owned, read, or mentioned. Though this extensive collection could authorize a connection between Twain's fiction and virtually any intellectual current of his day, the links between Twain's thought and science are particularly well documented. See especially Sherwood Cummings, *Mark Twain and Science: Adventures of a Mind.*

2. For discussions of Twain, science, and pseudo-science see Gribben, "Mark Twain, Phrenology, and the 'Temperaments'"; Poole, "In Search of the Missing Link"; Stern, "Mark Twain Had His Head Examined"; Waggoner, "Science in the Thought of

Mark Twain"; James D. Wilson, "The Monumental Sarcasm of the Ages"; and Zlatic, "Mark Twain's View of the Universe."

3. For Twain's direct references to phrenology, see Stern, "Mark Twain Had His Head Examined," and Gribben, "Mark Twain, Phrenology, and the 'Temperaments.'"

4. As Gribben notes, though contemporary usage of the word *temperament* does not necessarily imply a corresponding set of physical characteristics, for people in the nineteenth century "the term 'temperament' still possessed a connotation of physicality, of correspondence between mind and body, which has since been largely erased" ("Mark Twain, Phrenology, and the 'Temperaments'" 46).

5. Phrenology was popularized in the United States as a form of self-help. As Davies explains, the theory of cerebral location in its original form was not designed for wide practical application. It was Spurzheim who coined the term *phrenology* and began to promote the belief that the science could lead to human perfection. Though Gall had assigned thirty-seven different sections of the brain with a range of human tendencies, good and evil (he even labeled one organ "murder"), Spurzheim removed the negative labels and claimed that through "exercise" the wholly positive faculties of the brain could be strengthened and the organs enlarged. Thus phrenology promised human perfection through the diagnosis of character flaws and then systematic efforts of improvement. It was precisely this practical application that the Fowler brothers, Orson and Lorenzo, turned into a thriving business in the 1830s and 1840s.

6. As Knoper puts it, "The strain in phrenology of materialist science that reduced the incomprehensible human mind to the potentially mappable brain promised to sweep away the uncertainties of representation by certifying the reliability of physical transmission from cerebrum to cranium and from inner character to body type" (100).

7. The reading of character is phrenology's most powerful claim. Yet even Gall, the science's founder, became doubtful that character could be read from the skull: "I have never pretended to distinguish the influence, which modification of the forms of the cranium slightly mark, may have on the character, of how its corresponding shades may be traced. My first observations have only been made upon persons who were distinguished from other men, by some eminent quality or faculty. I easily perceived that it was only in such individuals, that I could find striking differences of the head, and that I could distinguish well marked protuberances" (qtd. in Davies 40).

8. "The Secret History of Eddypus" is one of Twain's later, unfinished works in which he imagines a future world run on the principles of Christian Science. "Eddypus" was Twain's play on the name of the founder of Christian Science, Mary Baker Eddy.

9. As Wilson notes, Twain also makes this critique in his *Autobiography*, where he remarks that every person who submitted to a phrenological examination in his town received the same flattering reading—their characters were in line with George Washington's.

10. Though this episode does not take place on the Mississippi, or during Twain's travels for *Life on the Mississippi*, he has included it, I would argue, in part because it serves to develop the theme of character and the ironies involved in reading it. Addition-

ally, Backus belongs to the category of figures in Twain's writing who impersonate and efface their own identities. Backus is a cousin to the tricksters in *Huckleberry Finn* and is part of the critical ground covered by Susan Gillman in *Dark Twins.*

11. See Adrienne Bond, "Disorder and the Sentimental Model: A Look at *Pudd'nhead Wilson,*" and Michael Orth, "*Pudd'nhead Wilson* Reconsidered, or the Octoroon in the Villa Viviani." Bond notes similarities between Twain's text and W. W. Brown's *Clotel, or the President's Daughter* (1853), Capt. Mayne Reid's *The Quadroon* (1856), Harriet Beecher Stowe's *Uncle Tom's Cabin* (1855), and Dion Boucicault's play *The Octoroon* (1859). Orth cites Reid, Boucicault, and Richard Hildreth's *Archy Moore, the White Slave* (1857).

12. This passage goes on to question the fixed testimony of visual symbols such as architectural decorations. In the next paragraph, Twain notes that the town's striped barber poles, were they in Venice, would signal the homes of nobility.

13. For a discussion of Twain's use of deadpan humor see chapter 2 of Randall Knoper's *Acting Naturally: Mark Twain in the Culture of Performance.*

14. This description touches upon standard attributes of the heroine of the tragic octoroon novel. Those heroines, according to Bond, are typically beautiful and virtuous, and their beauty is given as the outward sign of their virtue. However, they are not meek. Twain made this generically inappropriate addition because it subverts the inner/outer logic of the heroine's character in particular and of sentimental fiction in general.

15. As Twain notes, "But for the Sir Walter Scott disease, the character of the Southerner—or Southron, according to Sir Walter's starchier way of phrasing it—would be wholly modern, in place of modern and mediaeval mixed, and the South would be fully a generation further advanced than it is." He goes on to make the rather fantastic (as he himself admits) claim that "Sir Walter has so large a hand in making Southern character, as it existed before the war, that he is in great measure responsible for the war" (*Life on the Mississippi* 328).

16. Some critics have seen the twins' presence in the novel as distracting and unnecessary, or as a sloppy remnant of the story that Twain originally set out to write (published as *Those Extraordinary Twins*) in which they played a bigger part. I see the twins as foils to the aristocracy of Dawson's Landing who expose the town as provincial and highlight the emptiness of the performance of chivalry by its chief citizens.

17. A partial list includes Barbara Chellis, "Those Extraordinary Twins: Negroes and Whites"; Nancy Fredricks, "Twain's Indelible Twins"; Lee Clark Mitchell, "'De Nigger in You': Race or Training in *Pudd'nhead Wilson?*"; and Evan Carton, "*Pudd'nhead Wilson* and the Fiction of Law and Custom." James Kinney in *Amalgamation!* makes a forceful argument separating Twain from Roxy's assertion that black blood determines Tom's low character: "This overblown assertion goes unchallenged by the author because we are supposed to see the irony of having Roxy—the best character in the novel, the only match for Wilson in intelligence, and 'Tom's' self-sacrificing mother—be the one to offer the obvious racial explanation in such an exaggerated manner. Here, as elsewhere, Clemens uses exaggeration as a rhetorical clue to an intended irony" (221).

18. The tortured composition of the novel has led some to argue that it is inconsis-

tent and perhaps unworthy of consistent criticism. See especially Hershel Parker's essay "*Pudd'nhead Wilson:* Jack-leg Author, Unreadable Text, and Sense-Making Critics" in *Flawed Texts and Verbal Icons* (1984). However, the history of the manuscript rather fits my reading of the generic shifts. Tom first came into being when Twain was writing the story of Siamese twins, and he was a white character. Tom's lack of honorable behavior was designed to be a satire of the southern Cavalier long before he was rewritten as a mulatto. And when Twain removed the Siamese twins and turned his focus to the now mulatto Tom and his mother, he saw the center of his novel as the murder plot. Thus he became more interested in how guilt could be solidly located in the body of the accused.

19. As Brook Thomas argues in "Tragedies of Race, Training, Birth, and Communities of Competent Pudd'nheads," while contemporary critics tend to read the novel in terms of the late-twentieth-century nature/nurture binary, Twain's use of terms like "training" does not fall neatly into that binary. In fact, he explains that "within Twain's world the phrase 'training is everything' has repressive, not liberating connotations" (762).

20. See Lawrence Howe, "Race, Genealogy, and Genre in Mark Twain's *Pudd'nhead Wilson*" for a discussion of links between Twain and Poe and for a list of critics who explore the connections. See also James Cox's essay "*Pudd'nhead Wilson* Revisited."

21. See Michael Rogin's essay "Francis Galton and Mark Twain: The Natal Autograph in *Pudd'nhead Wilson*" for more on Twain's use of Galton.

22. He is also an expert at palmistry. In fact, Wilson demonstrates his extraordinary skill when he studies one twin's palm and then "maps out" his "character and disposition, his tastes, aversions, proclivities, ambitions and eccentricities" (51). The twins declare that Wilson's reading is "artistically drawn" and "correct" (51). The final testament to both Wilson's skill and to the power and accuracy of palmistry comes when he discovers evidence of an event in the past in which one twin had committed murder in self-defense and the twin confirms that the event actually happened. Tom, whose very social status depends on bodily invisibility, is rightly quite disturbed by Wilson's display: "Why, a man's own hand is his deadliest enemy! Just think of that—a man's own hand keeps a record of the deepest and fatalist secrets of his life, and is treacherously ready to expose him to any black-magic stranger that comes along" (52).

23. However, this example also enacts that which it seeks to criticize. Assumptions about gender work like assumptions about "character": for this experiment to work, one must accept the circumstantial testimony that women all sharpen pencils badly.

4. Howells and Chesnutt: The Racial Uses of Genre

1. Sundquist notes that to respond to this charge, "one would have to bear in mind that, as James Weldon Johnson would later contend in his provocative essay 'The Dilemma of the Negro Author,' it was nearly impossible for the minority writer to do otherwise" (12).

2. The quotation from chapter 3 of Warren's *Black and White Strangers* provided in

this paragraph does not do justice to the full scope of his argument. Ultimately, Warren concludes that the concept of character in Howellsian realism actually did much harm to the cause of social and political justice for African Americans in the period.

3. Critic Ellen Wright argues that while Howells was opposed to sentimental fiction, he believed that people exhibit a fair amount of what he called "sentimentalism" in their daily lives. For Howells, to sentimentalize means to observe the faces of others and construct stories to fit the features.

4. George Eliot's *Romola* (1863), often called a historical romance, describes the gradual decline in the character of its central figure, Tito Melema. Tito arrives in Florence knowing that his adopted father has been taken prisoner. Yet rather than spend time and resources trying to locate and free him, Tito works his way into Florentine society and marries the beautiful Romola. Mrs. Meredith obviously identifies with the novel's presentation of a failure of duty toward a family member as a sign of moral weakness. Furthermore, Edwin Cady remarks (in an editor's note to *An Imperative Duty*) that Howells viewed Romola's subsequent act of purifying self-sacrifice as "quixotic" and cited it as an example of the sentimental reverence of duty and renunciation that he found worthy of critique (147).

5. Jack Wilson develops an argument about how Howells uses the reading of character in fiction to characterize his characters. Wilson claims that several of Howells's "earnest" women characters of his novels of the 1880s are readers of *Romola,* including Alice in *April Hopes* and Miss Vance and Miss Carver in *The Minister's Charge.*

6. Although Howells's Olney holds a minority opinion on racial intermarriage, there were some contemporary scientists who recognized that miscegenation, like cross-breeding in animal and plant species, could have positive results. Joseph Le Conte admitted that "there are valuable qualities in the lower races which ought not to be lost, which ought to be incorporated into the perfect ideal humanity for which we hope; and this can be done only, or at least most directly, by mixture" (374). Nonetheless, Le Conte stopped short of endorsing interracial marriage; he argued that the mixture of radically different human types would not result in a stronger product. See the discussion of neo-Lamarckianism in chapter 1.

7. See also Brook Thomas's argument in "The Risky Business of Accessing the Economy of Howells's Realism in *The Rise of Silas Lapham*" for a discussion of the deliberate and ironic undermining of Olney's purely scientific standpoint.

8. Howells made jabs at Puritan fatalism and its ideological equivalent, absolute evolutionary determinism, in other novels. Though he apparently believed in the mechanism of evolutionary progress, according to Jane Marston he "embraced 'soft' evolution, which optimistically posited change as progress, as part of man's growth toward moral perfection" (232).

9. See Brook Thomas's discussion in "Risky Business" of the tendency for the progressive, Hegelian structures in Howells's fiction (the *Aufhebung*) to disrupt their own forward motion and throw off formal balance (as an example of Heidegger's *Verwindung*).

10. In fact, up until the point where they join their mother, Rena and John may have

been successfully passing for white to the reader, since Chesnutt has given no previous textual clues to their racial identity.

11. Eric Sundquist notes in *To Wake the Nations* that stories and interweaving genres appear often in Chesnutt's fiction. While the protagonists of *The House Behind the Cedars* use supposedly white genres in their self-fashioning, Chesnutt's fiction also makes creative use of black narrative traditions. His short stories in particular "offer an unparalleled bridge between the art of black folk vernacular and published literature" (13).

12. While Dixon and the white supremacists used the power of fiction to give the reading public an impression of black racial tendencies as they understood them, Howells's realism engaged in the recharacterization of whites.

13. Since Judge Straight comes to realize the social fiction of mixed race, Chesnutt seems to imply that the legal profession has the tools necessary to rethink race. In contrast, Dr. Green, an acquaintance of Tryon's, is a scientific racist. His speeches about white supremacy and black degeneracy are made ironic by the intelligence and character of John and Rena, suggesting that the medical perspective is inadequate.

5. Character and Black Art in *The Autobiography of an Ex-Coloured Man*

1. Most of Johnson's columns from the *New York Age* are reprinted in volume 1 of *The Selected Writings of James Weldon Johnson*, edited by Sondra Kathryn Wilson (hereafter abbreviated in the text as *SW*).

2. For Johnson's comments on how he wanted the novel to be received, see his letters to George A. Towns reprinted as "Letters to a Friend: Correspondence from James Weldon Johnson to George A. Towns," edited by Miles M. Jackson.

3. For this reason it is logical to see the narrator of the novel as Johnson's mouthpiece, as an individual who articulates and then strives to achieve the artistic goals that Johnson genuinely believed would help the racial situation in the United States. Yet many critics have also argued that the narrator is an ironic anti-hero whose opinions are to be looked on with suspicion. Robert Fleming, a chief proponent of the ironic reading, has argued that the novel as it is constructed is a "deeply ironic character study" (83).

4. Eugene Levy has suggested in his biography of Johnson that some critics use an ironic reading of the narrator as a way to avoid having to attribute some of the novel's expressed political or social opinions to Johnson. The fact is that Johnson held some opinions that do not sit quite right with contemporary thinking. In particular, his willingness to grant that white civilization is the superior goal toward which black people progress betrays an evolutionary thinking that predates more relativist understandings of culture.

5. See "A Note on the Text" in the Penguin edition edited by William L. Andrews (xxxi).

6. The passage Johnson evokes appears in Du Bois's essay "Of Our Spiritual Strivings": "After the Egyptian and Indian, the Greek and Roman, the Teuton and Mon-

golian, the Negro is a kind of seventh son, born with a veil, and gifted with second-sight in this American world,—a world which yields him no true self-consciousness, but only lets him see himself through the revelation of another world. It is a peculiar sensation, this double-consciousness, this sense of always looking at one's self through the eyes of others, of measuring one's soul by the tape of a world that looks on in amused contempt and pity. One ever feels his twoness,—an American, a Negro; two souls, two thoughts, two unreconciled strivings; two warring ideals in one dark body, whose dogged strength alone keeps it from being torn asunder" (5).

7. Eugene Levy suggests that both Frederick Douglass's *Life and Times of Frederick Douglass* and *Up From Slavery* were models for *The Autobiography*: "Both works are written in a simple, straight-forward prose style generally free of rhetorical flourishes; in both the narrator seems to detach himself from the experiences he describes; and both authors make frequent asides to comment directly on the significance of particular incidents to the American racial situation. It seems clear that *Up From Slavery,* more than any other literary influence, led Johnson to the use of the pseudo-autobiography" (*James Weldon Johnson* 130).

8. Roxanna Pisiak argues that in order for a main character to be ironized there must be an implied author who sends messages to the implied reader that are at odds with the messages associated with that character. She concludes that "because *The Autobiography of an Ex-Coloured Man* is a first-person account, it is difficult to determine when or how the implied author may be 'communicating' to the implied reader" (85). For this reason, questions about the amount and substance of irony directed at Johnson's narrator are extremely difficult to settle.

9. In *To Wake the Nations,* Eric Sundquist discusses the introduction of the cakewalk and ragtime to European audiences. He claims that both forms were artistically hybrid, but that they displayed something like the originality that Johnson insists upon: "Something outside the tradition of European ballroom dancing—something African American and southern—remained in the cakewalk, just as something alien to European rhythms appeared in the advent of ragtime, a culturally ambiguous form of music" (289). See also his footnote on Johnson with a list of important critical studies of ragtime (289–90).

10. There is a reference to Taine in the preface to *The Book of American Negro Poetry.*

11. The Hampton Institute was founded in 1868. Booker T. Washington received his initial education there, and its educational practices formed the basis for many of the innovations that he would employ in his own Tuskegee Institute.

12. Eric Sundquist notes the ironic links between the development of attitudes toward the South and the development of cakewalk-inflected American music: "Over several crucial decades in the development of American music (less so in the other arts), the nation became not just more Confederate in sympathy but also, consciously or not, more black and southern in the inflection of its cultural languages" (280).

13. As the narrator concludes, "In this respect I consider the conditions of the whites to be more deplored than the blacks. Here a truly great people that produced a majority

of the great historical Americans from Washington to Lincoln, now forced to use up its energies in a conflict lamentable as it is violent" (55).

14. Johnson does not name the authors, but the titles are *Birthright* (Century Company) and *White and Black* (Harcourt, Brace, and Company).

15. In *From Behind the Veil*, Robert Stepto has argued that Johnson directs irony at the narrator because he seems to understand himself through Du Bois's formulation in a grossly simplified way. Stepto demonstrates that the narrator's account of Du Bois's double-consciousness misses much of the doubleness of the formulation and reduces the "colored" point of view to a narrow, nearly inhuman position. It is possible that Johnson does not merely suggest that the narrator's instability in Du Bois's terms is his problem, but that his problems with his identity stem from a fundamental misreading of those terms.

Epilogue: Race and Representation

1. See especially Eugene Levy's "Ragtime and Race Pride: The Career of James Weldon Johnson."

Works Cited

Adams, John H. "Rough Sketches: A Study of the Features of the New Negro Woman." *Voice of the Negro* 1 (1904): 323–25.

Andrews, William L. "The Representation of Slavery and the Rise of Afro-American Literary Realism, 1865–1920." *African American Autobiography: A Collection of Critical Essays.* Ed. William Andrews. Englewood Cliffs, NJ: Prentice, 1993. 77–89.

Auerbach, Eric. *Mimesis: The Representation of Reality in Western Literature.* Trans. Willard R. Trask. 1953. Princeton: Princeton UP, 1968.

Bloomfield, Maxwell. "Dixon's *The Leopard's Spots:* A Study in Popular Racism." *American Quarterly* 16 (1963): 387–401.

Bogardus, Ralph F. "A Literary Realist and the Camera: W. D. Howells and the Uses of Photography." *American Literary Realism* 10 (1977): 231–41.

Bond, Adrienne. "Disorder and the Sentimental Model: A Look at *Pudd'nhead Wilson.*" *Southern Literary Journal* 13 (1981): 59–71.

Brinton, Daniel G. "The Aims of Anthropology." *Science* 2 (1895): 241–52.

Brooks, G. P., and R. W. Johnson. "Contributions to the History of Psychology: XXIV. Johann Caspar Lavater's *Essays on Physiognomy.*" *Psychological Reports* 46 (1980): 3–20.

Bruce, Philip A. *The Plantation Negro as a Freeman: Observations on His Character, Condition, and Prospects in Virginia.* New York: G. P. Putnam's Sons, 1889.

Bryce, James. "Thoughts on the Negro Question." *North American Review* 153 (1891): 641–60.

Cady, Edwin H., and Norma Cady. *Critical Essays on W. D. Howells, 1866–1920.* Boston: Hall, 1983.

Carter, Everett. *Howells and the Age of Realism.* Philadelphia: Lippincott, 1950.

Carton, Evan. "*Pudd'nhead Wilson* and the Fiction of Law and Custom." *American Realism: New Essays.* Ed. Eric Sundquist. Baltimore: Johns Hopkins UP, 1982. 82–94.

Chellis, Barbara. "Those Extraordinary Twins: Negroes and Whites." *American Quarterly* 21 (1969): 100–112.

Chesnutt, Charles. "The Future American: A Complete Race-Amalgamation Likely to Occur." *Boston Evening Transcript* 1 Sept. 1900: 24. Rpt. in *MELUS* 15.3 (1988): 95–107.

——. "The Future American: A Stream of Dark Blood in the Veins of the Southern Whites." *Boston Evening Transcript* 25 Aug. 1900: 15. Rpt. in *MELUS* 15.3 (1988): 95–107.

——. "The Future American: What the Race Is Likely to Become in the Process of Time." *Boston Evening Transcript* 18 Aug. 1900: 20. Rpt. in *MELUS* 15.3 (1988): 95–107.

——. *The House Behind the Cedars.* 1900. Athens: U of Georgia P, 1988.

——. *The Wife of His Youth.* 1899. Ann Arbor: U of Michigan P, 1968.

Combe, George. *Notes on the United States of North America During a Phrenological Visit in 1838–9–40.* Philadelphia: Carey, 1841.

Cook, Raymond Allen. *Fire from the Flint: The Amazing Careers of Thomas Dixon.* Charlotte, NC: Heritage, 1968.

Cox, James. "*Pudd'nhead Wilson* Revisited." *Mark Twain's "Pudd'nhead Wilson": Race, Conflict, and Culture.* Ed. Susan Gillman and Forrest G. Robinson. Durham: Duke UP, 1990. 1–21.

Cummings, Sherwood. *Mark Twain and Science: Adventures of a Mind.* Baton Rouge: Louisiana State UP, 1988.

Davies, John D. *Phrenology: Fad and Science.* New Haven: Yale UP, 1955.

Dawson, Marion L. "The South and the Negro." *North American Review* 172.2 (1901): 279–84.

Dixon, Thomas, Jr. *The Clansman: An Historical Romance of the Ku Klux Klan.* 1905. Lexington: U of Kentucky P, 1970.

——. *Dixon on Ingersoll: Ten Discourses, Delivered in Association Hall, New York.* New York: Alden, 1892.

——. *The Leopard's Spots: A Romance of the White Man's Burden—1865–1900.* 1902. New York: Wessels, 1908.

Douglass, Frederick. *Life and Times of Frederick Douglass, Written by Himself.* New York: Collier, 1962.

——. *Narrative of the Life of Frederick Douglass, An American Slave.* Ed. Houston A. Baker, Jr. 1845. New York: Penguin, 1986.

Du Bois, W. E. B. *The Souls of Black Folk.* 1903. New York: Penguin, 1989.

Edelman, Lee. "The Part for the (W)hole: Baldwin, Homophobia, and the Fantasmatics of 'Race.'" *Homographesis: Essays in Gay Literary and Cultural Theory.* New York: Routledge, 1994. 42–75.

Eliot, George. *Romola.* Ed. Andrew Sanders. 1863. New York: Penguin, 1980.

Fleming, Robert E. "Irony as a Key to Johnson's *The Autobiography of an Ex-Coloured Man.*" *American Literature* 43 (1971): 83–96.

Frederickson, George M. *The Black Image in the White Mind: The Debate on Afro-American Character and Destiny, 1817–1914*. Hanover: Wesleyan UP, 1971.

Fredricks, Nancy. "Twain's Indelible Twins." *Nineteenth-Century Literature* 43 (1989): 484–99.

Friedman, Lawrence J. *The White Savage: Racial Fantasies in the Postbellum South*. Englewood Cliffs, NJ: Prentice, 1970.

Gardiner, Charles. "The Future of the Negro." *North American Review* 189 (1884): 78–81.

Gates, Henry Louis, Jr. "The Trope of the New Negro and the Reconstruction of the Image of the Black." *Representations* 24 (1988): 129–55.

Gilliam, E. W. "The African Problem." *North American Review* 189 (1884): 417–30.

Gillman, Susan. *Dark Twins: Imposture and Identity in Mark Twain's America*. Chicago: U of Chicago P, 1989.

———. "'Sure Identifiers': Race, Science, and the Law in *Pudd'nhead Wilson*." *Mark Twain's "Pudd'nhead Wilson": Race Conflict and Culture*. Ed. Susan Gillman and Forrest G. Robinson. Durham, NC: Duke UP, 1990. 86–104.

Gilman, Sander L. "Black Bodies, White Bodies: Toward an Iconography of Female Sexuality in Late Nineteenth-Century Art, Medicine, and Literature." *Critical Inquiry* 12 (1985): 204–42.

Ginsberg, Elaine. "Introduction: The Politics of Passing." *Passing and the Fictions of Identity*. Ed. Elaine Ginsberg. Durham, NC: Duke UP, 1996. 1–18.

Godbold, E. Stanley, Jr. "A Battleground Revisited: Reconstruction in Southern Fiction, 1895–1905." *South Atlantic Quarterly* 73 (1974): 99–116.

Gossett, Thomas F. *Race: The History of an Idea in America*. Dallas: Southern Methodist UP, 1963.

Gould, Stephen J. *The Mismeasure of Man*. New York: Norton, 1981.

Greener, Richard T. "The Future of the Negro." *North American Review* 189 (1884): 93–95.

Gribben, Alan. Introduction. *Mark Twain's Library: A Reconstruction*. Comp. Alan Gribben. 2 vols. Boston: Hall, 1980.

———. "Mark Twain, Phrenology, and the 'Temperaments': A Study of Pseudoscientific Influence." *American Quarterly* 24 (1972): 45–68.

Haller, John S. *Outcasts from Evolution: Scientific Attitudes of Racial Inferiority, 1859–1900*. Urbana: Illinois UP, 1971.

Hampton, Wade. "The Race Problem." *Arena* 8 (1890): 132–38.

Harkins, E. F. *Little Pilgrimages Among the Men Who Have Written Famous Books*. Boston: Page, 1903.

Harris, Joel Chandler. *Uncle Remus: His Songs and His Sayings*. Ed. Robert Hemenway. 1880. New York: Penguin, 1986.

Harris, L. H. "A Southern Woman's View." *The Independent* 18 May 1899: 1354+.

Herskovitz, Melville J. *The American Negro: A Study in Racial Crossing*. 1928. Bloomington: U of Indiana P, 1964.

Hoffman, Frederick. *Race Traits and Tendencies of the American Negro*. 1896. New York: AMS, 1973.

———. "Vital Statistics of the Negro." *Arena* 29 (1892): 529–42.

Hofstadter, Richard. *Social Darwinism in American Thought.* 1944. New York: Braziller, 1959.

Hovenkamp, Herbert. "Social Science and Segregation before *Brown.*" *Duke Law Journal* 34 (1985): 624–72.

Howe, Lawrence. "Race, Genealogy and Genre in Mark Twain's *Pudd'nhead Wilson.*" *Nineteenth-Century Literature* 46 (1992): 495–516.

Howells, William Dean. *An Imperative Duty.* 1892. Ed. Edwin Cady. Albany: New College UP, 1962.

——. *The Rise of Silas Lapham.* 1885. New York: Vintage, 1991.

Jackson, Miles M., ed. "Letters to a Friend: Correspondence from James Weldon Johnson to George A. Towns." *Phylon* 29 (1968): 189.

Jefferson, Thomas. *Notes on the State of Virginia.* 1787. *The Heath Anthology of American Literature.* 3rd ed. Ed. Paul Lauter. 2 vols. Boston: Houghton Mifflin, 1998. 923–40.

Johnson, James Weldon. *Along This Way: The Autobiography of James Weldon Johnson.* New York: Viking, 1933.

——. *The Autobiography of an Ex-Coloured Man.* 1912. Ed. William L. Andrews. New York: Penguin, 1990.

——. *The Book of American Negro Poetry.* San Diego: Harvest, 1931.

——, ed. *The Books of American Negro Spirituals.* 1925 and 1926. New York: Da Capo, 1970.

——. *The Selected Writings of James Weldon Johnson.* Ed. Sondra Kathryn Wilson. 2 vols. New York: Oxford, 1995.

Johnson, Oliver. "The Future of the Negro." *North American Review* 189 (1884): 93–95.

Karcher, Carolyn. Introduction. *Hobomok and Other Writings on Indians.* By Lydia Maria Child. New Brunswick: Rutgers UP, 1986.

Kinney, James. *Amalgamation! Race, Sex, and Rhetoric in the Nineteenth-Century American Novel.* Westport, CT: Greenwood, 1985.

Knoper, Randall. *Acting Naturally: Mark Twain in the Culture of Performance.* Berkeley: U of California P, 1995.

Le Conte, Joseph. *The Race Problem in the South.* 1892. Miami: Mnemosyne, 1969.

Levy, Eugene. *James Weldon Johnson: Black Leader, Black Voice.* Chicago: U of Chicago P, 1973.

——. "Ragtime and Race Pride: The Career of James Weldon Johnson." *Journal of Popular Culture* 1 (1968): 357–70.

Lofgren, Charles. *The Plessy Case: A Legal-Historical Interpretation.* New York: Oxford UP, 1987.

Marden, Orison Swett. *Character: The Grandest Thing in the World.* New York: Cromwell, 1899.

Marston, Jane. "Evolution and Howellsian Realism in *The Undiscovered Country.*" *American Literary Realism: 1879–1910* 14 (1981): 231–41.

Michaels, Walter Benn. "The Souls of White Folk." *Literature and the Body: Essays on Populations and Persons.* Ed. Elaine Scarry. Baltimore: Johns Hopkins, 1988. 185–209.

Miller, Kelly. *As to the Leopard's Spots: An Open Letter to Thomas Dixon, Jr.* Washington: Rayworth, 1905.

Mitchell, Lee Clark. "'De Nigger in You': Race or Training in *Pudd'nhead Wilson?*" *Nineteenth-Century Fiction* 42 (1987): 295–312.

Morgan, John T. "The Race Question in the United States." *Arena* 10 (1890): 385–98.

Morgan, Lewis Henry. *Ancient Society. High Points in Anthropology.* Ed. Paul Bohannan and Mark Glazer. 2nd ed. New York: Knopf, 1988. 32–60.

"Mr. Thomas Dixon Jr., the Physiognomist." *Voice of the Negro* 2 (1905): 789–90.

Murch, A. E. *The Development of the Detective Novel.* London: Peter Owen, 1958.

Nelson, Dana. *The Word in Black and White: Reading "Race" in American Literature, 1638–1867.* New York: Oxford UP, 1992.

Orth, Michael. "*Pudd'nhead Wilson* Reconsidered, or the Octoroon in the Villa Viviani." *Mark Twain Journal* 14.4 (1969): 11–15.

Page, Thomas Nelson. *The Old South.* New York: Scribner's, 1892.

Panek, LeRoy Lad. *An Introduction to the Detective Story.* Bowling Green: Bowling Green State UP, 1987.

Parker, Hershel. "*Pudd'nhead Wilson:* Jack-leg Author, Unreadable Text, and Sense-Making Critics." *Flawed Texts and Verbal Icons.* Evanston: Northwestern UP, 1984. 115–45.

Pearsall, Derek. *The Canterbury Tales.* London: G. Allen & Unwin, 1985.

Pisiak, Roxanna. "Irony and Subversion in James Weldon Johnson's *The Autobiography of an Ex-Coloured Man.*" *Studies in American Fiction* 21 (1993): 83–96.

Pizer, Donald. "The Evolutionary Foundation of W. D. Howells's *Criticism and Fiction.*" *Philological Quarterly* 40 (1961): 91–103.

Poole, Stan. "In Search of the Missing Link: Mark Twain and Darwinism." *Studies in American Fiction* 13 (1985): 201–15.

Riggio, Thomas P. "*Uncle Tom* Reconstructed: A Neglected Chapter in the History of a Book." *American Quarterly* 28 (1976): 56–70.

Rogin, Michael. "Francis Galton and Mark Twain: The Natal Autograph in *Pudd'nhead Wilson.*" *Mark Twain's "Pudd'nhead Wilson": Race Conflict and Culture.* Ed. Susan Gillman and Forrest G. Robinson. Durham, NC: Duke UP, 1990. 73–85.

Shaler, Nathaniel Southgate. "Science and the African Problem." *Atlantic Monthly* 66 (1890): 36–45.

Shookman, Ellis. "Pseudo-Science, Social Fad, Literary Wonder: Johann Caspar Lavater and the Art of Physiognomy." *The Faces of Physiognomy: Interdisciplinary Approaches to Johann Caspar Lavater.* Ed. Ellis Shookman. New York: Camden, 1993. 1–24.

Skerrett, Joseph T., Jr. "Irony and Symbolic Action in James Weldon Johnson's *The Autobiography and an Ex-Coloured Man.*" *American Quarterly* 32 (1980): 540–58.

Smith, Geoffrey D. "Bartley Hubbard and Behavioral Art in William Dean Howells' *A Modern Instance.*" *Studies in American Fiction* 7 (1979): 83–91.

Smith, Henry Nash. Foreword. *Mark Twain's Library: A Reconstruction.* Comp. Alan Gribben. 2 vols. Boston: Hall, 1980.

Smith, William Benjamin. *The Color Line: A Brief on Behalf of the Unborn.* New York: McClure, Phillips, 1905.

Sollors, Werner. *Neither Black Nor White Yet Both: Thematic Explorations of Interracial Literature.* New York: Oxford UP, 1997.

Southern Society for the Promotion of the Study of Race Conditions and Problems in the South. *Race Problems of the South: Report of the Proceedings of the First Annual Conference.* 1900. New York: Negro UP, 1969.

Starke, Catherine. *Black Portraiture in American Fiction: Stock Characters, Archetypes, and Individuals.* New York: Basic, 1971.

Starke, D. *Character: How to Strengthen It.* New York: Funk, 1916.

Stepto, Robert. *From Behind the Veil: A Study of Afro-American Narrative.* Urbana: U of Illinois P, 1991.

Stern, Madeleine B. "Mark Twain Had His Head Examined." *American Literature* 41 (1969): 207–18.

——, comp. *A Phrenological Dictionary of Nineteenth-Century Americans.* Westport, CT: Greenwood, 1982.

Stocking, George W., Jr. *Race, Culture, and Evolution: Essays in the History of Anthropology.* 1968. Chicago: U of Chicago P, 1982.

Stowe, Harriet Beecher. *Uncle Tom's Cabin.* 1852. New York: Signet, 1981.

Straton, John Roach. "Will Education Solve the Race Problem?" *North American Review* 170 (1900): 785–801.

Sundquist, Eric. *To Wake the Nations: Race in the Making of American Literature.* Cambridge: Belknap, 1993.

Susman, Warren I. *Culture as History: The Transformation of American Society in the Twentieth Century.* New York: Pantheon, 1985.

Taine, Hippolyte-Adolphe. *History of English Literature.* 1871. Philadelphia: Altemus, 1908.

Thomas, Brook. "The Risky Business of Accessing the Economy of Howells's Realism in *The Rise of Silas Lapham.*" *REAL* 11 (1995): 229–53.

——. "Tragedies of Race, Training, Birth, and Communities of Competent Pudd'nheads." *American Literary History* 1 (1989): 754–84.

Tompkins, Jane. *Sensational Designs: The Cultural Work of American Fiction, 1790–1860.* New York: Oxford UP, 1985.

Twain, Mark. *Life on the Mississippi.* 1883. New York: Penguin, 1986.

——. *Mark Twain's Letters, Volume 1: 1853–1866.* Ed. Edgar Marquess Branch, Michael B. Frank, and Kenneth M. Sanderson. Berkeley: U of California P, 1988.

——. *Pudd'nhead Wilson and Those Extraordinary Twins.* 1894. Ed. Sidney E. Berger. New York: Norton, 1980.

——. "The Secret History of Eddypus." *The Science Fiction of Mark Twain.* Ed. David Ketterer. New York: Archon, 1984.

Waggoner, Hyatt Howe. "Science in the Thought of Mark Twain." *American Literature* 13 (1937): 357–70.

Warren, Kenneth. *Black and White Strangers: Race and American Literary Realism.* Chicago: U of Chicago P, 1993.

Washington, Booker T. *Up From Slavery.* Ed. William L. Andrews. 1901. New York: Norton, 1996.

Weaver, George Sumner. *Lectures on Mental Science According to the Philosophy of Phrenology.* New York: Fowlers, 1852.

Wiegman, Robyn. *American Anatomies: Theorizing Race and Gender.* Durham, NC: Duke UP, 1995.

Williamson, Joel. *The Crucible of Race: Black-White Relations in the American South since Emancipation.* New York: Oxford UP, 1984.

———. *New People: Miscegenation and Mulattoes in the United States.* New York: Free, 1980.

Wilson, Jack H. "Howells' Use of George Eliot's *Romola* in *April Hopes.*" *PMLA* 84 (1969): 1620–27.

Wilson, James D. "The Monumental Sarcasm of the Ages: Science and Pseudoscience in the Thought of Mark Twain." *South Atlantic Bulletin* 40 (1975): 72–82.

Wright, Ellen F. "William Dean Howells and the Irrational." *Nineteenth-Century Fiction* 38 (1983): 304–23.

Zelle, Carsten. "Soul Semiology: On Lavater's Physiognomic Principles." *The Faces of Physiognomy: Interdisciplinary Approaches to Johann Caspar Lavater.* Ed. Ellis Shookman. New York: Camden, 1993. 40–59.

Zlatic, Thomas D. "Mark Twain's View of the Universe." *Papers in Language and Literature* 27 (1991): 338–55.

Index